THE SPECULATIVE CITY

Emergent Forms and Norms of the Built Environment

Edited by Cecilia L. Chu and Shenjing He

The Speculative City explores property speculation as a key aspect of financialization and its role in reshaping the contemporary built environment. The book offers a series of case studies that encompass a range of cities whose urban fabrics have undergone significant transformation in recent years.

While the forms of these developments share many similarities, their trajectories and social outcomes were contingent upon existing planning and policy frameworks in addition to the historical roles assumed by the state and the private sector in housing and welfare provision. By paying close attention to the forces and actors involved in property development, this book underscores that the built environment has played an integral part in shaping new values and collective aspirations, while also facilitating the spread of financial logics in urban governance. The essays in this collection show that these dynamics represent a larger shift of politics and culture in the ongoing production of urban space and prompt reflections on future trajectories of finance-led property speculation.

CECILIA L. CHU is an associate professor in the Division of Landscape Architecture at The University of Hong Kong.

SHENJING HE is a professor and associate dean in the Faculty of Architecture at The University of Hong Kong.

The Speculative City

Emergent Forms and Norms of the Built Environment

EDITED BY CECILIA L. CHU AND SHENJING HE

UNIVERSITY OF TORONTO PRESS
Toronto Buffalo London

© University of Toronto Press 2022
Toronto Buffalo London
utorontopress.com

ISBN 978-1-4875-0719-0 (cloth)   ISBN 978-1-4875-3576-6 (EPUB)
ISBN 978-1-4875-2488-3 (paper)   ISBN 978-1-4875-3575-9 (PDF)

Library and Archives Canada Cataloguing in Publication

Title: The speculative city : emergent forms and norms of the built
   environment / edited by Cecilia L. Chu and Shenjing He.
Names: Chu, Cecilia L., editor. | He, Shenjing, editor.
Description: Includes bibliographical references and index.
Identifiers: Canadiana (print) 20210369116 | Canadiana (ebook) 20210369167 |
   ISBN 9781487524883 (paper) | ISBN 9781487507190 (cloth) |
   ISBN 9781487535766 (EPUB) | ISBN 9781487535759 (PDF)
Subjects: LCSH: Land speculation – Case studies. | LCSH: Urban renewal –
   Case studies. | LCGFT: Case studies.
Classification: LCC HD111 .S64 2022 | DDC 333.73/13 – dc23

Every effort has been made to contact copyright holders; in the event of an error or omission, please contact the publisher.

We wish to acknowledge the land on which the University of Toronto Press operates. This land is the traditional territory of the Wendat, the Anishnaabeg, the Haudenosaunee, the Métis, and the Mississaugas of the Credit First Nation.

University of Toronto Press acknowledges the financial support of the Government of Canada, the Canada Council for the Arts, and the Ontario Arts Council, an agency of the Government of Ontario, for its publishing activities.

 Canada Council for the Arts   Conseil des Arts du Canada

ONTARIO ARTS COUNCIL
CONSEIL DES ARTS DE L'ONTARIO
an Ontario government agency
un organisme du gouvernement de l'Ontario

Funded by the Government of Canada   Financé par le gouvernement du Canada

Contents

List of Figures vii

Acknowledgments ix

Introduction: Financialization, Speculation, and the Production of the Urban Built Environment 3
CECILIA L. CHU AND SHENJING HE

Section I. Mega Projects and Speculative Urban Development

1 Property Speculation: Causes and Consequences 21
SUSAN S. FAINSTEIN AND JOHANNES NOVY

2 The Financialization of Urban Redevelopment: Speculation and Public Land in Porto Maravilha, Rio de Janeiro 45
MAYRA MOSCIARO, ALVARO PEREIRA, AND MANUEL B. AALBERS

3 From Spectacular to Speculative Gulf Cities: A Tale of Dubai and Doha 70
ALI A. ALRAOUF

Section II. Reconfiguring the State: The Politics and Pragmatics of Speculation

4 Mega-Event Urbanism and the Politics of Speculative Urban Development in Shanghai 109
YUNPENG ZHANG AND SHENJING HE

5 Urbanization as Mass Speculative Event: Informal Finance and City-Making in Ordos, Inner Mongolia 134
MAX D. WOODWORTH

6 El Quiñón: Corruption and Speculative Development in the Spanish Financial Crisis   155
MARTA CATALÁN ERASO AND CECILIA L. CHU

Section III. Forms and Norms of Speculative Housing

7 Speculation in the London Housing Market: Flat Break-Ups, Loft Conversions, and Overseas Buyers   179
CHRIS HAMNETT

8 Speculative Subdivision of Private Rental Flats in Hong Kong   199
MANDY LAU

9 Contradictions of State and Household Investments in Public Housing in Singapore   221
CHUA BENG HUAT

Afterword   241
ALAN SMART

List of Contributors   253

Index   257

Figures

1.1	Map of Jersey City 30
1.2	View of downtown Jersey City 31
1.3	Map of Vienna 35
1.4	A view of Donau City 38
2.1	Perimeter of Porto Maravilha 50
3.1	Traditional settlements in the Gulf cities 73
3.2	The old parts of Doha 74
3.3	Main shifts in Gulf states' economic development 76
3.4	The first ever solar-powered plane taking off from Abu Dhabi 78
3.5	Aerial view of Dubai 82
3.6	Police supercars in Dubai 83
3.7	"Keep calm. There's no bubble" poster in Dubai 85
3.8	Cartoon depicting the aftermath of the 2008–2009 global financial crisis on Dubai's virtual economy 87
3.9	The evolution of Doha, 1937–2015 91
3.10	The growing population of Qatar 92
3.11	The contemporary skyline of Doha 93
3.12	The new Qatar National Museum 97
3.13	Smart KBUD: The case of Education City in Doha 98
3.14–3.18	Architectural and urban components of Education City in Doha 99–100
4.1	The planned area of the Expo Park before demolition, Shanghai 122
4.2	Redevelopment of the Expo site, Shanghai 126
6.1	View of El Quiñón 156
6.2	Entrance to the public park María Audena 165
6.3	Amenities in the buildings of El Quiñón 166
6.4	Aerial view of El Quiñón 167

Figures

7.1	Typical mansion block in London	184
7.2	1-10 Summers Street, London	189
7.3	The Ziggurat building, London	190
7.4	A Victorian school converted into apartments, London	191
7.5	The Jewish Soup Kitchen for the Poor converted into luxury loft apartments, London	192
8.1	A typical old building in the inner urban area of Hong Kong	205
8.2	New completions of Class A private domestic flats in Hong Kong, 2003–2016	207
8.3	Units that were leased among all newly completed Class A flats in Hong Kong, 2003–2016	209
8.4	Percentage of all lettings in each year located in the urban area, Hong Kong	210
8.5	Loss of Class A stock over the years due to demolitions in the urban redevelopment process, Hong Kong	211

Acknowledgments

The idea of *The Speculative City* originated from an interdisciplinary symposium at the University of Hong Kong with support from the Centre of Urban Studies and Urban Planning, Department of Urban Planning and Design, Department of Architecture, and the Faculty of Architecture. The preparation of the book was made possible with a publishing grant from the Department of Architecture at the University of Hong Kong. The authors would like to thank the three anonymous reviewers for their constructive feedback on the original manuscript, as well as Jodi Lewchuk, Breanna Muir, and Robin Studniberg for their assistance in the production of the book. Special thanks to Carolyn Zapf for her meticulous copyediting work. Finally, the authors would like to thank Marta Catalan Eraso, Calvin Liang, Yongshen Sam Liu, and Lillian Tam for their help in finalizing this project.

THE SPECULATIVE CITY

Introduction: Financialization, Speculation, and the Production of the Urban Built Environment

CECILIA L. CHU AND SHENJING HE

Recent scholarship in critical urban studies has explored the contested processes of neoliberalism, drawing attention to the entrepreneurialization of urban governance that increasingly caters to the logics of the market (Harvey, 1978, 2006; Rossi, 2013; Brenner, 2014; Rossi & Vanolo, 2015). Building on David Harvey's formulation of the secondary circuits of capital, numerous scholars have discussed the growing reach of financial capitalism and the concomitant increases in asset values and speculative housing practices (Aalbers, 2008; Moreno, 2012, 2014; Lapavistas, 2011). This literature highlights real estate as a central arena of financialization, abetted by the ongoing privatization of public goods and gentrification, as a key economic strategy adopted by governments around the world. The real estate and infrastructure that constitute the built environment have provided a geographical system for the redistribution of financial capital in which urban spaces are reproduced primarily as a means to fix, as well as to liquefy, financial capital (Harvey, 2006; Moreno, 2014; Rogers & Koh, 2018). These processes have hastened uneven development in both developed and developing economies, leading to increasing social inequality at the global, regional, and local scales (Pike & Pollard, 2010).

Despite the many critiques of neoliberal urbanization (especially after financial capitalism took an even more pervasive form following the 2008 global financial crisis), there have been fewer discussions of the ways in which the spatial and material processes of speculative property activities have shaped the forms of the built environment and their modes of production.[1] This oversight can partly be explained by

---

1 For a few exceptions to this view, see Gotham (2006), van Loon & Aalbers (2017), Smart & Lee (2003), and Moreno (2014).

the long-standing divide between the disciplines of architecture and planning and those of critical geography and urban studies, with scholars tending to focus on their preferred kinds of analyses. Likewise, the immense variety of urban spaces produced through institutional mediations in different countries has also made general theorization challenging. Notwithstanding its widespread influence, David Harvey's analysis of spatial production has been criticized as being overly encompassing with inadequate attention to existing institutional and cultural specificities (Robinson, 2006; Roy 2009; Brenner & Schmid, 2011). Given the deepening influence of financial capital in urban development across the globe in the twenty-first century, there is a pressing need for more detailed investigations into the evolving relationship between speculative capital accumulation and the ongoing production of urban space.

This book contributes to this investigation by exploring property speculation as a key aspect of financialization in recent years and examining its impacts on reshaping the forms and norms of the built environment. Speculation has always been a feature of global capitalism, and boom and bust cycles have been recurring patterns in the history of urban development in capitalist cities. A primary feature of speculative investment is the hope of significant and often rapid future financial gains primarily based on changes in asset prices, rather than through the slower accumulation of income over time. While the logic of speculation has shaped the spatial forms of most capitalist cities, the growing role of financial capital in fuelling global economic growth in the past several decades indicates a quantitative and qualitative shift in the way capital is being accumulated. The rise of what has been referred to as the "speculative city" can be seen as both a continuation of, but also a significant departure from, earlier forms of property investment, which, although including speculative elements, were tied more closely to the activities of the "real economy," from which their value derived, and to the "fixedness" of real estate. What distinguishes financialization from these earlier patterns of accumulation is that profits accrue primarily through financial channels rather than through trade and commodity production (Krippner, 2005). In the process, financialization circumvents "spatial fixity" and capital illiquidity by converting site-specific property assets into transparent securities that are tradable by (often distant) investors seeking rapid gains and efficient allocation of large sums of capital (Gotham, 2006; Aalbers, 2008). At the same time, the creation of new financial instruments has greatly increased the amount of capital available to real estate developers, leading to more speculation and risk-taking.

It is important to consider these aspects because they provide a context for understanding the broader processes of continuity and change in different cities and the ways in which states and societies become involved in speculative property markets in the era of financialization. We consider speculation, a practice that entails the anticipation of future gains and material improvement through asset accumulation, to be a productive process that generates new values, meanings, and aspirations at individual and collective levels. This perspective draws on recent anthropological studies of financialization, which argue that it should not simply be interpreted as a set of activities tied to global financial markets but as a contextually mediated process that operates within non-financial sectors of the real economy and interlocks financial networks with the lives of ordinary citizens (Allon, 2010; Martin, 2002).

This relational aspect of financialization is also emphasized by Philip Ashton and colleagues in their work on infrastructure finance, which has intertwined the public and private sectors in speculative development with significant impacts on the day-to-day lives of citizens. These dynamics have reconfigured the relations of power between the state and other institutional and social actors while facilitating the penetration of financial logics in urban governance (Ashton et al., 2016). Along with the realignment of the public and private sectors, the changing circuits of finance have also propagated increasing involvement of "shadow banking," which has blurred the boundaries between traditional lending for, and ownership of, development assets, as well as between formal and informal financial networks in the mediation of speculation.

Building on the insights of Fiona Allon, Ashton, and others, this book offers a series of case studies of speculative development that encompass a range of cities whose urban fabrics have undergone significant transformation in recent years. These developments exhibit similar physical forms and spatial patterns. They range from redevelopments in post-industrial cities, to new suburban settlements, to specific types of residential housing. While all were driven by sustained or short-lived property booms and shared the aim of facilitating investment flows and accumulation of capital, their development trajectories and social outcomes were contingent upon existing planning and policy frameworks as well as on the historical roles of the state and the private sector in housing and welfare provision. In most cases, speculative building was also reinforced by narratives that resonated with the entrepreneurial strategies adopted by developers and local governments. The rubric of competitiveness, for example, has propelled many city-branding campaigns in which the construction of exuberant architecture and infrastructure was deployed to instantiate property values and generate new demand for investment. Despite furthering gentrification and dispossession of poor households, images of spectacular built forms have helped to generate collective aspirations among ordinary citizens who desire to be part of a prosperous urban future represented by the "spectacle city" (Debord, 1967; Gotham, 2006; Chu & Sanyal, 2015). Importantly, architecture and urban landscapes play an active role, not only in shaping speculative aspirations but also in contributing to the normalization of property speculation through the mediation of global networks of finance and media.

Taking a vantage point of disciplinary and geographical diversity, the nine chapters of the book offer a critical perspective on speculative urbanism that scrutinizes the interfaces of divergent forces and actors involved in speculation at different scales, ranging from national, regional, and local (at both city and project levels). By presenting how the speculative city evolves physically and conceptually across space and time under financialization, the case studies also prompt reflections on the future trajectories of finance-led property speculation.

Megaprojects and Speculative Urban Development

The first section of this book focuses on the construction of large-scale speculative projects under different urban regimes. It begins with Susan Fainstein and Johannes Novy's chapter, which examines several mega mixed-used development schemes built under public-private partnerships (PPPs). The justification for PPPs, as Feinstein and Novy explain, fits well with the doctrine of neoliberalism, which asserts that marketization produces efficiency and flexibility and counters bureaucracy. Since the 1980s, such developments began to be initiated in major cities in Europe and America, many of which involved renewing former industrial areas and transforming them into mixed-use districts. The stated goal was to attract multinational businesses as well as to provide sites for new housing and cultural facilities for the city. Financing for these projects was typically provided by private investors, with the government switching from producers of housing to facilitators of its development. The financial risks of developers were, however, often displaced onto the public sector through tax-free bonds, tax exemptions, and other types of subsidies. While sponsors of these projects praise PPPs for strengthening competitiveness and producing modern and attractive cultural and residential spaces for the city, PPPs have also been criticized by social commentators for catering to the wealthy, exacerbating social inequality, and entrenching the corporate domination of the built environment. Nevertheless, as Fainstein and Novy illustrate in their comparison of the megaprojects in Jersey City and Vienna, the social impacts of these schemes are shaped by the extent of control assumed by the state over land use and planning. Although greater state involvement does not necessarily lead to better outcomes, it does carry potential for more equitable development.

The development of mixed-use megaprojects is not confined to the Global North, but also increasingly proliferates in developing economies in the Global South. This phenomenon is explored in the second chapter by Mayra Mosciaro and colleagues in their study on Porto Maravilha, a massive urban renewal project in a deprived neighbourhood near the central business district of Rio de Janeiro. The scheme was promoted as a necessary means to reintegrate an "urban frontier" into the city and to create a flourishing business district well connected with global businesses and international capital flows. Rapid implementation of the project was made possible by the creation of new policy tools and financial instruments that allowed the city government to raise upfront cash for financing urban improvements. Additional development rights were even traded as financial assets that in turn widened the scope of speculation. As Mosciaro and colleagues point out, Porto Maravilha represents a case of the financialization of real estate and urban governance in Brazil. It was portrayed as a happy marriage between the production of urban space and the possibility of fast and high economic returns through entrepreneurial governance that would release the city from using taxpayers' money. Like many other megaprojects initiated under the neoliberal agenda elsewhere, the scheme was conceived as a magic formula to revitalize the existing city. It was predicated heavily on the discourse of urban value creation through the valorization of property and anticipation of future gains. Central to its success was also the creation of speculative images of a vibrant mixed-use district with well-designed public spaces, cultural facilities, and corporate buildings. However, the project's execution necessarily entailed neglect of other social demands that were not perceived as helping property values to rise, thus leading to the displacement of low-income households in the existing site. In the process, the government became an active agent of city betterment and gentrification, and its leadership and redistributive role became largely subsumed to the rationale and interest of real estate prices at the expense of substantive social commitment.

The last chapter of the section by Ali A. Alraouf directs our attention to mega property developments in the Middle East, where the use of iconic architecture and infrastructure for generating speculative investment was employed to propel fast-tracked city building. Alraouf's focus is on Dubai and Doha, two cities in the Gulf region that have witnessed spectacular urban growth enabled by petroleum revenue since the 1980s. Building on an expanding body of critical writings on the so-called "Dubai model," Alraouf notes that, although Dubai has been successful in attracting external investment by offering both tax exemptions to foreign corporations and provision of impressive (and overscale) infrastructures, financing for these developments rapidly dried up after the financial crisis, leading to massive abandonment of hundreds of incomplete projects. Reflecting on the detrimental impacts of the crash, Alraouf argues that the financial crisis should be seen as a wake-up call for the Gulf states to conceive an alternative and more resilient urban model that focuses less on building superlative architecture but more on developing the knowledge economy for a post-carbon future (Alraouf, 2017). The need for this model, referred to as knowledge-based urban development (KBUD) with an emphasis on education, science, and innovation, has been increasingly accepted by Gulf state leaders as an appropriate path for the region to retain its competitiveness in the future. To this end, Alraouf posits Doha as a successful example that demonstrates such transition, thanks to strategic moves of the state to invest heavily in educational and cultural institutions aiming not only at attracting foreign knowledge workers but, more importantly, at building capacity for citizens. However, this inclusive and progressive vision has been seen by some critics to be necessarily limited because, after all, Qatar's political power continues to rest with the monarchy and elite families who control the economy. The study also makes the case that, despite all having benefitted from a sustained oil boom over the past decades, the development patterns of Gulf cities were not uniformly the same. To understand their divergent paths thus requires a closer investigation of the political, economic, and social equation that shapes the political legitimacy of each state.

Reconfiguring the State: The Politics and Pragmatics of Speculation

The chapters of the first section illustrate that, although the financialized production of megaprojects is part of an international pattern, their implementations were necessarily mediated by the state and the private sector in the development process, which in turn reconfigured the relationships between different institutional actors and other constituencies. These dynamics are explored in the second section.

Yunpeng Zhang and Shenjing He's chapter traces the transformation of Shanghai into a global city by focusing on the redevelopment of the post-Expo waterfront from an industrial to a mixed-used creative district. By detailing the specific interests of, and tensions between, the central and local states in its development, Zhang and He demonstrate how agents at different levels within the Chinese bureaucracy sought to promote economic growth via speculative urbanization, which is also taken as an effective strategy for government officials to accumulate social and political capital. This study thus challenges Harvey's monolithic view of the state and his underestimation of the complex negotiations and struggles entailed in the development process. Crucially, the chapter illustrates how the ascendance of the financial sector in China's transition towards a market-oriented economy has opened up new speculative opportunities for both state-controlled institutions and the private sector, while facilitating the penetration of financial logics in urban governance. As in other mega development projects, the promotion of post-Expo sites in Shanghai relied heavily on the projection of the spectacular architectural images of cultural centres, corporate towers, and luxury condominiums that were part and parcel of city branding. Despite leading to gentrification and furthering social inequality, the redevelopment has been widely discussed in government reports and the media as a beneficial move, boosting property values and elevating Shanghai's status as a world city.

The next chapter by Max D. Woodworth examines the case of Ordos, which saw ongoing redevelopment of existing towns and villages driven by a speculative building boom since the early 2000s. Complementing Zhang and He's analysis of the different state actors participating in speculation in China, Woodworth's study focuses on the role of informal finance in supplying capital to a broad range of speculators that include local industrialists, small-scale developers, members of the professional class, farmers, and blue collar workers. By tracing the financial mechanisms behind the spectacular development of Dongsheng and the Kangbashi New District, which saw the rapid emergence of massive scale infrastructure and property projects, Woodworth illustrates deep entanglements between formal and informal finance networks that range from interpersonal loans, to underground banks, to microfinance. Importantly, the study challenges the notion of state-led urbanization by revealing the blurred boundaries between state and market, legal and illegal, and formal and informal operations at the heart of urban development. The chapter also provides a much-needed explanation for the high acceptance of financial risk and the strong support for highly disruptive modes of development that have become a normative practice in the eyes of Chinese citizens. Such social consensus began to crack, however, with the onset of the lending crisis in 2011, when creditors sought to reclaim their capital from their borrowers, leading to mass panic and growing fear of bankruptcies, as well as to recriminations of widespread corruptive practices associated with speculation.

Marta Catalán Eraso and Cecilia Chu's chapter explores the intertwined economic, social, and political aspects behind the Spanish property bubble, which saw the biggest transformation of the nation's landscape in its history in the decade before the 2008 financial crisis. Although the patterns of speculative development in Spain followed those in other countries driven by financialization, they also exhibited elements that were specific to Spain's institutional and economic history, including the long-standing dependence of the national economy on the housing construction sector, the absence of effective legislative and administrative frameworks in town planning that encouraged irregular practices, and broad support for property ownership among the Spanish population, which was encouraged by the state since the Franco era (Romero et al., 2012; Muñoz & Cueto, 2017). Drawing from recent critical writings on the crisis, Catalán and Chu trace the conflicting dynamics in the development of El Quiñón, a huge speculative housing scheme targeted at middle-income working families on the outskirts of Madrid. Like many other speculative projects, the construction of El Quiñón was halted after the crisis and was transformed into "toxic assets." The housing units were eventually sold by the banks at hugely reduced prices to new homeowners. Despite its negative image and ongoing legal challenges, El Quiñón was gradually occupied over the past few years, and its current residents are generally content with their new environment. Despite all the vehement criticisms of corrupt officials and immoral speculators for causing the crisis in public discussions, there has been a marked absence of critiques linking such collapses with Spain's entrenched homeownership culture and the wide support for speculative projects by the populous during the boom years.

The chapters by Woodworth and Catalán and Chu bring to light some of the ways in which speculative practices are not only tied to the financial system and capital markets but also intersect with everyday social norms and ordinary people's concerns with their own stakes in real estate ownership. As noted by Allon and others, it is important to recognize that financialization is a process that operates within non-financial sectors of the real economy as much as within financial markets. Speculation is, after all, as much a cultural as an economic phenomenon (Allon, 2010; Palomera & Vetta, 2016; Langley, 2006). Blaming the financial crisis on the excesses of financial forces and the moral failings of speculators fails to recognize the cultural logics and economic rationality behind speculative developments and the collective attitudes that have developed towards specific financial practices over time. Likewise, the assertion that speculative bubbles of this sort were caused by an irrational mass mania does not account for the considered decisions made by developers, property owners, and the larger investment public in seeking out opportunities for asset accumulation in the capitalist system. The "rational choice" has, in many cases, been seen as including the opportunity to leverage and embrace financial risk as a way to improve one's standing and opportunities for the future.

Forms and Norms of Speculative Housing

The shaping of "speculative mentality" and how it, in turn, affects the forms of residential housing properties is discussed in the final section of the book. It begins with Chris Hamnett's chapter, which analyses various ways in which developers and property owners in London sought to maximize profits as new investment opportunities became available due to changes in the planning legislation and structure of the housing market. These include the "flat break-up" market that emerged in the 1960s, in which many institutional landlords owning residential rental apartments decided to sell their properties to speculative investors whose intention was to sell off as many of the individual flats as possible. These moves were incentivized by the growing "value gap" between the tenanted value of properties and their open market vacant possession value as a result of rapid property price inflation. A second example was the "loft conversion" movement that began in the 1980s, when ambitious developers started to convert rundown ex-industrial buildings into upmarket residential properties with significantly higher value. A third related case of transforming properties into higher value forms was the conversion of existing Victorian houses from single family homes to multiple apartments. While this process was in part a response to the growth of smaller households, its underlying rationale was financial, as many developers saw that they could generate significant financial gains by purchasing a house, splitting it into separate apartments, and then reselling them. Hamnett notes that, although all the cases cited in the chapter are examples of property speculation, it should be recognized that their social outcomes were not the same. The flat break-up process, for example, caused more harm than others because its operation often involved forcing existing residents to pay higher rents and service charges or inducing them to either buy or move out. By contrast, the loft conversion could be seen as beneficial to the city because it did not affect any existing residents but instead created much-needed new residential units "out of what was previously unused, or derelict, or low-value space."

The examples presented by Hamnett underscore how speculative housing practices are always contingent upon changes in land use legislation, planning policies, and the dynamics of the housing market, which together create new conditions of capital accumulation possibilities for property owners and developers. As William Baer (2007, pp. 313–14) points out in his discussion of speculative building in history, speculative developments, despite their seemingly "unplanned" nature, are in reality often built with considerably more "planning" than most people assumed. Much of this planning, however, is "invisible" in that it is based not on fulfilling specific planning and design visions but on rational investment decisions of individuals, predicated on the hope of making profits. Notwithstanding the damning label attached to speculative housing, it has been the main housing provider in almost all capitalist cities and has contributed significantly to their current urban forms and character. Criticisms of speculative housing, Baer further notes, are based on an implicit assumption that there is a better way to provide accommodation in a capitalist system, most notably through social housing, which offers a safety net to those who cannot afford to rent or purchase their own properties in the private market. Indeed, this perspective underlies many of the debates over housing provision and social equity in the past decades amid the accelerating retreat of the welfare state and the privatization of public assets across different countries. While critics from the left generally urge the state to retain a greater role in housing provision to protect the disadvantaged, pro-market commentators point to the failures of large-scale social housing as evidence that the private market offers better solutions.

Mandy Lau's chapter addresses the debates over the role of the state and the market in housing provision by focusing on Hong Kong, a city that has long been known for widespread property speculation but also, ironically enough, for having implemented one of the world's largest public housing programs (Smart & Lee, 2003). By examining the complex set of factors leading to the proliferation of speculative subdivided flats that have become the only housing option for many low-income households in the city, Lau challenges the dominant discourse that focuses on resolving housing needs by increasing the provision of public rental housing. The prime reason behind the growth of subdivided flats, Lau argues, is not so much due to insufficient supply of public housing but primarily to the imbalance in the private housing market, where major developers have preferred to build bigger, luxurious flats rather than smaller, affordable units over the past few years. The situation has pushed middle-income households into competition with low-income households for smaller rental flats. While the short supply of small flats has opened up opportunities for speculative landlords to maximize profits through subdivision, the government is implicated in the process through its refusal to intervene in the market and its reluctance to prioritize land allocation for non-luxury housing development. Lau's analysis of the symbiotic relationship between different segments of the private property market and the government's role in public housing provision supports the formulation of sociologist Lois Wacquant, who argues that "governments play a dual role through production of inequalities 'upstream,' while appearing to be busily alleviating inequality experienced 'downstream' by disadvantaged citizens" (Wacquant, 2013). Although housing has become an increasingly contentious issue in public discussion in Hong Kong in recent years, there is surprisingly little analysis of land use allocations and supply trends among different properties. The situation reflects inadequate problematization of the status quo by critics on both the left and right, who continue to perceive the housing problem as one caused by insufficient supply of public housing while remaining ambivalent on the issue of private property speculation.

As in Hong Kong, the success of the public housing program in Singapore has long been an important anchor for the state to maintain its political legitimacy. In Singapore, 90 per cent of its citizens live in flats provided by the Housing and Development Board (HDB), and among these, 85 per cent of households own their flats under a ninety-nine-year lease (Chua, 2011). The remarkable achievement in universal provision of affordable public housing, however, has not prevented speculative property activities from taking hold in the island nation. Chua Beng Huat's chapter deciphers the situation by examining the rationality of public housing homeownership in Singapore and the contradictions entailed in the implementation of its public housing program. A key aspect of the program is that, as an asset-based social welfare system, the People's Action Party (PAP) government is well aware that it must not allow the value of public housing units to fall; otherwise, the retirement needs of homeowners would be greatly jeopardized. To protect the financial interests of citizens and also, more importantly, its own political legitimacy, the PAP government is required to impose various administrative rules and regulations to control the property market, such as cutting the supply of available housing units and easing housing mortgages and loans. Ironically, these same rules and regulations are utilized by homeowners as instruments for their own capital accumulation, leading to fervent speculative activities within the public housing market. Chua contends that the PAP government is thus constantly engaged in balancing acts to address the competing demands in the housing system, where speculative gains are practically guaranteed by the state. It is worth noting that the growing financial burden borne by the government in order to sustain the increasingly hefty public housing sector also forces the city state to make its ends meet through colossal overseas speculation (for example the operation of Temasek Holdings Private Limited). In a nutshell, the domestic speculation within the public housing sector is indirectly sustained by the overseas speculation under state capitalism.

The Society of Speculation

Although the empirical cases presented in this book do not represent a full account of typologies of the speculative city, they together sketch out some of the major patterns of development of finance-led property regimes. By showing the ways in which different actors participate in speculative property practices, they make the case that financialization should not be approached simply as a structural determinant that subsumes all social relations and perpetuates inequality, but should also be seen as part of a larger shift of political and cultural rationalities behind the ongoing production of urban space. In particular, they illustrate how the ownership of property assets and the debt that such ownership implies have become increasingly associated with the accumulation of wealth and financial security. This shift also shows that the built environment has played an integral part in the generation of new values and social relations as well as in individual and collective aspirations.

The global financial crisis in 2008 has been seen by many commentators as a moment of awakening that revealed the excesses of financial forces and the failure of regulatory standards that were bound to lead to a crash. Such narratives of inevitability and tendencies to blame the crisis on "immoral speculators" have often been used to explain the rise of casino-style capitalism that corrupts the banking and real estate sectors. However, such an understanding, which sees the financial crisis as a result of corruption and moral decline, fails to account for the ways in which risk and speculation have always been part and parcel of economic activities in the capitalist system (Allon, 2010). More importantly, it does not consider how the everyday environment has been increasingly framed as a space of investment where citizens are required to secure their well-being and independence, not via state provision but through financial investments under neoliberal governmentality. Seen in this way, property speculation is associated not so much with financial exuberance but with emerging norms that centre on risk and calculation. From this perspective, it may be more productive to ask how the positive and negative aspects of such development might be contextualized within accelerating neoliberal urbanization.

This question raises the larger concern of the nature of the speculative city in the twenty-first century. While critics from the left tend to interpret unfettered speculation and growing social inequality as part of a historical process in which class conflicts intensify under capitalism, some economists argue that speculation is "endemic" to capitalist economies and that the recurring bursting of property bubbles is not an example of failure but of correction.[2] However, with the social contract under strain in many cities and nations where housing has become increasingly unaffordable, even the strongest advocates of free markets are recognizing that capitalism needs legitimacy to succeed. Despite renewed vigour in many real estate markets, many are concerned that economic mechanisms need to work differently to avoid another financial crisis. These concerns are furthermore bound up with growing awareness of the unsustainability of overbuilding resulting from speculation (Marcinkowski, 2015). The problem became more apparent after the financial crisis, which incited new critiques of the environmental and social costs of speculative urbanization and prompted calls to institute more effective control over speculation and its associated irregularities. From a regulationist perspective, certain forms of state intervention, or a mode of regulation, compatible with the prevailing accumulation strategies (regime of accumulation) are crucial to secure the economic base of the dominant mode of growth and also to tackle the inherent crisis of capitalism (He et al., 2020; Jessop, 2002; Smart, Afterword, this volume).

While the long-term environmental and social consequences of finance-led speculative development are yet to be seen, they have raised, and will continue to raise, new sets of ethical questions on the urban future. As Alan Smart asks in the concluding chapter in this volume, what modes of regulation will be needed to constructively channel an asset-based regime of accumulation? How may these shape social relations and ongoing transformation of the forms and norms of cities?

---

2 For example, see discussions by Ferguson (2008) and Glaeser (2013).

REFERENCES

Aalbers, M.B. (2008). The financialization of home and the mortgage market crisis. *Competition and Change, 12*(2), 148–66. https://doi.org/10.1179/102452908X289802

Allon, F. (2010). Speculating everyday life: The cultural economy of the quotidian. *Journal of Communication Inquiry, 34*(4), 366–81. https://doi.org/10.1177/0196859910383015

Alraouf, A.A. (2017). Interrogating Qatar's urbanity as a catalyst for building knowledge-based societies and economies. In R.G. Bertelsen, N. Noori, & J.-M. Rickli (Eds.), *Strategies of knowledge transfer for economic diversification in the Arab states of the Gulf* (pp. 53–66). Gerlach Press.

Ashton, P., Doussard, M., & Weber, R. (2016). Reconstituting the state: City powers and exposures in Chicago's infrastructure leases, *Urban Studies, 53*(7), 1384–1400. https://doi.org/10.1177/0042098014532962

Baer, W.C. (2007). Is speculative building underappreciated in urban history? *Urban History, 34*(2), 296–316. https://doi.org/10.1017/S0963926807004658

Brenner, N. (2014). Neoliberalism. In J. Self & S. Bose (Eds.), *Real estates: Life without debt* (pp. 16–26). Fulcrum.

Brenner, N., & Schmid, C. (2011). Planetary urbanization. In M. Gandy (Ed.), *Urban Constellations* (pp. 10–13). Jovis Verlag.

Chu, C., & Sanyal, R. (2015). Spectacular cities of our times. *Geoforum, 65*, 399–402. https://doi.org/10.1016/j.geoforum.2015.06.016

Chua, B. (2011). Singapore as model: Planning innovations, knowledge experts. In A. Roy & A. Ong (Eds.), *Worlding cities: Asian experiments and the art of being global* (pp. 27–54). Wiley-Blackwell.

Debord, G. (1967). *Society of the spectacle*. Buchet-Chastel.

Ferguson, N. (2008). *The ascent of money: A financial history of the world*. Penguin.

Glaeser, E.L. (2013). A nation of gamblers: Real estate speculation and American history. *American Economic Review, 103*(3), 1–42. http://www.jstor.org/stable/23469700

Gotham, K.F. (2006). The secondary circuit of capital reconsidered: Globalization and the US real estate sector. *American Journal of Sociology, 112*(1), 231–75. https://doi.org/10.1086/502695

Harvey, D. (1978). The urban processes under capitalism: A framework for analysis. *International Journal of Urban and Regional Research, 2*(1–4), 101–31. https://doi.org/10.1111/j.1468-2427.1978.tb00738.x

Harvey, D. (2006). *Spaces of global capitalism: A theory of uneven geographical development*. Verso.

He, S., Zhang, M., & Wei, Z. (2020). The state project of crisis management: China's shantytown redevelopment schemes under state-led financialization. *Environment and Planning A: Economy and Space, 52*(3), 632–53. https://doi.org/10.1177/0308518X19882427

Jessop, B. (2002). Liberalism, neoliberalism, and urban governance: A state–theoretical perspective. *Antipode, 34*(3), 452–72. https://doi.org/10.1111/1467-8330.00250

Krippner, G.R. (2005). The financialization of the American economy. *Socio-economic Review, 3*(2), 173–208. https://doi.org/10.1093/SER/mwi008

Langley, P. (2006). The making of investor subjects in Anglo-American pensions. *Environment and Planning D: Society and Space, 24*(6), 919–34. https://doi.org/10.1068/d405t

Lapavistas, C. (2011). Theorizing financialization. *Work, Employment and Society, 25*(4), 611–26. https://doi.org/10.1177/0950017011419708

Marcinkowski C. (2015). *The city that never was*. Princeton Achitectural Press.

Martin, R. (2002). *Financialization of daily life*. Temple University Press.

Moreno, L. (2012). Looking backward: Towards the critique of neo-modernity. *City, 16*(3), 345–54. https://doi.org/10.1080/13604813.2012.687876

Moreno, L. (2014). The urban process under financialised capitalism. *City, 18*(3), 244–68. https://doi.org/10.1080/13604813.2014.927099

Muñoz, S., & Cueto, L. (2017). What has happened in Spain? The real estate bubble, corruption and housing development: A view from the local level. *Geoforum, 85*, 206–13. https://doi.org/10.1016/j.geoforum.2017.08.002

Palomera, J., & Vetta, T. (2016). Moral economy: Rethinking a radical concept. *Anthropological Theory, 16*(4), 413–32. https://doi.org/10.1177/1463499616678097

Pike, A., & Pollard, J. (2010). Economic geographies of financialization. *Economic Geography, 86*(1), 29–51. https://doi.org/10.1111/j.1944-8287.2009.01057.x

Robinson, J. (2006). *Ordinary cities: Between modernity and development*. Routledge.

Rogers, D., & Koh, S. (2018). *The globalisation of local real estate: The politics and practice of foreign real estate investment*. Routledge.

Romero, J., Jiménez, F., & Villoria, M. (2012). (Un)sustainable territories: Causes of the speculative bubble in Spain (1996–2010) and its territorial, environmental, and sociopolitical consequences. *Environment and Planning C: Government and Policy, 30*, 467–86. https://doi.org/10.1068/c11193r

Rossi, U. (2013). On life as a fictitious commodity: Cities and the biopolitics of late neoliberalism. *International Journal of Urban and Regional Research, 37*(3), 1067–74. https://doi.org/10.1111/1468-2427.12063

Rossi, U., & Vanolo, A. (2015). Urban neoliberalism. In J.D. Wright (Ed.), *International encyclopedia of the social and behavioral sciences* (2nd ed., pp. 846–53). Elsevier. https://doi.org/10.1016/B978-0-08-097086-8.74020-7

Roy, A. (2009). The 21st-century metropolis: New geography of theory. *Regional Studies, 43*(6), 819–30. https://doi.org/10.1080/00343400701809665

Smart, A., & Lee, J. (2003). Financialization and the role of real estate in Hong Kong's regime of accumulation. *Economic Geography*, *79*(2), 153–71. https://doi.org/10.1111/j.1944-8287.2003.tb00206.x

van Loon, J., & Aalbers, M.B. (2017). How real estate became "just another asset class": The financialization of the investment strategies of Dutch institutional investors. *European Planning Studies*, *25*(2), 221–40. https://doi.org/10.1080/09654313.2016.1277693

Wacquant, L. (2013, 26 November). *Constructing neoliberalism: Opening salvo* [Plenary address]. The Australian Sociological Association, Brisbane. http://www.antoniocasella.eu/nume/Wacquant_constructing_neoliberalism_2013.pdf

SECTION I

Mega Projects and Speculative Urban Development

1 Property Speculation: Causes and Consequences

SUSAN S. FAINSTEIN AND JOHANNES NOVY

The wide-spreading social evils which everywhere oppress men amid an advancing civilization spring from a great primary wrong – the appropriation, as the exclusive property of some men, of the land on which and from which all must live. From this fundamental injustice flow all the injustices which distort and endanger modern development, which condemn the producer of wealth to poverty and pamper the non-producer in luxury, which rear the tenement house with the palace, plant the brothel behind the church, and compel us to build prisons as we open new schools.

– Henry George, 1912, VII.I. 20

We define speculation as a wager by private investors that the value of their property will increase beyond the value added by any investment they make in improvements. In other words, they are speculating that they will be able to collect an unearned increment, or what economists define as a rent.[1] Gains in value can result from a new locational advantage, such as that caused by government production of infrastructure, rezoning of a neighbourhood to permit higher densities, or increased demand for an area due to a change in attitudes regarding it. The latter may occur because previously disdained uses have been excluded (for example, by displacement of poor people or communities of colour;

---

1   Rent is any revenue received for non-produced inputs such as location. It includes both payments from tenants that exceed marginal costs and increases in value upon resale not attributable to improvements – for example, when a building changes hands for a price exceeding the cost of its production and maintenance. When a property owner "flips" a piece of unimproved land for a higher price than the seller originally paid, any profit is a pure rent, since it is not return on either labour or capital investment.

through deindustrialization and abandonment), because population growth in adjacent areas has increased demand, or because certain types of construction have become stylish (for example, industrial buildings, historic brownstones). When a developer invests in a property by constructing or remodelling a structure, the gains from development partly derive from investment inputs, but often large jumps in value simply reward a developer for anticipating the potential increased return from a change in use or occupancy.

Property development is inherently risky, and in a narrow sense, outside a totally government-controlled economy, any development project is speculative (Fainstein, 2001, chap. 3).[2] As noted in the introduction to this volume, boom and bust have long been the pattern in land markets under systems of private ownership of land and structures.[3] Within feudal systems, land was not alienable, but once capitalist markets in property were established, buying and selling real estate offered the potential for enormous profits. The demarcation of land into lots, along with the transformation of public land into freehold plots, essentially converted an immoveable object into a tradeable commodity. The danger of large losses arises because so many investors typically respond to the same expectations of growth in demand, leading to overinvestment in property. A crash happens when demand is insufficient to match the new supply, causing owners to default on their loan obligations, precipitating rapid deflation and foreclosures.

Most often cited as the underlying reason for the speculative character of property markets is the long time-horizon involved in major projects (Mills, 1980). At the moment a scheme is conceived, market conditions years in the future are unpredictable. Large front-end costs are typically covered with borrowed money, while returns on investment only come later. The success of a project depends on the demand for particular uses, on the general business cycle, and on unexpected events. Land within an urbanizing area gains value due to development around it, even if the owner makes no additional investment. The value of a site thus is partially independent of the actions of the owner.

The concept of the rent gap, developed by Neil Smith (1987), explains why a zoning change or new investment in the surrounding area can cause a property's value to shoot up. Essentially, the rent gap refers to the difference between the return on the present occupancy or use and the potential

---

2 Parts of this section are drawn from Fainstein (2016).
3 The United States set a precedent during the 1830s when it fell victim to a depression following a speculative property bubble stimulated by easy lending (Sellers, 1994).

return after a change of tenancy or type of use. Smith's (1979) theory of gentrification describes how rapid entry of capital can transform an area virtually overnight, displacing the original residents. David Harvey (1974) shows how the class character of neighbours, rather than simply the quality of the physical environment, determines the price of property. On the other hand, unanticipated problems like floods, terror attacks, changes in taste, and so on can cause the value of a property to plummet.

Despite the risks involved, the appeal of property investment is great. The construction of an apartment building where individual flats are sold separately, or the conversion of a rental building into condominiums, can produce a resale at a multiple of original costs (see Hamnett, Chapter 7, this volume). In the case of rental buildings, whether apartments, factories, or offices, expectations of future increases in value mean that the worth of the building upon resale can greatly exceed the present value of its rent roll. The use of non-recourse loans, which protect the assets of the owner when individual buildings fail to cover the debt on them, reduces individual risk while simultaneously introducing more risk into the system. Non-recourse loans mean that developers have few incentives for caution if financing is available. The extent to which speculation is heightened or dampened responds to state involvement through regulation, subsidization, and land banking. In the current period of neoliberalism, states have encouraged property development and largely withdrawn regulations that would discourage speculation.

In the twentieth century, and continuing to the present, various factors have led to an intensification of speculation. Perhaps most important has been the blurring of the distinction between property and other types of investment. As Mayra Mosciaro and colleagues (Chapter 2, this volume) describe, real estate holdings have become financialized; they now form a significant part of investment portfolios and are traded like any other asset. Syndicalization, real estate investment trusts (REITs), and mortgage derivatives have allowed investors to purchase interests in property without any involvement in its development and management. Property firms themselves may be listed on stock exchanges and traded by individuals and financial institutions.

The distinction between circuits of capital, if it ever existed, has essentially disappeared (Harvey, 1989; Beauregard, 1994). Restless capital – sometimes labelled "hot money" – is constantly seeking outlets. With interest rates at or near all-time lows and disappointing returns in other asset classes, capital is increasingly flowing into real estate, aptly dubbed *"Betongold,"* or "concrete gold," in Germany. Further, the enormous assets of pension funds, insurance pools, and sovereign wealth funds facilitate the construction of megaprojects and encourage the building of extremely expensive high-rise structures (Weber, 2016). Even when overbuilding is predictable, financial institutions continue lending if they cannot identify other, more promising outlets for their capital. As one developer observed, "money is the sine qua non. If you have money, you will build" (quoted in Fainstein, 2001, p. 67). Only after a slump actually occurs do credit markets seize up – then, no matter how worthy the project, no backing is available.

Private investors apply exchange values rather than use values to determine what gets built, the scale of projects, where building takes place, and how the existing building stock is treated (Logan & Molotch, 1987). The array of lenders has greatly broadened as non-bank financial institutions have entered the mortgage market. "Disintermediation," which refers to private developers selling their commercial paper directly rather than relying on banking institutions as primary lenders, broadens the options available to developers. Securitization, global banking, and internet and computer technology (ICT) allow financial specialists to make calculations based on rate of return. Given a range of choices, including purchase of real estate, art, equities, corporate bonds, and so on, the decision by investors to purchase an interest in property (which may be in the form of bonds, limited partnerships, mortgage securities, REITs, and the like) may put the purchaser at many removes from what is actually occurring in a particular place.

Furthermore, the explosion of the market in derivatives, which has allowed bondholders to hedge their purchases of debt instruments that are themselves bought and sold, has increased the amount of capital available to borrowers while introducing a new element of risk into the overall economy. In fact, it was these instruments that caused the global financial crisis of 2007–08:

> A variety of forces created an excess of global savings that, in turn, led to an excess supply of capital seeking higher returns than available in more traditional, secure investments. This meant that investors in mortgage-related securities were increasingly willing to pay a premium to invest in bonds backed by higher risk loans. The resulting "capital-push" nature of higher risk lending markets meant that loan originators were given an incentive to meet the appetite of Wall Street rather than respond to authentic demand from homebuyers and homeowners. (Immergluck, 2015, p. 274)

Megaprojects comprise the forms that potentially can produce the highest profits for developers. These projects typically cater to the needs of office-based businesses, high-income residents, tourism, and leisure services. Luxury residential condominiums are increasingly used as places for the global super-rich to sequester their assets, resulting in the proliferation of "ghost apartments" within major cities. The construction of sports venues (Long, 2014) or concert halls and art museums ("the Bilbao effect") as anchors for projects provides a means to market a city's identity (Plaza, 2008; Hamnett & Shoval, 2003). Renowned architects ("starchitects") often add an aura of glamour to the efforts (Ponzini & Nastasi, 2011). A striking physical similarity characterizes megaprojects, irrespective of the city in which they are located: despite a brief flirtation with postmodernist architecture during the 1990s, the majority of projects consist of glassy towers with little ornamentation, sometimes connected to low-rise buildings intended to produce some variety in scale. Historic preservation of some existing structures aims at providing texture, but the typically massive size of the schemes decontextualizes the projects from the adjacent city. At the same time, they differ in social outcomes and planning processes, reflecting the level of commitment that the host city has towards social equity.

Role of Government

Whether speculative development proceeds unhindered depends on the role of the state. If the state plays a significant role in use and location decisions, other criteria like community benefits may come into play. In the present era of global competition among local governments struggling with straitened resources, public officials see little choice but to compete for investment by lowering the costs of development through subsidies and regulatory relief. Moreover, nothing cheers up a politician more than the opportunity to be photographed putting a shovel into the ground or cutting the ribbon in front of a new project. New buildings constitute a trope for economic expansion, even if the production and jobs within the structure have only moved from somewhere else and do not constitute a net addition to the country's economy. Given the limited instruments at the disposal of local government for stimulating growth, promoting high-end property development offers the most immediate payback (as opposed to, for instance, improving education or building social housing).

Governments have encouraged construction through assuming much of the risk involved in property development. They have issued tax-free bonds, guaranteed loans, granted tax forgiveness, built infrastructure, and offered grants. They may also have loosened various planning restrictions regarding floor area ratios, setbacks, and parking requirements and offered other concessions. In return, developers may provide various forms of planning gain, such as some units of affordable housing, green amenities, or day-care facilities. Justification for the facilitating role of government and dominance by the private sector arises within neoliberal ideology, which claims that marketization produces efficiency, flexibility, and counters the bureaucratic rigidity of government. Where the state plays a more active regulatory role, it may require a percentage of affordable housing units, but the previous large role Western governments played in the direct production of housing for the working class has evaporated. Government has not removed itself from property development, but rather its function has switched from producer to entrepreneur and facilitator (Harvey, 1989).

Beginning in the 1980s, public-private partnerships (PPPs) have become the principal vehicle for the mounting of very large development projects in cities around the world and have been institutionalized through a variety of vehicles (Squires, 1989).[4] Some subsidies and loan guarantees are established by statute and apply automatically; others arise through negotiation. Frequently, semi-autonomous urban development corporations act as agents for government in making deals with private developers. The enterprise zone, originally conceived to jumpstart manufacturing in postcolonial developing countries, has been employed in wealthy countries to establish areas where property developers could escape taxation and regulation (Hall, 1982). Much governmental activity related to property proceeds on an ad hoc basis, with government responding opportunistically to developer proposals.

In the United States and Europe during the post-war years, pressure to clear away slums and blight constituted a further rationale for governmental involvement and resulted in the much-castigated urban renewal programs of the time. Now, in the West, governmental attention mostly falls on disused or vacant sites, where construction activity is not so disruptive or likely to provoke protest (Altshuler & Luberoff, 2003; Diaz Orueta & Fainstein, 2008). These projects in the West typically differ from their predecessors in that they minimize displacement through being located on obsolete industrial and port lands rather than intruding into residential areas.

---

4 Institutionalization of PPPs has a long history. In the nineteenth century, the US government subsidized railroad construction by selling public lands at below-market prices to private rail companies, which in turn profitably resold them. For more than a century, port and turnpike authorities have existed autonomously from normal government operations, providing a predictable framework for private development (for example, the Port of London Authority was established in 1908).

In the less developed world, demolition of occupied structures and their replacement by modernist office towers, expensive residential premises, and public institutions remains common and is justified in the name of slum removal and becoming modern. While such projects physically resemble those in developed countries, their political and economic contexts are quite different. In Western democratic polities with a history of controversy over development programs, many cities faced or continue to face population loss and economic disinvestment. Their governing bodies regard megaprojects as a means to confront the threat of decline and/or reassert their cities' allure and status. By contrast, in cities like Shanghai and Dubai, giant construction schemes symbolize their rise to power. Within Chinese cities, where land sales comprise the principal source of revenue for local governments, finding willing developers is crucial (Ren & Weinstein, 2013). Within Asia, the pattern set by the urban renewal programs of post-war America persists, with widespread demolition of structures housing poor people and small businesses and their replacement by public buildings, expensive residences, hotels, and office towers.

Effects of Speculative Development

Private control of the cityscape means that construction responds to anticipated profits, which skews development towards affluent users and ghettoizes poor people. In all capitalist countries, whether rich or poor, unless the state directly constructs public housing, the desirable parts of cities tend to be beyond the reach of the working class, and segregation of the poor results. In developing countries, concentrations of poverty usually occur on the periphery; in wealthy nations, they may be in the centre, as in many old American cities, or on the edge, as is characteristic of Europe.

Building for low-income residents is only profitable if construction is to a low standard and occupancy is at high levels of crowding. The large-scale development of informal housing in poor countries results from the impossibility of building to code and making money from it. Strong enforcement of housing codes inevitably means that private firms will not construct conforming affordable housing unless they receive subsidies or zoning bonuses. Private control also leads to gentrification, except where rent regulation prevents low-income residents from being priced out (Hamnett, 2003; Lees et al., 2013). Even when gentrification involves the reuse of old buildings rather than new construction, it incorporates speculative gains. In New York, a study showed that poor people were less likely to move from gentrifying neighbourhoods than from homogeneously poor areas, but the stabilizing factor was rent control (Freeman & Frank, 2004); without such regulation, the character of a neighbourhood can change rapidly. Gated communities are another manifestation of speculative property investment that segregates the well-to-do from others, regardless of whether they are centrally or peripherally located (Blakely & Snyder, 1997).

Three Examples: Jersey City, NJ; Donau City, Vienna; Singapore

In both Europe and the United States, PPPs are developing megaprojects on the urban periphery designed to accommodate large-floor-plate offices and high-rise residential structures. Asian cities likewise have sprouted such developments, both centrally and peripherally located. Their sponsors laud them for enhancing the competitiveness of their locations and for producing modern, accessible spaces answering the needs of contemporary, mobile workers and consumers. Critics have condemned them as sterile environments, in contrast to organically developed central areas, and have seen them as symbolizing corporate domination of development (Sennett, 1990, 2018; Kimmelman, 2019).

American property investment tends to be opportunistic, while European development is usually planned, but on both continents borrowed money provides the financial basis for construction. The US case of the Jersey City waterfront development and the European example of Donau City in Vienna, Austria, exemplify the similarities of speculative development but also the differences attributable to stronger state planning in Vienna. Both represent major office-commercial-residential complexes that have grown outside the traditional core over a period of more than thirty years. Singapore, to be discussed later, presents a contrasting case, where the government acts to dampen speculation and to retain gains in value for the public sector.

Both Jersey City and Donau City receive overflow from the pre-existing city centre and offer the advantages of more modern structures and lower costs. Despite their development under the auspices of differing governing institutions with differing conceptions of the role of the state in promoting welfare, the form of the built environment in the two areas is strikingly similar, and profits are largely kept by the private sector. We see their similarity as resulting from the influence in both places of property developers and of the triumph of neoliberal ideology. Both the New York/New Jersey (Jersey City is adjacent to New York City) and Vienna metropolitan areas compete with other cities in their vicinity that are seeking to attract business away from them, and in both places new, large structures are regarded as a means for meeting that competition.

Our discussion proceeds as follows: drawing on interviews with stakeholders and experts and an examination of both public documents and the secondary literature, we use the Jersey City and Donau City developments to reflect upon the complex patterns of variation and convergence that characterize the situations in Europe and the United States. Singapore provides a contrasting example, where direct state investment in housing and public facilities limits the role of private developers. We first recount the history of the projects under examination; then we contrast and evaluate the outcomes of development in terms of its physical and social impacts.[5]

Jersey City

Directly across the Hudson River from downtown Manhattan, Jersey City has mutated from a working class residential quarter surrounded by docks and manufacturing to become a heterogeneous area. A remarkable spurt of construction that began in the mid-1980s transformed the city into one of the nation's larger office centres. Its former planning director described the original government initiatives to stimulate development in this way:

> [It was a] "give away the store" process ... [after] decades of decline. Incentives were necessary to attract private investment in the uncharted land on the other side of the Hudson River [from New York]. New York City worked hard to dissuade companies from relocating, so Jersey City had to secure financial incentives to attract the first wave of private development. (Cotter & Wenger, 2015, p. 221; see also Lawless, 2002)

By 2012, the city could claim 1.27 million square metres (13.7 million square feet) of office space completed and another 418,000 square metres (4.5 million square feet) either approved or proposed, mostly

---

5 Unless otherwise indicated, information on Jersey City is drawn from interviews with Robert D. Cotter, Jersey City Planning Director; Douglas J. Greenfeld, Supervising Planner in the Office of the Mayor of Jersey City; Dan Frohwirth, Director of Real Estate for the Jersey City Economic Development Corporation. In Vienna, interviews were with Robert Schaar, "Wiener Entwicklungsgesellschaft für den Donauraum" (WED AG); Josef Guttmann, Bezirk Donau Stadt; Andrea Eggenbauer, MA 21 Stadt Wien; and Irmgard Taibl, Bürgerinitiative Kaisermühlen. In Singapore, Susan Fainstein served as a consultant to the Centre for Liveable Cities within the Urban Renewal Authority and participated over several years in discussions of planning with numerous actors. The authors wish to acknowledge the helpful and interesting information and insights provided by their informants.

30 Susan S. Fainstein and Johannes Novy

Figure 1.1. Map showing location of Jersey City. Source: Adapted from Google Earth.

along the Hudson River embankment (Jersey City Housing Authority, 2012).[6] Along with the office towers, around 16,000 new housing units and a giant shopping mall were constructed. Subsequently, patches of new development have sprung up away from the waterfront, but they are not of the same intensity. The development conforms to recent concepts of mixed uses as desirable. The new construction, much of which offers spectacular views of the Manhattan skyline, intersperses apartment towers for the relatively well-to-do with high-rise office buildings. The shopping mall houses chain stores, while nearby historic low-rise brownstone neighbourhoods, now occupied by gentrifiers, contain local shops. After a peak population of 316,715 measured in the 1930 Census, Jersey City's population declined to a low of 223,532 in 1980. Since then, however, reflecting its new wealth and the construction of thousands of apartments, population has grown, rising to over 292,000 in 2020 and producing an exceptionally high population density of over 17,000 persons per square mile

---

6 More recent data is not available, as the city seems to have ceased tabulating the amount of space constructed.

Figure 1.2. View of downtown Jersey City. Source: Photo by David Iliff. Licence: CC BY-SA 3.0.

(US Census Bureau, 2021).[7] Despite all the new investment, however, and reflecting the unevenness of development, the city's poverty level remained high, with nearly 19 per cent below the official poverty line in 2018, or 50 per cent more than the percentage for the United States as a whole.

In appearance the area mirrors the office and residential towers of Battery Park City on the Manhattan side of the river. Battery Park City, built over the last thirty-five years, conformed to strict design guidelines, and considerable effort was put into integrating its various elements; the underlying land remains in public ownership (Fainstein, 2001, chap. 8). Jersey City's components are not as integrated, and consequently it has less legibility and is more hostile to pedestrians. Its rather surprising expansion, while symbiotic with accelerated growth in the New York City property market, was generated by real estate entrepreneurs who had not previously worked in urban locations but rather had specialized in suburban, single-family home construction. Despite being separated from Manhattan only by a river, oversight of Jersey City's growth was the responsibility of the jurisdictions of the state of New Jersey and the municipal government of Jersey City, with New York State and City having no say in its development. Instead,

---

7 Jersey City has remarkable ethnic diversity. The most recent estimates of its demographic components show it to be 29 per cent Hispanic, 25 per cent Asian (mostly Indian), 24 per cent Black, and 21 per cent white. Over 40 per cent of the population was foreign born (US Census Bureau, 2021).

the absence of any overriding metropolitan authority caused New York and New Jersey to treat each other as rivals.

Retrospectively, Jersey City's conversion from derelict port and manufacturing area to thriving residential centre appears a natural outcome of New York City's increasing prosperity and limited housing availability during the last thirty years. Nevertheless, it was not an inevitable result of the heated property boom of New York; rather, pressures in New York presented an opportunity seized by a few major developers, who foresaw the possibility of giant profits. In the early 1980s, the Mack-Cali Realty Corporation undertook the conversion and rehabilitation of the giant Penn-Central warehouses into office space, while simultaneously a major bank built a back-office structure on the waterfront. Until then, Jersey City's office structures were relatively small, mid-rise buildings that exclusively served local needs. The bank's identification of Jersey City as a convenient place to locate space-consuming, routine functions spurred other speculative developers to see a future there for modern office and residential space.

The first residential investments, by the LeFrak Company, were in bland high-rise apartment buildings next to the Lincoln Tunnel that connects New Jersey to New York. Next came new office development along the disused waterfront, where Wall Street firms relocated their back offices to much cheaper spaces a short distance from their headquarters sites. Then the LeFrak Company, in partnership with Melvin Simon & Associates, a large developer of suburban shopping centres, launched an even bigger project on a derelict, environmentally degraded site. The company itself planned the entire layout – the role of government was to put in basic infrastructure and grant approvals. Samuel LeFrak, the founder of the firm bearing his name, describes his company's involvement:

> I had an opportunity of buying the land from the US government and developing what I had dreamed about all my life: a perfect balanced city which would be housing, jobs, shopping, all the important elements that were necessary at a price that people could afford to pay. (LeFrak Organization, c. 2007)

Characteristic of new megaprojects throughout the world, the detailed planning described by LeFrak was restricted to the project site rather than being integrated into a comprehensive scheme for the entire city.

A little later, the brownstone movement that swept New York City starting in the 1970s spread to the historic areas of Jersey City, where, as in Brooklyn's Park Slope, handsome low-rise town houses bordered tree-lined streets. Five designated historic districts have almost completely gentrified, and numerous old factory buildings have been recycled into apartments.

This spatial restructuring largely came as a surprise to public officials:

> The local state did not take the lead in identifying promising sites or proposing a plan for development; rather developers saw their opportunities, planned their projects with little coordination, and called on city and state government to provide support. The city government's main contributions were rezoning and facilitating a rapid response to development proposals. The extent of growth, however, was largely unanticipated: There was sort of a master plan for the waterfront ... done around 1973 ... It certainly didn't envision the massive growth we've seen there ... Over the years, we have adopted many diverse redevelopment plans that are the zoning for the area, but they are pretty much piecemeal efforts. (Email communication from Robert D. Cotter, Planning Director, 3 December 2012)

Thus, with minimal planning on the part of the municipality and the pass-through of some funds from the national government under the now-defunct Urban Development Action Grant (UDAG) program,[8] major investments in an area that few foresaw as an attractive address began. In fact, were it not for the scale of the new schemes, it is hard to imagine that businesses, residents, or shoppers would have been willing to go there. In this respect, it resembled London's Canary Wharf development, also constructed on land converted from derelict dockside uses in a peripheral part of the city regarded as extremely unattractive and lower class (Fainstein, 2001, chap. 9). In both places, only a total transformation of the area would have sufficed.

Although, in retrospect, proximity to the Manhattan financial district and excellent existing transportation connections[9] made Jersey

---

8 The UDAG program was launched by the Carter administration in 1978 and terminated by President Reagan in 1989. It offered federal matching funds to cities when private investors were willing to put in a greater amount of their own funds. It provided the template for public-private partnerships whereby government funding "leveraged" a larger sum of private money. LeFrak's Newport residential project received a $40 million grant, the largest that the program had granted at that time (Lawless, 2002, p. 1332).
9 Jersey City was already served by the Port Authority Trans-Hudson (PATH) subway trains that connected it to lower and midtown Manhattan and two expressways that linked it to New York through the Holland Tunnel. In addition, it was fifteen minutes away from Newark International Airport, and later it became connected to other New Jersey waterfront municipalities by light rail.

City appealing – it is only a three minute train ride away – the costs of conversion, the large number of poor immigrant residents, and the unsavoury reputation of the city made investment there extremely risky. Furthermore, within Manhattan itself, the downtown office market was struggling, as financial firms were increasingly seeking midtown locations that offered easier access to suburban Westchester and Long Island (Moss, 2005). Consequently, it was not a foregone conclusion that nearness to Wall Street was an advantage. Other old New Jersey municipalities (such as Bayonne, Elizabeth, and Newark), which also had proximity to New York, did not attract similar levels of interest.

Vienna: Donau City

In contrast to Jersey City, Vienna's Donau City project was sponsored by the Vienna city government, which, like many European municipalities, wanted to attract business investment while leaving its historic core intact (Giffinger & Wimmer, 2005). Located on the left bank of the Danube, the project's origins go back to the 1960s and 1970s. An International Garden Festival in 1963, along with the opening in 1979 of the Vienna International Centre, a building complex hosting the United Nations Office at Vienna (UNOV), as well as numerous infrastructural projects including extensive flood control works, began to change Vienna's relationship to the Danube. For centuries, Vienna had notoriously "turned its back" to the river, despite the latter's importance to its development, but now eyes increasingly looked to the riverfront for new development opportunities.

The site that would later become Donau City, located between the Reichsbrücke, one of Vienna's principal Danube crossings, and the Donaupark, where the above-mentioned Garden Festival had taken place, drew the interest of planners and policymakers. Until the late 1980s, unfavourable economic and demographic conditions prevented construction from beginning, but following the fall of the Iron Curtain in 1989 and the subsequent reordering of Europe, development accelerated. Local leaders initially hoped to fast-track growth by hosting the 1995 World Expo on the riverbank site, but a failed referendum in 1991 caused the city to withdraw its candidacy (Pirhofer & Simmer, 2007, p. 110). Trying to make a virtue out of an enormous public relations fiasco, the city turned to the already existing plans for the site's post-event use and put a newly established development corporation – the "Wiener Entwicklungsgesellschaft für den Donauraum" (WED AG) – in charge of coordinating the further development of the area. Composed of some of Austria's biggest banks and insurance companies, the

Figure 1.3. Map of Vienna. Source: Adapted from Google Earth.

WED AG emerged in the years that followed as a, if not *the*, key actor driving the area's transformation, reflecting the wider political shifts occurring in Vienna at the time. Prior to the 1990s, urban planning and development had been overwhelmingly a public sector affair. "Private initiative was the exception but not the rule in the material production of the city" (Novy et al., 2001, p. 137), and Vienna was synonymous with a "top-down, corporatist form of social-democratic urban governance" (p. 131) centred on a strong Fordist local welfare state. In line with David Harvey's (1989) description of a shift from urban managerialism to entrepreneurialism, this governance model was subject to profound changes in the course of the 1990s. Urban development strategies moved away from a primary focus on social redistribution and collective consumption towards providing favourable financial environments for private capital investment, and governance arrangements became more "fragmented, privatized, opaque and ad-hoc" (Novy et al., 2001, p. 131).

It was in this context that the idea to develop a "second city centre" (Seiß, 2008, p. 17), rivalling London's Canary Wharf or La Défense in Paris, began to take shape. Architects had long dreamed of transforming Vienna into a *"Doppelstadt"* (double city) and were enthused by the prospect to complement Vienna's historic centre with a second, modern core on the other side of the Danube. Elsewhere, the city's notoriously rigid planning and historic preservation guidelines blocked their ambitions: potent architectural gestures, including especially skyscrapers, that could shake off Vienna's reputation as a dreary city stuck in the past and transform it into a state-of-the-art metropolis (Pirhofer & Simmer 2007, p. 111). With this vision in mind, the WED AG commissioned a master plan for developing the site. In 1993, work began on the centrepiece of what was now called Donau City. The 17.4 hectares area would rest on the so-called Donauplatte ("Danube Platform") – a multilevel concrete deck covering large swathes of the riverbank and an adjacent motorway – and would contain a series of buildings and public plazas. In 1995, the deck was completed and, in what critics described as a sweetheart deal, sold to the WED AG. In the same year, the first office high-rise, the Andromeda Tower, went up on it. Other projects, both in Donau City itself or adjacent to it, such as the IZD (Internationales Zentrum Donaustadt) tower, soon followed. Mounting concern arose, however, that public amenities and infrastructure facilities promised by the WED AG when purchasing the site did not materialize, and its overall development fell far short of the high-quality urban environment the master plan had envisioned.

Significantly, the latter was neither legally binding nor very detailed. Instead, it left a lot of matters – for example, details relating to the height and form of buildings or the exact location and mix of uses – to later stages of development. The city government had from the outset taken a "back-seat" position. The WED AG thus dominated its trajectory as general developer, owner of the site since 1995, and negotiator with investors, prospective buyers, and tenants. Sluggish property prices and weak demand in the mid-1990s, meanwhile, meant that the aforementioned investors were often granted additional concessions to help spur development. As a consequence, several projects diverged, sometimes sharply, from the spirit of the original master plan with its emphasis on a broad and fine-grained mix of building types and uses as well as attractive public spaces and circulation routes across the site. While critics lamented the watering down of ambitions and standards for the sake of profit maximization (Seiß, 2008), the WED AG maintained that the scheme had to adapt to changing market conditions.

Following a competition for a new master plan in 2002, the future form of the area became fixed. Clearing the way for greater density, mass, and height to maximize development potential and land values, French architect Dominique Perrault won the competition and proposed to complete the Donau City's core area with an eye-catching pair of high-rises. Perrault's scheme was as spectacular as it was speculative:

spectacular because of its height, with the taller of the two towers to be Austria's tallest building, and speculative in that no prospective buyers or tenants were in place. Only in 2010 did a first anchor tenant commit to it and construction commence. Opening three years later with an occupancy rate of approximately 50 per cent, DC Tower 1 struggled to attract tenants, while DC Tower 2, the smaller of the two towers, remains (at the time of writing) unbuilt. Despite these problems and its failure to greatly improve the environmental character of the development, the WED AG presents the semi-completed scheme as a success – especially following the acquisition of DC Tower 1 by the German banking group DEKA in 2017. Detractors, however, view Donau City as an "example of the real estate market's inability to regulate itself and its unwillingness to even begin to create something like a city" (Seiß, 2017). Further, they regard it as indicating that property developers in Vienna today, as elsewhere, are less concerned with building for the "real property market, [than] for the global financial market" (Seiß, 2017) and consequently operate with different criteria for what constitutes success.

Still, the local government does continue to retain substantial involvement in housing provision. Almost all urban development projects of recent decades include at least some public or publicly subsidized housing units, and Donau City is no exception (see Rumpfhuber, 2012a, 2012b; Rumpfhuber et al., 2012). Hence, there is some truth to the slogan "Wien ist anders" ("Vienna is different") that the city used for years in its tourism campaigns and that Vienna's former secretary for housing and later chancellor of Austria, Werner Faymann, alluded to at a ribbon-cutting ceremony for one of the first housing projects on the site:

> This project illustrates the importance the City of Vienna and the developer, the Donau City Wohnbau AG, ascribe to social housing ... at a time [when] nothing else but private sector–led luxury projects would be possible at similar high-value locations in other large European cities ... Thanks to housing support programs, apartments on the Danube platform will be affordable to average income households. (quoted in OTS [1999]; translation by the authors)

Just how different Vienna truly is, however, remains a matter of debate. While Vienna is celebrated by many as a champion of affordable housing and a beacon of hope in the face of an emergent global crisis of urban housing affordability, the so-called Danube Flats, a new highrise construction slated for the emergent Donau City skyline, reveals an all-too-familiar pattern of urban redevelopment. Situated directly on the water and marketed as "unmistakable and immense," the project will

Figure 1.4. View of Donau City. Source: Robert F. Tobler, Licence CC-BY-SA 4.0.

consist of "600 privately financed flats and investment apartments ... high-end accommodation following international examples – such as in the thriving cities of New York, London, Singapore and Tokyo" (Soravia, n.d.). It was approved through a deal in which developer Soravia obtained development rights in return for a commitment to build around forty social housing units and invest in a school and kindergarten. Soravia may or may not fulfil these commitments, as the developer in early 2019 did not rule out reselling the project prior to construction.

State-Dominated Development: Singapore

Far different from these cases is Singapore, where state-sponsored housing development dominates the planning of the island nation (see Chua, Chapter 9, this volume; Fainstein, 2018). During the decades from the 1960s to the early 1990s, the government acquired most of the island's land, much of it already covered with low-rise structures, providing very low compensation to owners. The government's view was that landowners should not enjoy the benefits of increases in land prices that had accrued over the years. "It counseled the landowners to see this as their contribution to the welfare of society" (Chua, 2011, p. 44). Lee Kuan Yew, independent Singapore's founding father, spoke these words: "I saw no reason why private landowners should profit from an increase in land value brought about by economic development and the infrastructure paid for with public funds" (Lee, 2000, p. 119). The government's complete control of the polity allowed it to override any objections from landowners. Anne Haila, a Finnish scholar who has studied Singapore, notes the similarities between Singapore's land use regime and the ideas of Henry George, who argued for a tax that would confiscate all speculative gains from property ownership (Haila, 2016, pp. 76–7). Although Singapore, through its state-owned enterprises and its use of sovereign wealth funds, is an entrepreneurial state par excellence, within the property sector it remains a managerial entity (Harvey 1989).

Over 80 per cent of Singapore's resident population lives in Housing and Development Board (HDB) flats.[10] The HDB regulates the supply of new flats to ensure that the resale market does not become so tight as to cause a jump in prices producing windfall gains for sellers. Since 95 per cent of HDB households own their own flats, any speculative gain accrues to them rather than to entities within the development industry. Control of the buildings as well as the land under them remains with the HDB. Occupants are under substantial restrictions, as the HDB enforces stringent regulations upon them. Residents cannot sell their units for the first five to eight years of occupancy; they are limited in whom they can sell them to, as buildings are required to maintain an ethnic balance proportionate to the ethnic distribution of the entire Singapore population;[11] and they must abide by HDB rules that govern the management of the buildings. While some resident-owners have enjoyed speculative profits through reselling their units, increases in value have largely been in line with the general rate of inflation. In addition, the government provides a grant to cover the net deficit of the program. Although private real estate firms do build speculative housing, much of it intended for the very rich, they are allocated only a limited portion of the island's land area. Business premises are mostly privately owned and developed by speculative builders. Some gentrification is occurring in HDB structures within the most desirable locations, and the government has stopped constructing new HDB apartments in the central area, where speculative private development

---

10 About one third of Singapore's population consists of foreigners, who do not have the right to purchase HDB units.
11 In 1989, concerned that ethnic concentrations were forming in HDB complexes, the government established the Ethnic Integration Policy (EIP), which set limits on the maximum proportions that each ethnic group could encompass within each neighbourhood and block (Lee, 2010).

continues. Nevertheless, the state is able to dampen the property cycle for both residential and commercial investment through regulating the supply of land available.

Not only does the state act to prevent speculation and provide for a fairly even distribution of desirable residences across the city, but it insures the development of community facilities available to the entire population. Expansion to peripheral areas is in accordance with a planning doctrine that combines the garden city ideas of Ebenezer Howard with Le Corbusier's Radiant City. New developments are connected to transit, and all encompass large "hawkers' centres" and "wet markets," where inexpensive food, both cooked and uncooked, is available, as well as community centres, schools, libraries, shopping areas, and cinemas. Despite high population density, green space is ample and accessible. Except in conservation areas of historic structures, high-rise is the norm, and its visual impact is mitigated by lavish landscaping.

Conclusion

The commonality among all the cases described is speculative construction of most commercial premises (office, retail, hotel). They differ in the extent to which affordable housing is built and subsidies for lower-income occupants exist, with Singapore devoting more support to affordable housing than the others. The threat of severe slump varies among them, with Jersey City being the most vulnerable because government does not restrict construction. In American cities, if builders can obtain a loan, then they will build and typically can do so "as of right" (that is, if the project conforms to the zoning, it does not require planning permission). Limits on land availability in Vienna and Singapore mean that huge overhangs of vacant space are unlikely. In all three cities, private developers build for the affluent; public-private partnerships are the institutional form of speculative development; building appearances are similar; and the texture characteristic of old cities is lacking. In Singapore, the existence of "ghost apartments," owned by wealthy individuals who rarely inhabit them, has become increasingly common. The existence of the HDB does not wholly prevent gentrification in Singapore, but it is increasing much more quickly in Jersey City and Vienna.

In summary, the physical form of the speculative city does not vary much from place to place, and property speculation inevitably produces uneven development. When property markets are hot, small businesses and low-income people are pushed out. In slumps, vacancies and abandonment take hold. Control of the property cycle and the availability of affordable housing, however, differ according to the prominence of the state role. PPPs by definition incorporate private interests, but the extent to which the private sector dominates varies (Fainstein, 2016). In those places where the state owns the land, the potential for state control of development is much greater – although, as shown by Yunpeng Zhang and Shenjing He's depiction of development in Shanghai (Chapter 4, this volume), the state itself may act as a risk-taking entrepreneur. All property development is speculative in the sense that its occupancy depends on the level of demand at the time of completion. The state, however, has the power to regulate the supply of land to reduce the speculative element. Whether greater state involvement produces better outcomes depends on various factors: the existence of sensible design guidelines, the ideology defining the state role, the fiscal situation, among other considerations. Greater state involvement offers the potential for more generally equitable development but no guarantee.

REFERENCES

Altshuler, A.A., & Luberoff, D.E. (2003). *Mega-projects: The changing politics of urban public investment*. Brookings.
Beauregard, R.A. (1994). Capital switching and the built environment: United States, 1970–89. *Environment and Planning A: Economy and Space*, 26(5), 715–32. https://doi.org/10.1068/a260715
Blakely, E.J., & Snyder, M.G. (1997). *Fortress America*. Brookings.
Chua, B.H. (2011). Singapore as model: Planning innovations, knowledge experts. In A. Roy & A. Ong (Eds.), *Worlding cities: Asian experiments and the art of being global* (pp. 29–54). Wiley-Blackwell.
Cotter, R.D., & Wenger, J. (2015). Jersey City on the rise. http://global.ctbuh.org/resources/papers/download/2462-jersey-city-on-the-rise.pdf
Diaz Orueta, F., & Fainstein, S.S. (2008). The new mega-projects: Genesis and impacts. *International Journal of Urban and Regional Research*, 32(4), 759–67. https://doi.org/10.1111/j.1468-2427.2008.00829.x
Fainstein, S.S. (2001). *The city builders* (Revised ed.). University Press of Kansas.
Fainstein, S.S. (2016). Financialisation and justice in the city: A commentary. *Urban Studies*, 53(7), 1503–8. https://doi.org/10.1177/0042098016630488
Fainstein, S.S. (2018). State domination in Singapore's public-private partnerships. *Journal of Urban Affairs*, 43(2), 270–87. https://doi.org/10.1080/07352166.2017.1406787
Freeman, L., & Frank, B. (2004). Gentrification and displacement: New York City in the 1990s. *Journal of the American Planning Association*, 70(1), 39–52. https://doi.org/10.1080/01944360408976337

George, H. (1912). *Progress and poverty*. Doubleday, Page & Co. http://www.econlib.org/library/YPDBooks/George/grgPP27.html

Giffinger, R., & Wimmer, H. (2005). Cities between competition and cooperation in Central Europe. In R. Giffinger (Ed.), *Competition between cities in Central Europe: Opportunities and risks of cooperation* (pp. 6–19). Road.

Haila, A. (2016). *Urban land rent: Singapore as a property state*. Wiley-Blackwell.

Hall, P. (1982). Enterprise zones: A justification. *International Journal of Urban and Regional Research*, 6(3), 416–21. https://doi.org/10.1111/j.1468-2427.1982.tb00389.x

Hamnett, C. (2003). Gentrification and the middle-class remaking of inner London, 1961–2001. *Urban Studies*, 40(12), 2401–26. https://doi.org/10.1080/0042098032000136138

Hamnett, C., & Shoval, N. (2003). Museums as "flagships" of urban development. In L.M. Hoffman, D. Judd, & S.S. Fainstein (Eds.), *Cities and visitors* (pp. 219–36). Blackwell.

Harvey, D. (1974). Class-monopoly rent, finance capital and the urban revolution. *Regional Studies*, 8(3–4), 239–55. https://doi.org/10.1080/09595237400185251

Harvey, D. (1989). From managerialism to entrepreneurialism: The transformation in urban governance in late capitalism. *Geografiska Annaler. Series B. Human Geography*, 71(1), 3–17. https://doi.org/10.1080/04353684.1989.11879583

Immergluck, D. (2015). A look back: What we now know about the causes of the US mortgage crisis. *International Journal of Urban Sciences*, 19(3), 269–85. https://doi.org/10.1080/12265934.2015.1044460

Jersey City Housing Authority. (2012). Retrieved 3 September 2017 from *Statistics* http://www.jcha-gov.us/sites/sites.aspx.

Kimmelman, M. (2019, 14 March). Hudson Yards is Manhattan's biggest, newest, slickest gated community. Is this the neighborhood New York deserves? *New York Times*. https://www.nytimes.com/interactive/2019/03/14/arts/design/hudson-yards-nyc.html

Lawless, P. (2002). Power and conflict in pro-growth regimes: Tensions in economic development in Jersey City and Detroit. *Urban Studies*, 39(8), 1329–46. https://doi.org/10.1080/00420980220142664

Lee, H.L. (2010, 26 January). Singapore to keep HDB flats affordable. [Address by Prime Minister Lee Hsien Loong to the International Housing Conference]. Government of Singapore, Government Monitor. https://www.pmo.gov.sg/Newsroom/address-prime-minister-lee-hsien-loong-gala-dinner-international-housing-conference

Lee, K.Y. (2000). *From third world to first, the Singapore story: 1965–2000*. Marshall Cavendish.

Lees, L., Slater, T., & Wyly, E. (2013). *Gentrification*. Routledge.

LeFrak Organization. (c. 2007). 20th anniversary of Newport film. Retrieved 31 July 2017 from http://www.newportnj.com/overview/history

Logan, J.R, & Molotch, H.L. (1987). *Urban fortunes*. University of California Press.

Long, J.G. (2014). *Public-private partnerships for major league sports facilities*. Routledge.

Mills, D.E. (1980). Market power and land development timing. *Land Economics*, 56(1), 10–20. https://doi.org/10.2307/3145825

Moss, M. (2005). The redevelopment of Lower Manhattan: The role of the city. In J. Mollenkopf (Ed.), *The contentious city* (pp. 95–111). Russell Sage Foundation.

Novy, A., Redak, V., Jäger, J., & Hamedinger, A. (2001). The end of Red Vienna: Recent ruptures and continuities in urban governance. *European Urban and Regional Studies*, 8(2), 131–44. https://doi.org/10.1177/096977640100800204

OTS. (1999, 12 March). Wohnungsübergabe im wohnpark Donaucity. [Press release]. www.ots.at/presseaussendung/OTS_19990312_OTS0098/wohnungsuebergabe-im-wohnpark-donaucity

Pirhofer, G., & Simmer, K. (2007). *Pläne für Wien. Theorie und praxis der Wiener stadtplanung von 1945 bis 2005*. Stadt Wien.

Plaza, B. (2008). On some challenges and conditions for the Guggenheim Museum Bilbao to be an effective economic re-activator. *International Journal of Urban and Regional Research*, 32(2), 506–17. https://doi.org/10.1111/j.1468-2427.2008.00796.x

Ponzini, D., & Nastasi, M. (2011). *Starchitecture*. Umberto Allemandi.

Ren, X., & Weinstein, L. (2013). Urban governance, mega-projects, and scalar transformations in China and India. In T. Roshan Samara, S. He, & G. Chen (Eds.), *Locating right to the city in the Global South* (pp. 107–26). Routledge.

Rumpfhuber, A. (2012a). Introduction: The Vienna model of housing provision in times of austerity. *dérive, Zeitschrift für Stadtforschung*, 46, 3–9. http://www.iut.nu/wp-content/uploads/2017/03/The-Vienna-Model-of-Housing-Provision-in-Times-of-Austerity.pdf

Rumpfhuber, A. (2012b). Vienna's housing apparatus and its contemporary challenges: Superblock turned Überstadt. *dérive, Zeitschrift für Stadtforschung*, 46, 25–9. https://derive.at/texte/vienna-s-housing-apparatus-and-its-contemporary-challenges-superblock-turned-uberstadt/

Rumpfhuber, A., Klein, M., & Kolmayr, G. (2012). Almost all right: Vienna's social housing provision. *Architectural Design*, 82(4), 88–93. https://doi.org/10.1002/ad.1435

Seiß, R. (2008). *Wer baut Wien? Hintergründe und motive der stadtentwicklung Wiens seit 1989*. Anton Pustet.

Seiß, R. (2017, 25 August). Grosses Theater an der Wien oder die architektonische abschaffung der stadt. *Neue Züricher Zeitung*. https://www.nzz.ch/feuilleton/

donau-city-grosses-theater-an-der-wien-oder-die-architektonische-abschaffung-der-stadt-ld.1312402

Sellers, C. (1994). *The market revolution: Jacksonian America, 1815–1846*. Oxford University Press.

Sennett, R. (1990). *The conscience of the eye*. Knopf.

Sennett, R. (2018). *Building and dwelling*. Farrar, Straus and Giroux.

Smith, N. (1979). Toward a theory of gentrification: A back to the city movement by capital, not people. *Journal of the American Planning Association*, 45(4), 538–48. https://doi.org/10.1080/01944367908977002

Smith, N. (1987). Gentrification and the rent gap. *Annals of the Association of American Geographers*, 77(3), 462–5. https://doi.org/10.1111/j.1467-8306.1987.tb00171.x

Soravia. (n.d.) Ein neues landmark an der Donau. https://www.soravia.at/project/danubeflats

Squires, G.D. (Ed.). (1989). *Unequal partnerships*. Rutgers University Press.

US Census Bureau. (2021). QuickFacts, Jersey City, New Jersey. https://www.census.gov/quickfacts/jerseycitycitynewjersey

Weber, R. (2016). *From boom to bubble: How finance built the new Chicago*. University of Chicago Press.

2 The Financialization of Urban Redevelopment: Speculation and Public Land in Porto Maravilha, Rio de Janeiro

MAYRA MOSCIARO, ALVARO PEREIRA, AND MANUEL B. AALBERS

Introduction

There is a long debate in urban studies on the role of real estate in capitalist development. Real estate plays a central role in the urban studies sub-literatures on growth machines and coalitions, capital switching and the spatio-temporal fix, entrepreneurialism and neoliberalism, megaprojects and starchitecture, and more recently, financialization and assetization. We will not try to summarize these literatures here, but rather focus on three key contributions relevant to our argument.

First, although real estate investment is more than a "kind of last-ditch hope for finding productive uses for rapidly overaccumulating capital" (Harvey, 1985, p. 20), one of the roles of real estate is that it is frequently considered a safe haven for capital accumulated in other economic sectors (Fernandez & Aalbers, 2016). Real estate is an investment channel in its own right (Aalbers, 2007; Beauregard, 1994; Charney, 2001; Fainstein, 2001; Feagin, 1987; Haila, 1991) that competes for financing in the general capital market. Actors in financial markets move capital from low-yielding products or places to higher yielding products or places (Leitner, 1994).

Second, changes in contemporary economies and societies, including urban economies and societies, are increasingly debated in terms of financialization. An inclusive definition of financialization would be the following: "the increasing dominance of financial actors, markets, practices, measurements, and narratives, at various scales, resulting in a structural transformation of economies, firms (including financial institutions), states and households" (Aalbers, 2017). Financialization demands that commodities become more liquid, enabling them to be compared to other investments and traded as such. Investors increasingly conceptualize real estate investments as "just another asset class"

(Van Loon & Aalbers, 2017). Land is key to the development of financialized capitalism, not only in an urban context but also in rural contexts, performing both coordinating and transformative roles in the transition from industrial to financial capitalism (Harvey, 1982; Kaika & Ruggiero, 2016).

Third, as a result of the two trends above, not only real estate but also the underlying land is increasingly treated as a financial asset. In some cases, the development of real estate is seemingly unnecessary as land can be traded as a financial asset without the intention of development (Savini & Aalbers, 2016). Both land and real estate are commodities in tension. The risk of investment in the production of urban space is related to the fact that this commodity is immobile but today tradable on global markets as a liquid asset (Aalbers, 2008; Gotham, 2006; Rutland, 2010). Real estate properties have become one of the major commodities that strengthen corporations' portfolios and increase their capacity to leverage (Savini & Aalbers, 2016). Furthermore, cities are increasingly accommodating real estate development as an attractive financial asset that can compete with other investments and is expected to fuel economic growth (Hebb & Sharma, 2014; Molotch, 1976; Tasan-Kok, 2010; Weber, 2015).

In this context, local governments may be acting based more on "potential" than "need" (Van Gent & Boterman, 2019), reminiscent of a wider shift from urban managerialism to urban entrepreneurialism (Harvey, 1989). The state, and the local state in particular, can of course act under multiple guises. It may be a regulator, facilitator, or sponsor of real estate development – often more than one at the same time. Politically, decision-making processes have moved largely into "the 'in-between' spaces of governance that exist outside, alongside or in-between the formal statutory scales of government" (Haughton et al., 2013, p. 220), where private and public technocrats operate outside democratic control (Oosterlynck & Swyngedouw, 2010; Raco, 2014; Vainer, 2011). Building on Agamben's (2005) work on "states of exception," we can think of the spaces created through regulatory frameworks to be *outside* of the "normal" spaces of regulation as "spaces of exception."

Bringing these debates together, we can see financialization as a specific current within entrepreneurial urbanism leading to a situation in which "entrepreneurial strategies are increasingly realized through financially mediated means and in conjunction with credit market actors, agencies, and intermediaries" (Peck & Whiteside, 2016, p. 5). We are now in a situation where municipal budgets increasingly rely on creative financial engineering, for instance by monetizing future tax income from urban redevelopment and infrastructure (Aalbers, 2020;

Weber, 2010). It is sometimes argued, either explicitly or implicitly, that these developments are typical of cities in the Global North or, more specifically, North America and Western Europe. So-called peripheries within the Global North as well as the entire Global South are then considered to be less financialized or not financialized at all, whether for reasons of political instability, poverty, the underdevelopment of financial markets, or because real estate investment is considered too risky or insecure to function as a financial asset.

This chapter will discuss the case of Porto Maravilha in Rio de Janeiro. It will serve as an illustration of the financialization of the real estate and urban governance in Brazil. The Porto Maravilha project intends to redevelop an area of 5 million square metres (500 hectares) near the city's central business district (CBD). When looking into a project of this magnitude, many aspects are worth investigating. Our main interest in this chapter is to look into the use of an urban redevelopment instrument, called Urban Operation, and a financial product, called Certificate of Additional Building Potential (CEPAC[1]), which consists of a municipally issued tradable non-interest yielding asset, an urban planning and financial market tool facilitating and sponsoring the financialized speculation of public land. The use of CEPACs in Urban Operations can be seen as a funding scheme similar to both tax increment financing (TIF), an instrument that allows municipalities to raise upfront cash for financing urban improvements (see, for example, Weber, 2010), and tax anticipation notes (TANs), a similar, but short-term scheme used in the United States, issued by municipalities or states as a way to upfront funds (Weber & Goddeeris, 2007). This new urban redevelopment scheme that had been pioneered by the city of Sao Paulo was incorporated into national urban policy regulations with the enactment of the City Statute of 2001. It is not a pattern that can be witnessed throughout Brazil, but we see parallel developments in Belo Horizonte (Canettieri, 2017) and Curitiba (Neto & Moreira, 2013; Stroher, 2017), among other big cities. But even if we take Porto Maravilha as a case in and of itself, rather than as a representative example of such processes in Brazil, it still articulates national and international trends through one of the largest development projects in the world, representing how the built environment is also becoming increasingly financialized outside the Global North.

In the Brazilian urban studies literature, the policy of Urban Operations is considered to be one representing neoliberal managerial urban

---

[1] CEPAC is the abbreviation for Certificado de Potencial Adicional de Construção, the name of this financial asset in Portuguese.

governance strategies (Carlos, 2001; Fix, 2003; Massonetto, 2003; Siqueira, 2014). Up until now, Porto Maravilha is the largest and most expensive representation of this policy instrument. There have been several attempts to "revitalize" the area since the 1980s, all of them unable to trigger major transformations. In a changing political environment, the City of Rio de Janeiro implemented an urban planning strategy that incorporated a novel set of financial engineering tools.

Different from previous attempts, the ongoing project was entirely conceived by a group of private real estate developers. Their proposal not only included a comprehensive urban renewal plan but also the institutional arrangement and financial engineering that should be adopted. The city only needed to approve it and create the legal and official structures to begin the works.

The backbone of Porto Maravilha consists of three basic elements. First was the adoption of the Urban Operation financing scheme, meaning that the necessary capital for the completion of the project would come from the sale of CEPACs. Second, public land had to be assembled as a resource for investment (Li, 2014) in order to attract developers and investors to the project, since public plots represent around 75 per cent of the land that could be developed. The third element only became known after the auction of the CEPACs. The monopolistic buyer of the CEPACs is a federal public fund, called *Fundo de Garantia do Tempo de Serviço* (FGTS). The complex web of relations, capital, and interests that needed to be articulated in order to put the project into motion will be discussed in the next sections.

In order to reveal the financial structure and rationale behind Porto Maravilha, this chapter relies on multiple sources. We analysed regulations and official documents from the Porto Maravilha Urban Operation. As this is an ongoing intervention, new regulations and official documents became available during the data gathering phase of our study (2013–17). Another useful source of information was in-depth, semi-structured expert interviews with seven key actors, including managers, directors, and CEOs of CDURP (*Companhia de Desenvolvimento Urbano da Região Portuária*) and other institutions directly related to the project (2014 and 2016). In our analysis, we constructed a narrative that brings together these different documents and interviews in order to understand the workings of the Urban Operation and, in particular, the CEPACs.

This chapter is structured in the following way. The next section will contextualize the Porto Maravilha area. Then, the concepts of Urban Operation and CEPAC will be explained in depth. The fourth section will look into the financial engineering behind Porto Maravilha. Finally, some concluding remarks will shed light on the speculative mechanism created to foster major urban projects in Brazil. Furthermore, we will try to make sense of the underlying rationalities that support this financialized pattern of urban space production and to understand how these "spaces of exception" impact the broader city development.

A New Urban Frontier in the Old Harbour of Rio de Janeiro

Porto Maravilha (Wonderful Port) is a project that intends to redevelop 5 million square metres of space in the Port of Rio de Janeiro (see Figure 2.1). According to the goals presented in the official discourse, the aim is to develop a mixed-use neighbourhood that will bring new life to the area. Corporate AAA towers, luxury housing, services, and tourist attractions will be developed side by side in order to change the urban environment within this neglected portion of the city. The envisaged interventions to transform the area are very broad, ranging from basic infrastructure provision to the development of large office towers, alongside luxury apartment blocks, museums, shopping malls, and a set of new touristic venues.

Two of the key selling points of the project are its territorial scale and the claim that it will bring new life not just to the area but to the city as a whole. The size of the project is used as a central marketing device to attract investors. The project includes many infrastructural improvements, including 70 kilometres of new streets, 17 kilometres of cycling lanes, and 4 kilometres of traffic tunnels, a light rail network, and cable cars to Morro da Providência (a favela in the middle of the area). All these infrastructural investments are paramount to the development of the project, since the area has been neglected for decades.

The goal of this section is not to provide a vast historical account of the area, but to contextualize and present the basis of what is happening today in Rio's port area. The port of Rio has suffered serious setbacks since the beginning of the twentieth century. The story is not that different from many other port cities around the world, but some peculiarities of this case are relevant to understand how the project was conceived.

In the first decades of the twentieth century, Rio went through a major reform of its downtown area, including the port. Together with other symbols of the colonial past, the old port experienced a comprehensive modernization process. The works promoted in the area included the rectification of the coastline, which involved the construction of landfills on the Guanabara Bay. The federal government, responsible for redesigning the coast, became the owner of the plots in the newly created areas along the docks. This arrangement set the current land ownership

Figure 2.1. Perimeter of Porto Maravilha. Rio's main central business district is located southeast of Porto Maravilha and west of Santos Dumont airport. Source: Adapted from Google Earth by the authors.

structure in the port, where the federal government is a major actor. The specificity of the local land market is a key point to understand the financial engineering of the Porto Maravilha redevelopment project, as will be discussed below.

For a long time, this area was part of one of the most important industrial and logistics complexes in the country. However, it gradually lost its importance. First, the port infrastructure set up in the early twentieth century is no longer compatible with current demands, and very few interventions have happened since. Second, Rio's port has progressively lost its prominence with the development of other ports in Brazil.

The growing obsolescence of the port, associated with the land use and ownership structure, set favourable conditions for a comprehensive urban regeneration project. First, land was relatively abundant and cheap due to the economic decay of the area. Second, the vast majority of the plots inside the perimeter of intervention were distributed in large parcels, mostly belonging to one of the three governmental levels of the Brazilian administrative structure (municipal, state, and federal). This land ownership structure reduced transaction costs, since it prevented developers from having to deal with a multitude of small private owners, a common feature in regeneration projects promoted in or near urban centres. The concentration of land in a few hands facilitated transactions. For example, the municipal government could directly lobby the federal government to ease its access to strategic plots. Moreover, the fact that the three governmental levels were committed to the success of this project made them willing to relinquish their properties below market value, when necessary. As is also mentioned by Susan Fainstein and Johannes Novy (Chapter 1, this volume), "the potential for state control of development is much greater" if the state owns the land. However, it is important to mention that, in the case of Porto Maravilha, this sort of negotiation was only possible because there was an atypical convergence of interests and alliances between the municipality, the state, and federal authorities when Porto Maravilha started in 2009. In a different context, public land could have become an obstacle for real estate development.

The cityscape of this area is composed of many empty warehouses and abandoned public sites. There are also many smaller properties, used as houses or for small businesses. In addition, people who used to work in the docks and ship crews have inhabited this area since colonial times. The concentration of people related to the naval industry (sailors, low-skilled workers, prostitutes, urban slaves, and so on) contributed to the creation of the area's bad reputation in other parts of the city. The arrival of poor residents and marginalized social groups was intensified in the wake of a huge modernization process inspired by Haussmann's reforms in Paris at the beginning of the twentieth century (Abreu, 1997). The aggressive interventions in the central area of Rio resulted in massive displacement. As a result, many people who had lost their homes moved to peripheral neighbourhoods near the city centre, including the port area. The favela that is currently known as Morro da Providência received many of the displaced affected by the early twentieth century reforms. This area used to be known as Morro da Favela in the nineteenth century, but the place-specific name became genericized once this sort of informal settlement became more common in Rio (Abreu, 2014; Valladares, 2000).

The stigma of the port area was aggravated in the twentieth century as the city started to expand southwards. Middle and upper middle class groups left the city centre and its surrounding residential neighbourhoods in search of "better" and "cleaner" neighbourhoods (Abreu, 1997, 2014), leaving the downtown area to poorer inhabitants. According to the latest Census, 5,000 people live in Morro da Providência. However, due to the recurrent improvement reforms that have been taking place in the favela since the early 2000s, it is estimated that at least one-third of the residents has been, or is, at risk of being displaced (Faulhaber & Azevedo, 2015; Sanchez & Broudehoux, 2013). CDURP estimated that, in 2012, 30,000 people were residing within the Urban Operation perimeter. Regardless, in the imaginary of many of the city's inhabitants, the neighbourhoods situated within the project's perimeter barely exist; many people assume it is a completely abandoned place that should be reintegrated into the city. The municipality is using this imaginary to develop a discourse in which a comprehensive intervention such as Porto Maravilha is necessary in order to reincorporate this valuable and historically rich area into the city. One of the city's chief urban planners, during a presentation of the project, stressed that Porto Maravilha is not a new frontier; he claimed that it is downtown Rio, as if to say that people just do not know it, and therefore the project serves to reclaim the area for the city.

Even though this urban planner claims "frontier" is not the right term, what can be observed from the official discourses is exactly the opposite. The status of a deprived area, together with the discourse that this is a natural area of expansion of Rio's central business district, composes the "urban frontier" picture portrayed by Neil Smith (1996). According to Smith, the urban frontier imagery perceives the inner-city population as a natural element of their physical surroundings, an element of wilderness in opposition to civilization: "The frontier discourse serves to rationalize and legitimate a process of conquest, whether in the eighteenth-century and nineteen-century West, or in the late twentieth-century inner-city" (p. xv). Despite the managerial discourse claiming there is no frontier, this image is very clear in the political discourse, as can be confirmed by the following quote from Eduardo Paes, the former mayor of Rio, who implemented the project:

> Our focus is the port area. Rio de Janeiro has always fled going west. Is the center degraded? Go to Copacabana. If it's over, go to Ipanema, then Leblon. Afterwards, they invented Barra da Tijuca. Now, for the first time in history, there is a willingness to return to the center, to revitalize an area of 5 million square meters ... *The government is looking for new frontiers, so we created Porto Maravilha.* (Pereira, 2015, p. 164; our translation, emphasis added)

Even though the former mayor seems to present the project as a unique and innovative strategy, the goal to redevelop this area is not new. Over the past decades, a series of intentions to "revitalize" this part of the city have been considered. However, only in 2009 was a particular conjunction of favourable conditions achieved. With the alignment of the different governmental interests and the country's economic boom, the Porto Maravilha project could rapidly be put in motion. It took three years for the project's structure to be defined, implemented, and financed, allowing construction and interventions to begin, an unusually fast development for a project of this size.

The regulatory framework behind Porto Maravilha was central to the plan's rapid implementation. It is mainly based on the combination of an Urban Operation, a public-private partnership to build urban infrastructure and operate public services, and the creation of a company with the specific purpose of coordinating the implementation of the project. Taking advantage of experiences previously tested in other cities and further developing them, this regulatory framework allowed the coordination of public and private agents' efforts and the gathering of a critical mass of capital to kick-start the envisaged transformations in the area. In the next section, we will provide a brief overview of the history of Urban Operations in the country and then explain the specific arrangement for Porto Maravilha.

Urban Operations: A New Pattern of Urban Redevelopment

Urban Operations have become an emblematic regulatory tool employed by large Brazilian cities to promote urban redevelopment in the context of the alleged fiscal retrenchment of the state. The general mechanism behind an Urban Operation consists of the financing and implementation of a set of improvements within a delineated area in the city through the sale of additional development rights inside its perimeter. The acquisition of additional development rights is done through the purchase of tradable non-interest yielding assets issued by the municipal government, known as CEPACs.

The CEPAC is fundamentally a title of fictitious capital issued by the state, in which it capitalizes on future expectations. It does not consist of a public debt title that would give the holder the right to claim interest or future revenue streams. But it is an asset, which can only generate the envisaged returns for an investor if there is market demand for it and while the Urban Operation lasts.[2] The valorization of these assets is ultimately dependent upon the increase of real estate prices within the perimeter. The issuance of CEPACs is a way of anticipating virtual revenues that would be collected in the future if a market demand for the purchase of additional development rights in the area actually existed. By capitalizing upon future expectations, the government raises

---

2 The law that creates an Urban Operation also defines a time frame in which the exceptional urban conditions applied to its perimeter will last. If a CEPAC ends up not being employed within this period, its holder will not recover the investment that was made to purchase it.

upfront cash and uses it to foster the demand for CEPACs by investing these resources in a way that results in the effective increase of real estate prices.

The first attempts to promote large-scale urban interventions based on this mechanism can be traced back to the beginning of the 1990s, when a renewal project for an area in downtown Sao Paulo was launched. However, the Urban Operation Anhangabaú, created in 1991 by a left-wing municipal government, did not thrive (Fix, 2003). The first effective experience involving its use only took place in 1995, when Sao Paulo's municipal government, then controlled by a right-wing coalition, launched the Urban Operation Faria Lima. Contrasting with the preceding case, which was an urban project of moderate territorial scale located inside an area that had previously faced economic decline, the Urban Operation Faria Lima consisted of a huge intervention project located in an area already targeted by high-end real estate developers. While the Anhangabaú project intended to offset current trends in the real estate market and foster reinvestment in the inner city, the Faria Lima project was conceived to accelerate developments in an area that was already a main focus of real estate activities, illustrating the trend "from need to potential" under entrepreneurial governance, as discussed in the introductory section.

The rising importance of Urban Operations as a model of urban governance has tempted Fix (2001, 2009) to see them as a contemporary Brazilian expression of "growth machines" (Logan & Molotch, 1987). The use of this regulatory tool has been diffused to other locations of market interest within the city of Sao Paulo as well as to other state capitals and some medium-sized cities. It would be precipitous, however, to present Urban Operations as a generalized pattern of urban regulation in Brazilian cities. Not only do Urban Operations merely exist in a limited number of cities, they are also limited to areas that fulfil a very specific set of conditions, more spaces of exception than spaces of generalizability. It is this specific set of conditions to which we now turn.

Since Urban Operations are regulated by the City Statute (Federal Law no. 10.257/2001), their implementation requires the approval of a specific law by the local government defining some of the main aspects. This law addresses issues like the perimeter of the intervention, the zoning rules applied inside it, the aggregate stocks of additional development rights, the conditions for negotiating these rights, the general guidelines for the improvement program, and the basic governance framework to manage the project – all things that set the Urban Operation apart from general urban development regulations.

The establishment of relatively flexible zoning rules inside the perimeter of the Urban Operation is one of the key elements of its financial engineering. In a general sense, this mechanism works as follows. The zoning rules applicable to the Urban Operation define basic and maximum floor area ratios (FARs). A developer is allowed to carry on a project in which the total built area does not exceed the basic development rights, defined by multiplying the plot's size by the FAR. Then comes the innovation: projects that exceed the basic development rights are admissible, as long as the builder purchases additional development rights. The total of additional development rights cannot exceed a certain limit, defined by a sort of "FAR+." In this case, the builder is supposed to purchase additional development rights to meet the difference between the FAR and the FAR+.

The Urban Operation's law defines the total amount of CEPACs that can be issued along its implementation. It also sets different parameters for the conversion of CEPACs into development rights, establishing their spatial distribution inside the project area. Generally, these ratios are more permissive for residential projects than for commercial and other kinds of developments. In a hypothetical example, one single CEPAC can be converted into 1 square metre of additional building right in the case of a commercial project located in Sector A, or 1.5 square metres in a residential project in the same Sector A, or 2 square metres in a commercial project located in Sector B, or 3 square metres in a residential project in Sector B, and so on.

The CEPACs are issued by the municipal government and sold through public auctions carried out at the stock exchange. These financial assets are tradable securities that can be bought by, and resold to, anyone, without necessarily being attached to a specific project. An investor, whose purpose is trading in a secondary market rather than using them to get a project approved, can also purchase them. Often CEPACs are sold gradually. Cities organize successive auctions in which they sell a certain amount of CEPACs that would allow them to raise funds to accomplish a certain step of the redevelopment project. The issuance of the CEPACs and the management of the Urban Operations are monitored by the *Comissão de Valores Mobiliários* (Securities and Exchange Commission of Brazil, or CVM), the independent authority that regulates capital markets in Brazil. Like the TIF scheme in the United States, the CEPACs are also a way for the municipality to raise upfront cash to promote major urban interventions. In both mechanisms, the transactions occur in a securitized form. However, the returns from CEPAC and TIF come from different sources. In the Brazilian case, the returns come from the sale of additional building rights, whereas in the

United States, the capital is raised through the sale of expected property tax revenue increases. Nevertheless, in both cases, the ultimate expectation is an increase in real estate prices in a predetermined area of the city, with the support of the local state.

The sale of additional development rights is a practice that does not apply exclusively to Urban Operations. Indeed, it is a widespread mechanism used by local administrations in Brazil to boost municipal revenues and support urban policies and improvements. However, there are two aspects involved in its use within Urban Operations that help to create spaces of exception (Vainer, 2011), delimitating areas where flexible regulations and specific fiscal conditions are applied.

The first is that all the funds raised through the sale of the CEPACs must be reinvested inside the perimeter of the Urban Operation. It is significantly different from the use of the same financial mechanism outside Urban Operations, where the municipality can reinvest the funds raised in other parts of the city. By tying the resources to the Urban Operation, this mechanism curtails the possibility of using such funds for cross-subsidization purposes and comprehensive redistributive urban policies (Massonetto, 2003).

The second important difference relates to the securitized form assumed by the additional development rights. Outside Urban Operations, an agent intending to undertake a project that exceeds the basic development rights of a plot simply pays the fee to the municipality in order to get it approved. By contrast, in the case of an Urban Operation, development rights are traded independently from any connection with a specific project. These rights are turned into a financial asset with autonomous value, a condition that widens the room for speculation in the field of urban development.

The Financial Engineering behind Porto Maravilha

Before Porto Maravilha, the financing of Urban Operations was always carried out through sequential auctions of CEPACs, in which the overall stock of additional development rights was gradually sold. The amount of CEPACs issued before each individual auction used to be defined according to the estimated expenses of a specific phase of the project, and the titles were offered at a minimum value that would allow the municipal government to meet the costs of interventions, even if the lot was sold at its minimum price. Formerly, the price of the CEPACs was set at the stock exchange and sold to multiple agents, but this pattern has changed with the implementation of the Porto Maravilha Urban Operation.

To understand the local configuration, we first need to introduce two organizations: CDURP and FGTS. The *Companhia de Desenvolvimento Urbano da Região Portuária* (CDURP) is a *publicly owned company* established under *private law*, owned by the municipality and created to manage the Porto Maravilha project. Its main function is to coordinate the different agents that take part in the operation (public sector, private investors, residents, the consortium hired to carry on the works, and so on). The *Fundo de Garantia do Tempo de Serviço* (FGTS) is a *semi-public fund* that centralizes mandatory deposits made by employers, corresponding to 8 per cent of the wages of formal employees in the country (Pereira, 2017). It is a kind of mix between a pension fund and an unemployment insurance system. The deposits of the fund are almost entirely invested in real estate developments, mainly in low- and middle-income residential projects. More recently, it was allowed to invest in urban development activities.[3]

In the Porto Maravilha Urban Operation, all CEPACs were sold in one transaction to a single buyer rather than through sequential auctions and to multiple buyers. After a process of negotiation involving CDURP, potential buyers, and consultants, FGTS purchased all CEPACs: a total of 6,436,722 certificates, encompassing up to 4,089,502 square metres of additional development rights. CDURP agreed to sell the CEPACs to a single buyer on the condition that the buyer would cover all the costs of the Urban Operation. The full cost includes the public-private partnership contract with Porto Novo S.A. (around R$7.6 billion) and the estimated managerial costs of CDURP itself (around R$400 million), making an estimated total of R$8 billion (just over US$2.5 billion at the time of writing).[4]

For the public authorities, selling all CEPACs in a single transaction at a price covering the total estimated costs of the Urban Operation was regarded as a convenient opportunity: (1) it guaranteed what was their main concern – paying off the expenses of the Urban Operation; (2) it seemed easier and cheaper to sell all the CEPACs at once; and (3) it would give clear signs to construction firms, developers, and investors that the total amount of resources needed to implement the project was already available rather than being dependent on uncertain future

---

3 For a more detailed explanation about the functioning of FGTS and its relations with the real estate sector, see Royer (2009); in English but less detailed, see Mosciaro and Aalbers (2020).

4 These were the nominal values of the mentioned obligations by the time the sale of the CEPACs was concluded in June 2011. In current values, the total expenses of the Urban Operation are around R$10 billion (over US$3 billion at the time of writing).

demand for CEPACs. For the FGTS, purchasing all CEPACs granted the fund the monopolistic control over development rights within the Urban Operation, allowing it to orchestrate the entire redevelopment project in terms of type and volumes of development as well as the mixing of uses within the project. In short, the purchase enabled FGTS to control the overall strategy, which in the fund's view made the project likely to become a profitable undertaking.

However, there was one aspect that troubled the willingness of any single buyer to assume such a huge obligation, which had to be countervailed if the transaction were to be carried out on this basis: the land ownership structure within the area and the likelihood of private agents to be able to mobilize it for development purposes. Most of the land within the port area was public and owned by different state agencies. Different layers of the state, primarily the federal but also the local and state governments, held most of the public land. Part of the land owned by the federal government was directly controlled by it, while a public-private joint stock company called Docas S.A. controlled the other part.

If the CEPACs could only be used on privately owned plots, only about one quarter of the CEPACs would be utilized. The other three quarters of the CEPACs would become virtually useless assets if the publicly owned land was not available for real estate development. Moreover, the biggest and best located plots of land were predominantly publicly owned. These plots were considered crucial for the project to succeed, but it was not easy to include them within the developable land. By the time the proposal was conceived, there was a strong alignment of local, state, and federal governments. They were all willing to make Porto Maravilha a successful story, assuring that the management of public land would be conducted in a way to facilitate the implementation of this project. However, there was no guarantee that this political situation would last, and there was nothing preventing an eventual political shift in any of these governmental spheres from jeopardizing the ability of developers to access land within the area. Besides the political risks, there were also legal complications involved. Brazilian public law establishes a set of requirements and specific procedures for the use and alienation of public goods that could make the sale of these plots a difficult, long, and conflicting process.

In view of this situation, FGTS established an additional condition for buying the CEPACs at the price of the overall cost of the Urban Operation: CDURP should acquire the ownership of public plots that would suffice for the employment of at least 75 per cent of the CEPACs and offer the fund options to buy these plots for the same price. In addition, the price of the land would be deducted from the total price of the CEPACs. In short, the final deal consisted of FGTS agreeing to fund the entire Urban Operation and being compensated by receiving the total stock of additional development rights embodied in the CEPACs as well as a set of public plots that would enable it to utilize at least 75 per cent of the certificates.

We are presenting here a simplified explanation of this contractual relationship. Technically, the deal was not struck between CDURP and FGTS directly, but between two real estate investment trusts (REITs) created with the specific purpose of functioning as contracting parties for the transaction, both of them controlled by the respective parties: Região Portuária REIT, owned by CDURP, and Porto Maravilha REIT, owned by FGTS. Another important aspect to be mentioned relates to the timing of payments. In reality, FGTS did not pay upfront for the estimated costs of the Urban Operation; payments are conditional on CDURP delivering plots that are eligible for implementing the additional building rights owned by FGTS. The key aspect here is that public land became the central issue of the financial flows of this urban redevelopment project.

With this arrangement, CDURP was charged with the complicated task of reassembling a set of public plots and transferring them to FGTS without attaching any political or legal conditions. These contractual obligations virtually impeded governmental bodies from allocating public land within the Urban Operation for any other purpose than offering buying options to FGTS and, by doing so, having the right to charge this fund for the costs of the public-private partnership. In a general sense, the regulatory framework developed in this project enhanced a trend that had already been observed in other, smaller Urban Operations: the use of public assets to foster market dynamism and the insulation of public institutions from political and democratic control being stitched into a kind of neoliberal straitjacket (see, for example, Hodkinson, 2011).

Most of the land acquisitions required had been accomplished by CDURP by March 2016.[5] Most of the previously publicly owned land is now being employed in a way consistent with the interests of FGTS, which is heavily dependent upon the valorization of property prices to pay off its liabilities and enable it to make returns on the capital

---

5 According to CDURP's quarterly reports (http://www.portomaravilha.com.br/relatorios_trimestrais), the plots already acquired by the company allowed the employment of 62.7 per cent of all CEPACs.

invested. FGTS is allocating its assets based on a long-term business strategy. Rather than selling them to developers to raise cash to afford the expenses of the Urban Operation, the fund is using plots and CEPACs to establish partnerships and acquire stakes in projects. The reason behind such behaviour is the expectation of making higher returns in the long run by converting these assets into claims upon future revenue streams coming from real estate developments in the area rather than selling them at their current value, supposedly lower than the level they may attain after the improvements reach a more advanced stage. By doing so, the fund is also taking on higher risks. According to an FGTS manager we interviewed, the adoption of this business strategy reflects their confidence in the future of the area.

In order to leverage the entire project, FGTS, CDURP, and other governmental bodies are striving to create an image of Porto Maravilha as a flourishing business district, a site connected with global businesses and international capital flows. Many features can be highlighted as representative of this place marketing strategy, such as the invitation of "starchitect" offices to design museums and corporate buildings (Ponzini & Nastasi, 2011), the establishment of partnerships with real estate developers recognized as relevant players in global markets, or the hiring of specialized international consultancy firms to oversee the whole development process and provide technical advisory. We can mention some emblematic examples, such as the corporate buildings designed by Norman Foster, a museum designed by Santiago Calatrava, the towers developed by Tishman Speyer and GTIS Partners, or even the presence of Hines as a general consultant.

The envisaged changes, however, cannot take place without entailing conflicts with existing uses. In spite of the efforts of all the agents involved in the implementation of this redevelopment project to qualify it as an inclusionary urban policy, and as something that will benefit the population of the city as a whole, squatters and favela inhabitants are being displaced (Faulhaber & Azevedo, 2015; Rolnik, 2015; Sanchez & Broudehoux, 2013). Low-income households and small commercial activities are being forced to leave the place due to the pressures imposed by real estate market dynamics, steered by the neoclassical principle of the "highest and best use" of land. Even if minor inclusionary measures are being promoted, in a general sense, the overall logic underlying this project leads public and semi-public institutions to act as agents of gentrification, as also demonstrated in the case of Sao Paulo (Carlos, 2001; Fix, 2001; Maricato & Ferreira, 2002; Siqueira, 2014). According to the official sources, the area currently has 30,000 inhabitants, and the goal is to increase this number to 100,000 by 2025, mostly residing in the yet-to-be-developed residential buildings. The municipality claims that they want to create a "lively downtown," where one can live, work, and have fun; nevertheless, all of this already happens in the area. Apparently, the current uses – or more precisely, the current users – of the area are not considered suitable by the coalition promoting the project.

Discussion and Conclusion

Large-scale urban redevelopment projects are a mechanism through which globalization becomes urbanized, and through them we can understand how the global, national, and local interplay in particular urban contexts (Klink & Souza, 2017; Moulaert et al., 2005). In this chapter, we have analysed the case of Porto Maravilha in order to demonstrate how such relations are being shaped in Brazil. To understand why and how Porto Maravilha developed, we have presented an analysis that considers historical, political, social, and economic aspects. Not all elements can be grounded in local or national developments; international trends also play a significant role in the consolidation of entrepreneurial urban management discourse and practice. However, the local sphere is unequivocally key to understanding the nuances and particularities of the case. In Rio de Janeiro, we focused on a depreciated port and mixed-use area located in the inner city, representing the possibility of fast and high economic returns. The temporality of the unique political and economic circumstances in the city and country facilitated the approval and implementation of the Urban Operation Porto Maravilha.

The political economy underlying the rationale of an Urban Operation is particularly representative of the financialized production of urban space. By capitalizing upon future expectations, the government raises upfront cash and uses it to foster the demand for CEPACs by investing these resources in a way that results in the effective increase of real estate prices. The CEPAC is fundamentally a title of fictitious capital issued by the state in which it capitalizes on future expectations. It is currently assumed in speeches made by enthusiastic policymakers, real estate developers, and even scholars that such a regulatory tool enables city governments to carry out developmental plans without spending budgetary resources. It has been frequently portrayed as a kind of "magic formula" that provides means for the implementation of large-scale urban projects at the same time as releasing city governments from using taxpayers' money to afford them (Fix, 2003). Caught up in an entrepreneurial logic, the state ends up assuming roles that are barely distinguishable from that of developers and speculators (Pereira, 2017). Indeed, "[public] authorities act simultaneously as enablers, partners, and clients" (Moulaert et al., 2005, p. 251), putting all their efforts towards the pursuit of a continued increase in real estate prices. An inevitable outcome of this regulatory and financial configuration is that the city government becomes prone to neglect social claims that do not play a positive role in helping property values rise. For example, the state may become directly engaged in the displacement of low-income households and become an active agent of gentrification (Fix, 2001; Mosciaro & Pereira, 2019; Weber, 2010). Urban Operations exhibit many aspects in common with other regulatory tools related to an entrepreneurial or neoliberal approach to urban governance (Harvey, 1989). CEPACs become a tool that enables the commodification and financialization of building rights, while real estate investments become more mobile and liquid, effectively turning them into financial assets. It follows the same logic of tax increment financing (TIF), a regulatory tool that has become increasingly popular in US cities since the 1980s (see, for example, Weber, 2010). TIF consists of a mechanism in which city governments raise upfront cash for financing urban improvements through the sale of future increments on property tax revenues within a specific district. Despite the differences concerning where the returns on TIF bonds and CEPACs come from, they both represent a bet on increasing real estate prices in a specific part of the city. For governments, they both represent the means of anticipating expected future revenues and using the raised funds to promote urban improvements that can lead to the fulfilment of expectations concerning increases in property prices in a circumscribed area. In both cases, urban policies end up being confined in a straitjacket in which any intervention that does not help boost valorization becomes virtually excluded (Hodkinson, 2011; Raco, 2013). By promoting urban projects and attracting private investments, local governments end up being almost completely overwhelmed by the rationale and the interests of these agents.

Undermining the ability of the state to promote goals other than those related to the growth of real estate prices can go even further. As studies concerning Urban Operations in Sao Paulo have demonstrated (Fix, 2003; Maricato & Ferreira, 2002), it is a common trend that the overall costs involved in their implementation end up not being completely met by the sale of CEPACs alone and therefore require additional public investments. Since the exchange value of a CEPAC depends on expectations among market agents about real estate prices, municipalities commonly undertake duties to stimulate a process of change in the urban environment in order to provide the required signals for potential investors and thus leverage the whole project. Like an osmotic effect, public funds collected elsewhere may freely flow into an Urban Operation perimeter, but restrictions are imposed to constrain funds flowing out of the Urban Operation. Also in this sense, the Urban Operation is a space of exception (see Agamben, 2005; Vainer, 2011), that is, a space created *through regulatory frameworks* to be outside of the "normal" spaces of regulation.

In simple terms, Urban Operations are implemented where there is money to be made on the redevelopment of urban land, that is, where a "rent gap" exists (Smith, 1996). The regulatory and financial configuration of Urban Operations makes them likely to deepen existing patterns of uneven development. The mandatory reinvestment of funds raised through the sale of CEPACs inside its perimeter pushes this development in two interconnected ways. First, it curtails the possibility of cross-subsidization based on the transfer of resources that have been collected in areas where the interest of private agents in promoting developments already existed into places unlikely to receive such investments. Second, it leads to a cumulative concentration of investments within certain parts of the city, which commonly unfolds into gentrification and intensifies speculation within it, widening socio-spatial inequalities. The regressive nature of Urban Operations is aggravated by the speculative rationale of their financial engineering. In spite of the alleged alleviation of public investment, putting a financial mechanism of this kind in motion and keeping it running usually requires additional public investment that will absorb a significant amount of public resources that could be employed elsewhere, or with purposes other than securing property valorization.

The practices adopted by FGTS in this project also give clear signals of its financially driven motivations as well as demonstrate how public land is central to the financial flows of this urban redevelopment project. As FGTS is a fund that was created to guarantee welfare provision and enhance the savings of workers, one could argue that a profitable implementation of the Porto Maravilha project would ultimately result in higher returns for employees benefitting from the fund. However, in order to achieve these profits, FGTS, along with other (semi-)public authorities, is undertaking actions that go against the class interests of workers. Pension funds are typically prone to cope with pressures to push wages down in order to enhance profits of the companies in which they own stocks. In a similar way, the FGTS displaces low-income households for the sake of higher profits. From the very beginning of its involvement in the project, FGTS has followed a development strategy that is similar to those of the structural speculators described in Logan and Molotch's (1987) classical study. It consists of mobilizing huge amounts of capital in the area and orchestrating the entire redevelopment process through a quasi-monopolistic control of both land and CEPACs – in other words, creating monopoly rent on top of differential rent (Harvey, 2002; Ward & Aalbers, 2016). The strategy of the FGTS is to create higher returns through establishing a quasi-monopoly, but the flipside of this speculative strategy is that it also means a concentration of development and financial risks in one central actor.

The fact that the main investor in Porto Maravilha is a semi-public fund could potentially be a good thing, as it could allow for different urban redevelopment and investment practices. The case of the FGTS, however, suggests that it works primarily according to a speculative, financialized strategy that prioritizes shareholder value over public goals (Lazonick & O'Sullivan, 2000). In the end, the strategies and practices of FGTS contribute to a deeper integration of real estate and financial activities. The local government of Rio does not appear to act as a counterweight against the interest of FGTS and, by extension, real estate developers and financial investors. It has facilitated FGTS all along and has created a privately run entity, CDURP, to deal not only with the urban planning challenges in a neglected port area but also with assembling the plots of public land owned by different state agencies and opening the way for their privatization. The local state has willfully created a space of exception for the Porto Maravilha project and, in particular, for its key player, FGTS, and the local planning agency, CDURP, that operates outside of normal democratic control mechanisms.

In conclusion, land ownership and development, urban redevelopment and planning, finance, and various arms of the local and federal state have become entangled in a speculative logic. This logic preys on, but also furthers, uneven development in Rio's metropolitan area (Mosciaro & Pereira, 2019), resulting in the displacement and selective channelling of investments into areas designated for commercial/office activities, as well as into residential areas for the rich. The case of Porto Maravilha shows how land and development is no longer treated only *metaphorically* as a financial asset (à la Harvey) but also that land development rights are *literally* treated as just another financial asset. The peculiar deal between FGTS and CDURP allowed the municipality to raise funds for improvements within the perimeter of the Urban Operation, which were needed to enable the valorization of the real estate within the Porto Maravilha project. CEPACs – and by extension urban redevelopment – were treated as pure financial assets. The multilayered chain of abstractions, in which the issuance of these assets is based, turned additional development rights into instruments of speculation. This approach might curtail the responsiveness of political institutions to other social claims and eventually turn them into active agents of gentrification, indicative of a wider shift from managerial to entrepreneurial and financialized urban governance. Porto Maravilha is an ongoing project and its final effects remain to be seen. However, it is unequivocal that the increasing insertion of financial tools in the production of the built environment is not limited to the Global North and is taking quite extreme forms in projects developed under the Urban Operation policy framework in Brazil.

REFERENCES

Aalbers, M.B. (2007). Geographies of housing finance: The mortgage market in Milan, Italy. *Growth and Change, 38*(2), 174–99. https://doi.org/10.1111/j.1468-2257.2007.00363.x

Aalbers, M.B. (2008). The financialization of home and the mortgage market crisis. *Competition & Change, 12*(2), 148–66. https://doi.org/10.1179/102452908X289802

Aalbers, M.B. (2017). Corporate financialization. In D. Richardson et al. (Eds.), *The International encyclopedia of geography: People, the earth, environment, and technology.* https://onlinelibrary.wiley.com/doi/10.1002/9781118786352.wbieg0598

Aalbers, M.B. (2020). Financial geography III: The financialization of the city. *Progress in Human Geography, 44*(3), 595–607. https://doi.org/10.1177/0309132519853922

Abreu, M. (1997). *A evolução urbana do Rio de Janeiro.* Iplanrio.

Abreu, M. (2014). *Escritos sobre espaço e história.* Gramond.

Agamben, G. (2005). *Spaces of exception.* Chicago University Press.

Beauregard, R.A. (1994). Capital switching and the built environment: United States, 1970–89. *Environment and Planning A: Economy and Space, 26*(5), 715–32. https://doi.org/10.1068/a260715

Canettieri, T. (2017). A produção capitalista do espaço e a gestão empresarial da política urbana: O caso da PBH Ativos S/A. *Revista Brasileira de Estudos Urbanos e Regionais, 19*(3), 513–29. https://doi.org/10.22296/2317-1529.2017v19n3p513

Carlos, A.F. (2001). *Espaço-tempo na Metrópole: A fragmentação da vida cotidiana.* Contexto.

Charney, I. (2001). Three dimensions of capital switching within the real estate sector: A Canadian case study. *International Journal of Urban and Regional Research, 25*(4), 740–58. https://doi.org/10.1111/1468-2427.00342

Fainstein, S.S. (2001). *The city builders.* University Press of Kansas.

Faulhaber, L., & Azevedo, L. (2015). *SHM 2016: remoções no Rio de Janeiro Olímpico.* https://issuu.com/morula/docs/smh2016_issuu

Feagin, J.R. (1987). The secondary circuit of capital: Office construction in Houston, Texas. *International Journal of Urban and Regional Research, 11*(2), 172–92. https://doi.org/10.1111/j.1468-2427.1987.tb00045.x

Fernandez, R., & Aalbers, M.B. (2016). Financialization and housing: Between globalization and varieties of capitalism. *Competition and Change*, 20(2), 71–88. https://doi.org/10.1177/1024529415623916

Fix, M. (2001). *Parceiros da exclusão: Duas histórias da construção de uma "nova cidade" em São Paulo: Faria Lima e Agua Espraiada.* https://books.google.be/books?id=tTtHAAAAYAAJ

Fix, M. (2003). A fórmula mágica da parceria: Operações urbanas em São Paulo. *Cadernos de Urbanismo*, 3, 1–15. http://www.labhab.fau.usp.br/wp-content/uploads/2018/01/fix_formulamagicaparceria.pdf

Fix, M. (2009). Uma ponte para a especulação: Ou a arte da renda na montagem de uma "cidade global. *Caderno CRH*, 22(55), 41–64. https://doi.org/10.1590/S0103-49792009000100003

Gotham, K.F. (2006). The secondary circuit of capital reconsidered: Globalization and the U.S. real estate sector. *American Journal of Sociology*, 112(1), 231–75. https://doi.org/10.1086/502695

Haila, A. (1991). Four types of investment in land and property. *International Journal of Urban and Regional Research*, 15(3), 343–65. https://doi.org/10.1111/j.1468-2427.1991.tb00643.x

Harvey, D. (1982). *Limits to capital.* Verso.

Harvey, D. (1985). *The urbanization of capital: Studies in the history and theory of capitalist urbanization.* Blackwell.

Harvey, D. (1989). From managerialism to entrepreneurialism: The transformation in urban governance in late capitalism. *Geografiska Annaler. Series B. Human Geography*, 71(1), 3–17. https://doi.org/10.2307/490503

Harvey, D. (2002). The art of rent: Globalization, monopoly and the commodification of culture. *Socialist Register*, 38, 93–110. https://socialistregister.com/index.php/srv/article/view/5778/2674

Haughton, G., Allmendinger, P., & Oosterlynck, S. (2013). Spaces of neoliberal experimentation: Soft spaces, postpolitics, and neoliberal governmentality. *Environment and Planning A: Economy and Space*, 45(1), 217–34. https://doi.org/10.1068/a45121

Hebb, T., & Sharma, R. (2014). New finance for America's cities. *Regional Studies*, 48(3), 485–500. https://doi.org/10.1080/00343404.2013.843163

Hodkinson, S. (2011). Housing regeneration and the private finance initiative in England: Unstitching the neoliberal urban straitjacket. *Antipode*, 43(2), 358–83. https://doi.org/10.1111/j.1467-8330.2010.00819.x

Kaika, M., & Ruggiero, L. (2016). Land financialization as a "lived" process: The transformation of Milan's Bicocca by Pirelli. *European Urban and Regional Studies*, 23(1), 3–22. https://doi.org/10.1177/0969776413484166

Klink, J., & de Souza, M.B. (2017). Financeirização: Conceitos, experiências e a relevância para o campo do planejamento urbano brasileiro. *Cadernos*

Metrópole, 19(39), 379–406. https://revistas.pucsp.br/metropole/article/view/2236-9996.2017-3902

Lazonick, W., & O'Sullivan, M. (2000). Maximizing shareholder value: A new ideology for corporate governance. *Economy and Society*, 29(1), 13–35. https://doi.org/10.1080/030851400360541

Leitner, H. (1994). Capital markets, the development industry, and urban office market dynamics: Rethinking building cycles. *Environment and Planning A: Economy and Space*, 26(5), 779–802. https://doi.org/10.1068/a260779

Li, T.M. (2014). What is land? Assembling a resource for global investment. *Transactions of the Institute of British Geographers*, 39(4), 589–602. https://doi.org/10.1111/tran.12065

Logan, J.R., & Molotch, H.L. (1987). *Urban fortunes: The political economy of place*. University of California Press.

Maricato, E., & Ferreira, J.S.W. (2002). Operação Urbana Consorciada: Diversificação urbanística participativa ou aprofundamento da desigualdade? In *Estatuto da Cidade e Reforma Urbana: Novas perspectivas para as cidades brasileiras*. http://cidadesparaquem.org/textos-acadmicos/2002/7/1/operao-urbana-consorciada-diversificao-urbanstica-participativa-ou-aprofundamento-da-desigualdade

Massonetto, L.F. (2003). Operações Urbanas Consorciadas: A nova regulação urbana em questão. *Revista Da Procuradoria Geral Do Município de Porto Alegre*, 16(17), 101–18. http://www2.portoalegre.rs.gov.br/pgm/default.php?reg=6&p_secao=502

Molotch, H. (1976). The city as a growth machine: Towards a political economy of place. *American Journal of Sociology*, 82(2), 309–30. https://doi.org/10.1086/226311

Mosciaro, M., & Aalbers, M.B. (2020). Asset-based welfare in Brazil. *Housing Studies*, 35(2), 376–89. http://dx.doi.org/10.1080/02673037.2017.1364712

Mosciaro, M., & Pereira, A. (2019). Reinforcing uneven development: The financialization of Brazilian urban redevelopment projects. *Urban Studies*, 56(10), 2160–78. https://doi.org/10.1177/0042098019829428

Moulaert, F., Rodriguez, A., & Swyngedouw, E. (2005). *The globalized city: Economic restructuring and social polarization in European cities*. Oxford University Press.

Neto, P.N., & Moreira, T.A. (2013). Operação Urbana Consorciada da Linha Verde: Limites e oportunidades à luz da gestão social da valorização da terra. *Cadernos Metrópole*, 15(30), 583–603. https://doi.org/10.1590/2236-9996.2013-3010

Oosterlynck, S., & Swyngedouw, E. (2010). Noise reduction: The postpolitical quandary of night flights at Brussels Airport. *Environment and Planning A: Economy and Space*, 42(7), 1577–94. https://doi.org/10.1068/a42269

Peck, J., & Whiteside, H. (2016). Financializing Detroit. *Economic Geography*, 92(3), 235–68. https://doi.org/10.1080/00130095.2015.1116369

Pereira, A. (2015). *Intervenções em centros urbanos e conflitos distributivos: Modelos regulatórios, circuitos de valorização e estratégias discursivas* [Doctoral dissertation, Universidade de São Paulo]. https://teses.usp.br/teses/disponiveis/2/2133/tde-19052016-111952/publico/AlvaroPereiraTeseDoutorado.pdf

Pereira, A. (2017). The financialization of housing in Brazil: New frontiers. *International Journal of Urban and Regional Research, 41*(4), 604–22. https://doi.org/10.1111/1468-2427.12518

Ponzini, D., & Nastasi, M. (2011). *Starchitecture: Scenes, actors and spectacles in contemporary cities*. Umberto Allemandi.

Raco, M. (2013). The new contractualism, the privatization of the welfare state, and the barriers to open source planning. *Planning Practice and Research, 28*(1), 45–64. https://doi.org/10.1080/02697459.2012.694306

Raco, M. (2014). Delivering flagship projects in an era of regulatory capitalism: State-led privatization and the London Olympics 2012. *International Journal of Urban and Regional Research, 38*(1), 176–97. https://doi.org/10.1111/1468-2427.12025

Rolnik, R. (2015). *A guerra dos lugares: A colonização da terra e da moradia na era das finanças*. Boitempo.

Royer, L. de O. (2009). *Financeirização da política habitacional: Limites e perspectivas* [Doctoral dissertation, Universidade de São Paulo]. http://www.teses.usp.br/teses/disponiveis/16/16137/tde-19032010-114007/en.php

Rutland, T. (2010). The financialization of urban redevelopment. *Geography Compass, 4*(8), 1167–78. https://doi.org/10.1111/j.1749-8198.2010.00348.x

Sanchez, F., & Broudehoux, A.-M. (2013). Mega-events and urban regeneration in Rio de Janeiro: Planning in a state of emergency. *International Journal of Urban Sustainable Development, 5*(2), 132–53. https://doi.org/10.1080/19463138.2013.839450

Savini, F., & Aalbers, M.B. (2016). The de-contextualisation of land use planning through financialisation: Urban redevelopment in Milan. *European Urban and Regional Studies, 23*(4), 878–94. https://doi.org/10.1177/0969776415585887

Siqueira, M.T. (2014). Entre o fundamental e o contingente: Dimensões da gentrificação ontemporânea nas operações urbanas em São Paulo. *Cadernos Metrópole, 16*(32), 391–415. https://doi.org/10.1590/2236-9996.2014-3205

Smith, N. (1996). *The new urban frontier: Gentrification and the revanchist city*. Routledge.

Stroher, L. (2017). Reestruturação da Metrópole Periférica e o impasse da Reforma Urbana em Curitiba. *Revista Latinoamericana de Estudios Urbano Regionales, 43*(128), 273–94. https://doi.org/10.4067/S0250-71612017000100012

Tasan-Kok, T. (2010). Entrepreneurial governance: Challenges of large-scale property-led urban regeneration projects. *Tijdschrift Voor Economische En Sociale Geografie, 101*(2), 126–49. https://doi.org/10.1111/j.1467-9663.2009.00521.x

Vainer, C. (2011). Cidade de exceção: Reflexões a partir do Rio de Janeiro. *Anais Do XIV Encontro Nacional Da ANPUR, 14*. http://anais.anpur.org.br/index.php/anaisenanpur/article/view/635/622

Valladares, L. (2000). A gênese da favela carioca: A produção anterior às ciências sociais. *RBCS, 15*(44), 5–24. https://doi.org/10.1590/S0102-69092000000300001

Van Gent, W., & Boterman, W.R. (2019). Gentrification of the changing state. *Tijdschrift voor Economische en Sociale Geografie, 110*(1), 35–46. https://doi.org/10.1111/tesg.12331

Van Loon, J., & Aalbers, M.B. (2017). How real estate became "just another asset class": The financialization of the investment strategies of Dutch institutional investors. *European Planning Studies, 25*(2), 221–40. https://doi.org/10.1080/09654313.2016.1277693

Ward, C., & Aalbers, M.B. (2016). "The shitty rent business": What's the point of land rent theory? *Urban Studies, 53*(9), 1760–83. https://doi.org/10.1177/0042098016638975

Weber, R. (2010). Selling city futures: The financialization of urban redevelopment policy. *Economic Geography, 86*(3), 251–74. https://doi.org/10.1111/j.1944-8287.2010.01077.x

Weber, R. (2015). *From boom to bubble: How finance built the new Chicago.* University of Chicago Press.

Weber, R., & Goddeeris, L. (2007). *Tax increment financing: Process and planning issues.* https://www.cdfa.net/cdfa/cdfaweb.nsf/ord/dee466796291554d8825793600641312/$file/goddeeris-weber-financing.pdf

3 From Spectacular to Speculative Gulf Cities: A Tale of Dubai and Doha

ALI A. ALRAOUF

In the last two decades of the twentieth century, Gulf urbanity was mainly characterized by a commitment to use oil revenues to allow primitive, small, and simple Gulf cities rapidly transform from traditional settlements into cities with modern status. It was a process of massive transformation of the endless deserts into real estate megaprojects, coupled with qualitative upgrade of cities' infrastructure to prepare for a new modern condition. Gulf cities have become a worldwide brand for speculation due to the unique logic of urban growth. Considerable research has been generated to make sense of these recent urban forms (Dubai, Doha, Abu Dhabi) or their less "spectacular" but equally petroleum-revenue engineered adjacent neighbours (for example, Manama or Kuwait City). In this chapter, influential paradigms concerning the evolution of contemporary Gulf cities will be discussed. The aim of the discussion is to provide an analysis of the current paradigmatic shift from building spectacular urbanism to speculating on the future of Gulf cities, particularly in the post-carbon era. With a focus on the most controversial cities in the Gulf, Dubai and Doha, the chapter illustrates how a full reliance on iconic development and spectacular urbanism, as a development approach, should be revisited. Observing the urban scene in the Gulf through the last two decades, Dubai's spectacle has by far dominated the whole picture. While other significant Gulf cities, like Manama in Bahrain, Kuwait in Kuwait, or Riyadh in Saudi Arabia, were slow in their commitment towards a tangible change in their urbanity, Doha emerged slowly yet aggressively with the help of oil and liquefied natural gas (LNG) revenues to achieve a radical change. Doha was the only Gulf city, as will be elaborated later, that overcame the impact of the global financial crisis, and by 2010 the state cultivated its gradual progress by winning the bid for hosting the FIFA World Cup in 2022, an incident that dramatically alerted Dubai to a newcomer that might threaten its superiority in the Gulf and within the whole Middle East.

The impact of the global financial crisis in 2008 will be analysed to evaluate its consequences on creating the Dubai spectacle. A decade ago, the productive nature of the spectacle was very evident in marketing Dubai as an urban brand both regionally and internationally. Additionally, the chapter aims to shed light on the emerging new urbanity in other Gulf cities, particularly Doha, to answer the need for essential change in developing a sustainable future for cities that were created with unlimited carbon revenues. The chapter suggests that Doha resorts to a new interpretation of spectacular urbanism based on a knowledge economy and the generative principles for planning knowledge and creative cities. Emergent forms and models of the Gulf built environments are diversified and subjected to particular forces that have resulted from each Gulf state's speculative position and understanding of future urban growth. Such practical forces include the relative financial power of Gulf states. Hence, not every Gulf city can use the narrative of a creative or expensive spectacle as an image for the city or a manifestation of its global identity. The ethnic diversity in Gulf states like Bahrain and Kuwait also requires a more rational approach in creating developmental strategies. The chapter aims to illustrate how the two cities, Dubai and Doha, while being grouped within contemporary Gulf cities, provide radically different models of development and future growth. Therefore, the principles of the knowledge economy were declared as the backbone in all Gulf states' future visions, including Bahrain 2030, Dubai 2030, Abu Dhabi 2032, Qatar 2030, Kuwait 2035, and Riyadh 2025. Recently, notions as important as the knowledge economy and the related knowledge-based urban development (KBUD) concept are seen as strategically important for the future development of Gulf cities (Alraouf, 2017, 2016). Emerging knowledge cities in the Gulf, mainly Doha, Dubai, Abu Dhabi, and more recently Riyadh, are trying, in different capacities, to transform themselves from their previous status as oil-producing economies to cities celebrating education, research, and innovation, while attracting knowledge workers. For this process to thrive, a different kind of urbanism is required. The needs of the global knowledge workers and the creative class moving to Gulf cities will change the spatial contents, boundaries, and qualities of these cities.

The chapter suggests that examining cases from the contemporary Gulf cities illustrates two main interpretations concerning the juxtaposition of the spectacular and the speculative. The first interpretation is centred on how economic prosperity tempted Gulf cities to use their unprecedented financial revenues from oil to invest heavily in real estate speculation. More significantly, the interpretation focuses on the trend associated with such speculative processes: resorting to spectacular architectural and urban forms. Such a trend has resulted in a substantial move, with relative degrees of aggressiveness, towards real estate fantasies and iconic development being adopted in all main Gulf capitals and major cities. The second interpretation stems from a commitment towards speculating on the future in a more expansive sense, which considers the most recent events and transformations in the Gulf context. Hence, the chapter speculates on the future of contemporary Gulf cities in light of decreased oil prices, a post-carbon paradigm, the blockade against Qatar by its close neighbours and members of the Gulf Cooperation Council (GCC), the inhumane war against Yemen, and finally the speculation about the fate of the GCC as a shattered dream for Gulf states' unity and solidarity.

The Evolution and Contemporary Status of Gulf States

At one time just quiet desert tribes, the Gulf states of Saudi Arabia, Oman, the United Arab Emirates (UAE), Qatar, Bahrain, and Kuwait now exert unprecedented influence on international platforms, the result of their almost unimaginable riches obtained from oil and gas. Miller (2016) provides an account of the achievements of these countries since the 1973 global oil crisis. In the 1970s, one of the most hot and harsh regions in the world burst onto the international stage. The discovery and subsequent exploitation of oil allowed tribal rulers of the Gulf states to dream big (Cooke, 2014). The unprecedented financial revenues substantially helped simple nomads, fishermen, and pearl divers to catch up with the rest of the modernized world. Cooke (2014) also investigates how the insightful Arab Gulf rulers, who have overcome crisis after crisis, meet the external and internal challenges of the approaching future. Observing skylines of cities in the Gulf or tracing their geographical boundaries during the last two decades will show what diverse researchers have considered an unprecedented momentum of development (Al Qassemi, 2013; Kamrava, 2013; Gray, 2013; Davidson, 2008; Alraouf, 2008).

The common understanding in terms of the planning and evolution of cities suggests that they develop organically over hundreds of years. However, Gulf cities provide a solid example that contradicts this conceptual interpretation of gradual urban development. In the last few decades, contemporary Gulf cities have expanded rapidly in terms of size, buildings, infrastructure, and population. In particular, over the last decade, Gulf cities have become magnets of attraction for people coming

Figure 3.1. All the Gulf cities were once simple traditional settlements, which were subjected to an unprecedented pace of change in a short time frame. Source: Author.

from almost every part of the world to generate more income and secure their future. Yet, a major misunderstanding about the evolution of global cities has characterized the attempts of some Middle Eastern cities, mainly in the Gulf, to claim they are globalized. As numerous researchers suggest, Gulf cities, in their attempt to gain a place on the global stage, have focused on the imagery nature of globalization (Al-Nakib, 2016; Alraouf, 2017, 2010; Wippel, 2014; Fromherz, 2012; Wiedmann, 2010; Al Hathloul, 2004). Hence, as the focus was more on the image, the construction of skyscrapers similar to the ones in New York and Chicago was more important than investing in the real components that would create a global city. While cities like New York, Chicago, and Hong Kong are full of skyscrapers, their skyline is not the reason they are placed on top of the list of global cities. Planners and decision-makers in the Gulf were not able to see the other layers, clearly described in Sassen's (1991, 2002) research, that are needed to label a city as global. The urban image is crucial. However, for a positive speculation about any city and its global nature, many factors have to be considered, such as its economic prosperity and its ability to attract people, attain different levels

Figure 3.2. The old parts of Doha, where its history as a traditional settlement should be preserved and perceived as an authentic component of the city's spectacle. Source: Author.

of connectivity, be located in a unique geographical position, and maintain a mature activation of freedom and democracy.

While the only constant component in the matrix of contemporary Gulf states' development is the unprecedented rapid development, the current crisis alludes to the shifting sands that they sit upon. Urban development is not only in a constant state of fluidity in the region, but the adopted strategies also differ in the wake of the post-oil future. Much of the continuing urban development of the Gulf region rests on the oil economy. But it seems that the typical threat of what would happen when the oil runs out is not the prime concern. The need for oil will slow down in the future, with the inevitable outcomes of extensive research into alternative sources of energy that suggest more clean, reliable, and cheap sources. The new urban development strategies for Gulf states should highlight how architecture and urbanism might be developed to generate new urban settings that are economically viable and environmentally sustainable. More alarming, since the unfolding of the Arab Spring, concrete signs suggest that the Gulf Cooperation Council (GCC) is swiftly approaching an anticipated collapse. GCC, which was seen in the Arab world as the only successful form of Arab solidarity, was subjected to deep fractures due to the opposing positions of its states' leaders towards significant issues like people's right to revolt and the severe intra-Gulf states competition, particularly between Qatar and the UAE. Such disputes resulted in the imposition of an unprecedented blockade against Qatar, which will be analysed in the coming sections of the chapter in order to confirm the contemporary fragility of Gulf development and solidarity.

The Inevitable Paradigm: Knowledge-Based Urban Development

In the face of the growing competition between countries, cities, organizations, and individuals, a new way of thinking is required if all are to achieve economic success. To date, only some of the Middle Eastern countries have been fortunate. They are oil-rich states, although reserves are dwindling, and they have been able to use oil revenues to develop projects to diversify their economies. The grand plan for most of these economies is to become knowledge-based. Particularly during the last five years, major Gulf cities have emerged as rapidly growing knowledge economy localities as they realize the inevitability of the need to go beyond the oil-based economy (Ulrichsen, 2011). The Gulf region has become an East–West hub for travel, tourism, sport, culture, trade, and finance. Yet, this hub's sustainability needs stability. The consequences of the Arab Spring and Gulf conflict have challenged the autocratic regimes' ability to maintain stability at home and influence abroad as they deal with the demands of social and democratic reform. Miller (2016) considers an array of factors – Islamism, terrorism, the Arab Spring, volatile oil prices, global power dynamics, and others – to assess future possibilities. Within the contemporary Gulf states, the objective of developing a knowledge-based economy is clear and well declared, as stated in their strategic visions. The plans of the GCC states bank on the diversified and knowledge-intensive economies. Principally, the emerging Gulf cities, namely Kuwait City (Kuwait), Manama (Bahrain), Doha (Qatar), Abu Dhabi, Dubai, Sharjah (UAE), and Muscat (Oman), have exhibited a relative commitment towards adopting the knowledge economy principles.

Consequently, the need for governments to educate and nurture local talent will become paramount, and they will need to encourage people to think differently. In other words, shifting towards a knowledge-based economy is becoming a necessity rather than an optional development direction. Gulf countries are constructing a clear case for the relevance of

Figure 3.3. Main shifts in Gulf states' economic development and the inevitability of a move towards a knowledge economy. Source: Author.

knowledge-based development in the post-oil paradigm, using the outstanding oil revenues that have accumulated in the Gulf countries due to unprecedented increases in oil prices. More critically, some main cities and states in the Gulf, including Bahrain and Dubai, have already experienced depletion in oil resources. Coupled with such alarming signs is the fact that the world is moving towards other sources of energy, which may lead to the irrelevance of oil to the global economy. Hence, there has been a decline in oil prices to levels that would not be able to sustain Gulf states' economies or guarantee the distinguished lifestyle that Gulf people currently enjoy. When the price of a barrel of oil reached US$70 in 2005, the way was paved for an economic revolution that started with the Gulf's real estate boom. In addition, a lot of the Gulf financial capital savings in American and European banks were withdrawn and redirected locally as a consequence of 9/11's culture of fear. Fear of embargo, freezing of assets, or severe punishments on Arabs and Muslims has urged a considerable number of the Gulf's richest people to invest locally. Real estate was an ideal answer to the presence of exceptional levels of liquidity in Gulf/Arab modern history (Alraouf, 2008). These projects are the most recent packaged residential environments in the Gulf. Their different themes and design concepts, as well as the different amenities and services, allow inhabitants to engage in an exclusive lifestyle. Hertog (2017) illustrates how the GCC oil monarchies have been using their oil wealth to buy the accoutrements of "good citizenship" and "progressiveness" in the international arena through costly policy projects that involve urban interventions like the building of international museums, universities, and "zero-carbon cities" – urban enclaves with an audience that is almost exclusively international. This interpretation is valid for some Gulf states, particularly the Emirate of Dubai. The megaprojects reflect a desire to gain international recognition via exhibiting full adoption of Western norms and influential principles.

Knowledge-based urban development (KBUD) is a new development paradigm. The KBUD concept first emerged in the urban planning and development discourse during the last decade of the twentieth century as a promising paradigm to support the transformation process of cities into knowledge cities and their societies into knowledge societies (Ergazakis et al., 2006). In the Gulf states context, the concept aims to increase the region's competitive edge, attract highly skilled human resources and investments, and support the people of the region in reaching a high standard of living and welfare. KBUD is based on the premises of knowledge economy, which play a crucial role in the improvement of competitiveness among cities and urban regions (Yigitcanlar, 2011). Knight (2008) argues that KBUD is a social learning process in which the knowledge capital is utilized in the development of a sustainable urban region. Kunzmann (2008) characterizes the KBUD concept as a collaborative development framework that provides guidelines to the public, private, and academic sectors in terms of the make-up of future development strategies to attract and retain talent and investment, as well as guidelines for the creation of knowledge-intensive urban and regional policies. Yigitcanlar (2011) looks upon KBUD in the era of the global knowledge-based economy as a novel development paradigm, which is designed to create economic prosperity, social order, a sustainable environment, and appropriate municipal governance. As evidence in the last decade suggests that Gulf states are quite rapidly moving into the post-oil paradigm, speculation about the future is based on a mature reliance on the conceptual pillars of KBUD. The conceptual structure of KBUD rests on an integrated set of pillars (Carrillo et al., 2014; Yigitcanlar, 2011; Alraouf, 2008). The economic development pillar is aimed to set the knowledge capital in the centre of economic activities because, according to this concept, knowledge is not a supplementary factor of development but rather a key resource. The sociocultural pillar aims to improve people's knowledge to a level that results in a knowledge-based society, with the main characteristics of strong

Figure 3.4. The first ever solar-powered plane took off from Abu Dhabi for a world tour marking the inevitability of the post-carbon era. Source: Courtesy of Masdar Institute of Technology, Masdar City.

human capital, acceptance of diversity, and social equality. This latter pillar is crucial for Gulf states, as the unique demographic situation and the existence of expatriates require different and creative approaches for social inclusivity. The third pillar of KBUD is the environmental and urban (enviro-urban) development, which aims to find a level of harmony between preservation and improvement of the built and natural environments. Positive spatial, sustainable development in KBUD emphasizes the quality of life and place, as it aims to guarantee the spatial quality needed to attract knowledge workers and to establish a knowledge milieu. The environmental and urban pillar reflects the dimension of sustainable urban development and the creation of quality of life.

The Post-Carbon Era: A Need for an Alternative Urbanism

Speculating on the future of the Gulf states is no longer a question of relying on maintaining a dynamic real estate market sustained by oil revenues, as was demonstrated by all the consequences of the oil crisis during the last five years. All Gulf states came to the conclusion that a focus on development strategies for a post-carbon paradigm is essential. The decline in oil prices during the last five years, from US$100 per barrel to less than US$40, suggests a swift change in the way Gulf states envision their future. The oil reserves are limited and will be exhausted in the near future. To secure wealth and further economic prosperity, the Gulf cities rely, among other prospects, on knowledge-driven industries and well-educated knowledge workers. In the case of Qatar, its national development strategy clearly asserts this path. As stated in the *Qatar National Development Strategy, 2011–2016*, the main goal for a better future is to build on knowledge: "As Qatar's economy diversifies more from its reliance on gas and oil, success will increasingly depend on the ability to compete in a global knowledge economy. Educating and training Qataris to their full potential will be critical to continuing progress" (QSDP, 2011, p. 122). In the *Dubai Strategic Plan 2015*, two knowledge-based aims are described: (1) "preparing Dubai's workforce for the high-value, knowledge-driven economy, which requires attracting and retaining highly skilled employees, improving Nationals' qualifications and increasing their motivation;" and (2) "turning Dubai into a vibrant science and technology hub in targeted sectors, by supporting the development of existing sectors, and establishing the right environment for nurturing the post 2015 economy" (Dubai Strategic Plan, 2007, p. 22).

In the previous sections, my attempt was to construct a well-founded case supporting the realization of a new development paradigm in the evolution of contemporary Gulf cities. In the coming sections, using the two distinguished cases of Dubai and Doha, I will analyse and consider, in particular, KBUD and how each city is adopting a different model of urban development. I argue that each of the two cities in question has a different perception of how its image should be constructed both regionally and globally. The hypothesis examined suggests that Dubai is still obsessed with the manufacturing of a city image based on spectacular urbanism. In such an understanding, real estate triumphed, and speculation still supports the famous slogan of the city's evolution narrative: "Build It and They Will Come." Alternatively, Doha, after falling into the trap of regional rivalry in trying to imitate Dubai in the early 2000s, resorted to a development strategy that transcends the Dubaification process of contemporary Gulf and Middle Eastern cities.

The Case of Dubai, UAE

The Multiple Façades of Dubai: The Spectacle of Urbanity

Even though Dubai is not a classic example of a global city such as New York, Paris, and London, its rise in the past century is notable and significant. In the late twentieth century, Dubai became an urban spectacle rising from the desert, envisioned by its rulers as the new blueprint for creating a utopian territory within the Middle East (Kanna, 2011). Dubai – one of the seven emirates that make up the UAE – has built a reputation as the pre-eminent business hub in the Middle East, with an open economy that welcomes companies and individuals from around the world. Additionally, in the first decade of the twenty-first century, the city exploded onto the world stage. A balanced assessment of Dubai's reinvention as a city, a global trade centre, and an experiment in urban planning is a major task in understanding the evolution of the city as a regional urban brand. Narrating a critical account of Dubai requires us to consider the Emirate outside the dominant portraits and to shed light on other well-constructed narratives and interpretations of the city's evolution. Such interpretation becomes fundamentally relevant as Dubai has been a dominant development model for a number of Gulf and Middle Eastern cities in the recent decade (Davidson, 2008; Alraouf, 2016).

Dubai is one of the cities where multifaceted readings can be provided to better understand the identity of the city and its development mechanism. While Elsheshtawy (2010, 2015) illustrates a vision of the other Dubai, which extends beyond the flashy image, my intention is to provide a third reading, which would transcend both the spectacular and the other Dubai. The suggested account in the context of this chapter seeks to shed light on Dubai's exclusive narrative of constructing a brand that is not only based on spectacle but also on advocating for a social and cultural lifestyle that would not necessarily survive any real test. The most typical perception of Dubai stems from the extensive presence of spectacular architecture, which starts from the time of the construction of the World Trade Center by John Harris and encompasses a critical presentation of spectacular achievements such as the skyscrapers of Sheikh Zayed Road, the Palms, the Atlantis Resort, and the Burj Khalifa Tower. Another stimulating component in Dubai's urbanity is the coloured retail landscape composed of a number of mega thematic shopping malls, such as the Mercato, Dubai, Emirates, and Ibn Battuta Malls. More controversially, it encompasses a ski resort on the edge of the desert. The exaggerated sizes and the visually attractive theming of real estate projects, and the speed of urbanization, are all part of the top-down approach to swiftly create the new city brand. The result is an unparalleled interpretation of the ways in which the built environment shapes – and is shaped by – the experience of globalization and neoliberalism in a diverse, multinational city. As Kanna (2013) observes, the visually attractive aspects of architecture should be placed within a holistic view of the city that takes in the less sensational elements, such as worker camps and informal urban spaces. Therefore, it is inevitable for a holistic assessment of Dubai's superlative and spectacular model that we situate the city's urbanism in its contexts of architecture, urban planning and design, and historical and cultural processes.

Dubai really started thinking about prospective planning in the 1960s, and its city-building dreams accelerated in the 1980s with the oil boom. Since then, Dubai has grown rapidly, riding the globalization wave. Its urban plans have consistently aimed at making Dubai an international city and a transport, trade, and commerce hub. Dubai has therefore consistently been working to reinvest the income from the oil industry and to seek revenue from prime real estate. Most of these projects are built on the knowledge that oil will eventually dry up and Dubai must diversify its economy and become a major centre for leisure, trade, and commerce. Dubai has invested in iconic architecture projects and global infrastructure projects geared towards the future. It is becoming a "city of cities," encompassing as it does Dubai Media City, Dubai Internet City, Dubai Sports City, Healthcare City, and International City. This status has attracted developers and investors from around the globe. Dubai is also famous for its flashy real estate megaprojects, such as the Burj-al-Khalifa complex, Palm Jumeirah, and Dubai Marina. Dubai can also be described as one huge "megaproject" – the city has grown in just half a century from a regional town to an international city with over two million inhabitants today.

Regionally, in the last two decades, Dubai's urbanity has emerged as a model for urban development, a model that is based on spectacular megaprojects and iconic developments from palm-shaped gigantic real estate to the highest building on earth. Such a model was the result of a top-down approach, which, as Keshavarzian (2016) rightly argues, praised the narrative of rulers who were represented as captains steering these remarkable projects. Within this perspective, Dubai constructs an interesting experience, and its cityscape has emerged through the implementation of a set of developmental models that emphasize the global objectives and aspirations of the city. The creation of icons in Dubai, or iconic development, seems to be the governing strategy for all its current and upcoming projects. Hence, projects and buildings are becoming urban brands waiting to be exported and then consumed by other Arab and Gulf cities in their race to join the global paradigm. Most of the major Arab cities have been competing to imitate Dubai in its unprecedented effort to construct the tallest and the largest ever built architectural and urban statements (Wippel, 2014; Wiedmann, 2010). One problem of the explosion of growth in cities like Dubai and its followers is the creation of what Frey (2010) calls "gated regions" – places like New York, London, and Tokyo – in which both the city and many of the surrounding suburbs have become unaffordable for all but the very wealthy. Such developments tend to contradict the main principles and promises of knowledge cities, as the

Figure 3.5. An aerial view of Dubai shows its emergence as a new urban brand within the context of the Gulf and the Middle East by relying on constructing iconic developments and real estate fantasies. Source: Author.

spread of such gated regions and communities is in antithesis to the commitment to create knowledge cities. Such social disparity and segregation has transformed some cities, with all their spectacle urbanity, into an exclusive urban territory where available lucrative financial resources are the only way to enjoy the city and experience its distinguished narrative.

Elsheshtawy (2010) discusses the relatedness of the same concept and suggests a closer examination of the actual content of the model: architectural forms, processes, and the relationship between investors and planning. The echoing alarm bell was clearly heard during the 2008 financial crisis and its severe results, which left Dubai devastated and almost vacant, its expatriate workforce fleeing in desperation to escape the crushing debt accumulated during the boom years (Elsheshtawy, 2010, 2015, 2019). The financial crisis that hit the world in 2008 left a huge impact on Dubai. While the main lesson learned was the inevitable need to avoid a virtual economy resulting from speculation in real estate, the city resorted once more, and in a swift manner, to the same urban norms and development policies (Davidson, 2008). Once the impact of the crisis resolved, particularly with the substantial financial support given by Abu Dhabi, Dubai has continued the process

From Spectacular to Speculative Gulf Cities   83

Figure 3.6. The obsession for using all aspects of branding to construct the city's global fame was extended to its police fleet. Dubai has gained recognition for giving supercars to its police force, including models such as Ferrari, Porsche, Bentley, McLaren, Bugatti, and Lamborghini. Source: Author.

of constructing its urban brand as a city with iconic real estate developments and a focus on shopping and consumption. While Dubai may have shown a desire to move towards a knowledge- and creativity-based economy, limited credible and tangible efforts have been geared towards this developmental strategic alternative. In the meantime, Abu Dhabi has gradually acknowledged the inevitable move beyond oil (Davidson, 2009). Consequently, substantial investment has been geared towards a knowledge-based infrastructure that includes foreign universities such as the Sorbonne, museums like the Louvre, and major research institutes like Masdar.

Admirers of Dubai were shocked in the aftermath of the 2008 global financial crisis. Resituating the Dubai spectacle was illustrated in the published work, which transcends the glittering global – almost utopian – image and scrutinizes the holistic aspects of the city's development model. Hence, as Kanna (2011, 2013) and Elsheshtawy (2010) look behind this seductive vision, the reality of Dubai's model emerged once the role of cultural and political forces that shaped both the image and the reality of Dubai were analysed. Yet, any honest observer would realize that, in the past several years, Dubai has exploited its impressive infrastructure and unique projects to regain the needed development momentum, albeit at the expense of the city's social and urban integrity. The 2008 financial crisis helped Dubai to look critically at some of the projects underway and gave it the opportunity to revisit some or even cancel them. In some other cases, projects were controlled in order to allow better use of the financial resources in more feasible investments. In all its efforts, Dubai, using its spectacle images to construct positive speculation regarding its future, aspired to be the ideal model and move from having regional to having global impact. Yet, particularly in the last two years, clear evidence has emerged suggesting that the spectacle created needs to be holistically scrutinized. On the city level, it was clearly realized that creating such a glitzy spectacle facilitated different negative symptoms, including fragmented urbanity, the loss of substantial segments of the city's traditional quarters, and non-stop gentrification. Guided by a neoliberal approach, Dubai has not developed as a place for all, or as an inclusive urbanity. The speculative mindset can be seen to have manifested itself in the numerous degraded, gentrified, and excluded spaces that dominate the city's urbanity. The city is moving towards more spectacular megaprojects, while other projects are not completed (Elsheshtawy, 2019). More demolition is taking place to pave the way for more spectacular additions in the hope that it will increase the speculation value of the future real estate (Reuters, 2014). For instance, most of the 200 fabricated islands off Dubai's coast, which are laid out in the shape of a world map, clearly symbolize the 2008 property market crash, as many remain empty after state-owned developer Nakheel's near debt default in 2009 (Molotch & Ponzini, 2019).

The intention here is to invite the reader to determine from a one-dimensional interpretation the increasing impact of Dubai's model. Learning from Dubai is possible if it is structured around rejecting the mere perception of the city as a prototype for Gulf and Middle Eastern urbanism. Rather, the city should be perceived as a utopia imagined by Dubai's rulers and merchant elite, who have had the opportunity to be financially backed up by the neighbouring emirates in the event of failure and financial crisis.[1] Dubai's urban planning approach is more project-based. The plans are flexible, so they can be moulded to the next big project on the market. In such circumstances, the comprehensiveness of Dubai's plan becomes questionable. Even though the plan documents

---

1 The Emirate's near economic collapse in the financial crash of 2008 to 2009 resulted in the subsequent debt bail-out by Abu Dhabi.

Figure 3.7. "Keep calm. There's no bubble" proclaimed a giant poster advertising a property-finding portal on a forty-storey building overlooking a Dubai highway. That may have been true at the time, but the risks are rising. Source: Provident Estate.

have some wider aims and objectives, it is no exaggeration to say that urban planning in Dubai is more project- than goal-based. Most of these projects cater to a foreign market in the hope of attracting investment. Hence, the obvious priorities for the government are its nationals (10 per cent of the population) and foreign investors. Without doubt, a share of these financial transactions would qualify as "money laundering." Politically and financially speaking, the short-term analysis of the immediate post–Arab Spring consequences reveals a considerable flow of cash towards Dubai. Yet, the cash was mainly sourced from members of the autocratic regime circles who fled their countries in the wake of the Arab Spring. As documented, they found a safe haven for their illegal assets in UAE banks, where the money was smoothly accepted and often directed towards real estate investment and expenditures without any questions asked regarding sources or legitimacy. Dudley (2019) describes Dubai as a "money-laundering paradise." Citing investigations by the Organized Crime and Corruption Reporting Project (OCCRP) and the Center for Advanced Defense Studies (C4ADS), Transparency International (2018b) said that real estate worth millions of pounds can be bought in Dubai in exchange for cash with few questions ever being asked. Gambrell (2018) discusses the findings of a report that describes Dubai real estate as a money-laundering haven. The report alleges that war profiteers, terror financiers, and drug traffickers sanctioned by the United States have used Dubai's real estate market in recent years as a haven for their assets.[2] The report by the Washington-based Center of Advanced Defense Studies (CADS), relying on leaked property data from the city-state, offers evidence to support the in-depth stories about Dubai's real estate boom. Whether of suspicious or clean origin, foreign investment has produced a large share of the city's empty buildings. (Before the 2008 financial crisis, more than 50 per cent of apartments were empty.) It can be inferred from this fact that Dubai's development is more geared towards speculation than inhabitation.

Like other Gulf countries, the UAE has also attracted expatriate workers and investors by offering a consistent policy of zero income tax – something now under threat as oil prices fall – and even Saudi Arabia is showing a massive budget deficit. Tax-free incomes would tempt expatriates to reside temporarily in Dubai or other Gulf states, but will never create a stable social mass with an authentic sense of belonging, spatial bonds, and citizenship. The most notable statistic is that about 90 per cent of Dubai's population are immigrants. These immigrants arrived in order to participate in Dubai's growth story. However, with the market reigning over everything else, key questions remain over social and environmental impacts (ISOCARP, 2016). The immigrants and expats work hard to afford a decent life. For many, with low wages and high competition, it remains a dream, as most of the services are market-based. With market speculation raising housing prices way beyond their reach, social justice and inclusiveness are absent.

CONTESTING DUBAI AS A REGIONAL OR GLOBAL URBAN BRAND

The new reading of Dubai's spectacular narrative provided in this chapter has emerged from the gradually fractured image of the city resulting from the current, unfolding Gulf crisis, which resulted from a blockade on the neighbouring state of Qatar by a coalition of Saudi

---

[2] Despite Dubai's shortcomings, the UAE is the best rated country in the Middle East and North Africa region when it comes to corruption. In the 2018 Corruption Perceptions Index, it is ranked 23 out of 180 countries, with a score of 70 points, closely followed by its near neighbour – and regional rival – Qatar, which is ranked 33 overall, with 62 points (Transparency International, 2018a).

Figure 3.8. The aftermath of the 2008–2009 global financial crisis on Dubai's virtual economy was depicted in cartoons published globally. Source: Author.

Arabia, the UAE, and Bahrain, starting on 5 June 2017.[3] This new face of Dubai substantially contradicts the perspective that Elsheshtawy (2010) suggests as to how the city represents a nexus of capital accumulation, real estate speculation, and political power structures, all of which converged to create a city that is representative of the twenty-first century and may have the potential to become the blueprint for our future. Yet, the Gulf crisis resulting from the blockade against Qatar showed clearly that the rosy picture painted of Dubai as a centre for tolerance and an ideal place for accommodating a global population might be questioned. This point is crucial, as it was stated that Dubai is a model for the Arab world, not just through its megaprojects but because it accommodates multiple nationalities, a fact that may contribute to its unique response to globalizing conditions (Elsheshtawy, 2010, p. 275). But of course, this perspective poses the question of urban governance and access to citizenship, an issue that the author does not specifically discuss. More damage to Dubai's global image has resulted from the

---

3 In the early hours of Monday, 5 June 2017, three countries from the Gulf Cooperation Council (GCC), including Saudi Arabia, the United Arab Emirates, and Bahrain, joined by Egypt, decided to mount a total blockade and impose trade and travel bans on Qatar due to major political disputes.

severe contradiction between actual deeds and superficial slogans.[4] The 2017 Gulf crisis also illustrated that, while the UAE is the only country on earth with a ministerial position in the cabinet for happiness and one for tolerance,[5] these ministerial positions have never prevented the UAE from punishing its own people when they are seen to show any level of sympathy towards their relatives and family members in Qatar. Yet again, it was realized that the UAE appointed these new ministers of "tolerance" and "happiness" as part of a cabinet reshuffle in an attempt to cement its position as the Arab world's most eye-catching nation, but not as a catalyst for transforming the country and the city into a platform for human rights, tolerance, acceptance, and, more significantly, freedom. The hostile behaviour of Dubai towards its neighbour and close member in the GCC, Qatar, was analysed as a contradiction to its publicized advantages: primarily tolerance and happiness. Dubai was not able to provide a convincing argument that would justify not only imposing a total blockade against Qatar but also punishing its own people if they showed any form of empathy towards their longtime neighbours, relatives, and family members in Qatar.

Dubai went on a building spree as it headed towards the 2020 World Expo (McGinley, 2015). Several megaprojects added millions of square feet of luxury residential and retail space. However, what the role of this infrastructure will be in the long-term development of the city and *all* its residents is uncertain. Like most of the Gulf cities, Dubai's cycles of masterplans proved irrelevant to a different pace of urbanization. The new vision, titled *Dubai Masterplan 2020*, failed to provide answers to issues like sustainability, social justice, or climate change challenges (Municipality of Dubai, 2014). Projects that are more controversial than most of the megaprojects in contemporary Dubai, including the massive

---

4 There is also no freedom of the press, and academics such as British research Matthew Hedges, a PhD candidate at Durham University in the United Kingdom, visited the Gulf country to carry out research for his doctorate. He was detained at Dubai International Airport. After enduring five months in solitary confinement, he was accused by the UAE government of spying on behalf of an unnamed foreign agency. In November 2018, Hedges was sentenced to life imprisonment in the UAE on charges of espionage in state security. The UAE issued a pardon as part of a series of orders on the country's National Day anniversary. However, a spokesman said Mr. Hedges was "100% a secret service operative" (see BBC News, 2018).

5 Sheikh Mohammed bin Rashid, vice president and ruler of Dubai, announced at the beginning of February 2016 that new positions would include a minister of state for happiness, who will have the responsibility to "align and drive government policy to create social good and satisfaction," and a minister of state for tolerance, who will "instill tolerance as a fundamental value in UAE society" (The National, 2016).

new city called Mohammed Bin Rashid City, are not carried out under any guidance of a master plan that regulates growth (Elsheshtawy, 2019). There are important lessons to be learned from Dubai. The city is an enviable economic growth story and a reminder of humanity's power to build a successful city in a desert. The result is more about a good return on investment, rather than a liveable and sustainable community. This fact reminds us of the importance of comprehensive planning and policies for inclusive planning and environmental betterment. The looming possibility that the world is on a path to accelerated climate change casts a shadow on Dubai's past achievements and future viability. Indeed, Dubai's growth has also had a major impact on its environment. The structural plan in the 1990s made no mention of sustainability, a global buzzword in that era. These impacts have both local and global repercussions, as Dubai has one of the largest carbon footprints in the world. The government is beginning to realize these impacts, but positive action is awaited. It should also be noted that the city is a role model to several other cities in the Gulf region. They emulate what Dubai does, but in some cases they are without a need to duplicate its mistakes, as seen in the recent case in Cairo with the unjustified Dubai by the Nile or the New Capital City (Alraouf, 2018).

In some cases, the image of Dubai as a happy, tolerant, and idealistic place was damaged by a lack of respect for intellectual property, particularly in spectacle projects like the new Dubai Frame. As Wainwright (2018) illustrates, the city of Dubai, home to the tallest skyscraper, the largest shopping mall, and the longest driverless metro system in the world, added a new landmark, as the city officials label it. The new addition to Dubai's spectacle was called the biggest picture frame on the planet. The building, which is creating a lot of controversy due to its scale, internal emptiness, and sense of incompleteness, added one more crucial aspect. The objective was to design a "tall emblem structure to promote the new face of Dubai." The Mexican architect Fernando Donis, whose frame proposal won an international competition in 2008 that was organized in collaboration with the International Union of Architects, claimed that Dubai took his project, changed the design, and built it without his presence, as reported in *The Guardian* (Wainwright, 2018). The architect added that he received a contract from the Dubai municipality that limited his involvement to an advisory role. It demanded that he hand over his intellectual property, never visit the construction site, and never promote the project as his own work, while the municipality could terminate the agreement at any point (Wainwright, 2018). Some planners have argued that a project-based planning approach has led to fragmented planning. The city itself is fragmented into megaprojects that are not accessible to everyone. It is also based on zoning for the separation of functions, which increases car use and urban segregation. The outcome is isolated communities, surrounded by large car parks and vacant pieces of land separated by multilane highways. The massive scale of development, lack of walkways, and the hot, dry climate have also made cars necessary. The city's public transport is used by just 9 per cent of the population. Those who cannot afford cars are usually limited to the informal parts of the city, which present quite a contrast to the high-rise glitzy development. These areas have time and again been threatened by market-driven projects eyeing their land. Some have succumbed, while others persist. This situation points to a general lack of comprehensive planning towards a common social good. Unfortunately, Dubai cleverly managed to create its own niche on the global stage. Dubai constructed an unprecedented spectacle within the context of the Gulf states and the whole Middle East. Such a spectacle would have been a guarantee for speculation on a prosperous future for Dubai. Yet, the spectacle constructed has proved limited and unable to act as a catalyst towards a holistic, sustainable, and resilient future in a just and tolerant city.

The Case of Qatar

A Paradigm Shift from a Resource to a Knowledge Economy

It has been several decades since the British left Qatar, and much has changed during the last four decades. Hydrocarbons have replaced pearls as Qatar's main source of revenue, bringing previously unimagined wealth to the former British protectorate, as White (2010) rightly argues. With a per capita income of US$83,000, second highest in the world, the leaders of Qatar are building a new future for their country. In the last decade, Qatar managed to provide a stimulating yet provocative development model within the Gulf and the Middle East. As Roberts (2017) claims, rarely has a state changed its character so completely in so short a period of time. Previously content to play a role befitting its small size, Qatar was a traditional, risk-averse Gulf monarchy until the early 1990s. In 1995, an emerging leader with a progressive vision for the future came to power. Financed by gas exports, Qatar diversified its foreign relations, established the satellite broadcaster Al Jazeera, assumed a leading role in international mediation, and hosted a number of top-level sporting tournaments, culminating in the successful FIFA World Cup 2022 bid. Qatar, while developing its vision for the future, decided to adopt the knowledge economy as the new pillar

Figure 3.9. The evolution of Doha from a fishing-based, traditional settlement in 1937 to an expanded metropolitan city, as documented in 2015. Source: Author.

for its economy and development. For that reason, the case of Doha is stimulating, as such interventions are made to pave the way for a new development vision structured on the value of knowledge economy and knowledge-based urbanity. Yet, for a more holistic understanding, one cannot merely see all the cultural and educational projects in all Gulf cities as part of the spectacle construction process and as a catalyst for global recognition. Such projects are used to create a different kind of spectacle not dependent on the virtual economy of real estate and the speculative mechanisms of unsustainable development.

Establishing Qatar as a Regional Hub for Knowledge and Research

With the full realization that a new development identity is needed, Qatar has shifted to a new growth policy that transcends the typical model used in Gulf states. By any measure, Qatar's growth is phenomenal; in the past decade, the population has trebled, and the size of metropolitan Doha's built environment has increased fourfold (Alraouf, 2017). From its humble origins as a fishing and pearling village, Doha has emerged as a growing world city, where ambition and means are

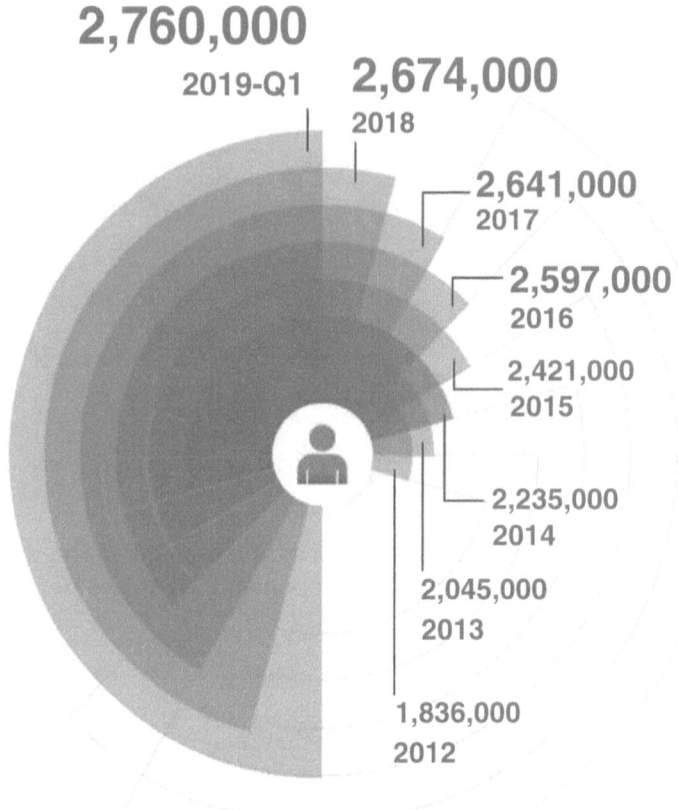

Figure 3.10. The growing population of Qatar, despite the recent blockade that was activated in June 2017. Source: Data from Ministry of Development Planning and Statistics.

fueling exciting experiments in education, health, sports, and culture (Fromherz, 2012; Kamrava, 2013; Alraouf, 2008, 2016, 2017). The need to diversify the state's economy and to shift from a hydrocarbon-based economy to a knowledge-based one is a key stipulation of the *Qatar National Vision 2030* (QSDP, 2009), the *Qatar National Development Strategy 2011–2016* (QSDP, 2011), and the updated version covering the time frame 2016–32 (Ministry of Municipality and Environment, 2016). Central to the state's vision is the recognition that, as plentiful as Qatar's

Figure 3.11. The contemporary skyline of Doha, suggesting its attempt to be placed on the global stage. Source: Author.

natural resources may be, their value will one day be significantly diminished by the emergence of sustainable forms of energy production (Woodman, 2008; Ouroussoff, 2008). More significantly, the country's long-term development plan is aimed at reducing dependency on hydrocarbons and creating a diversified economy driven by the principles of knowledge economy. Such choices should be scrutinized, not only from architectural and urban points of view but also from a social perspective. No city in the world, including Doha, can be transformed into a knowledge and creative city without a legitimate framework that allows city dwellers, locals, and expatriates to be engaged, considered, and gain a sense of belonging.

The combination of a massive labour deficit and the abundance of discretionary wealth cemented the necessity for a new alternative for development and investment. Qatar's national vision of transitioning towards a knowledge-based economy is rooted in developing the state as a regional and increasingly global leader in terms of research and development. The government has gradually strengthened the human and capital resources required to achieve this goal through the transformation of its education systems and by means of major investments in developing an advanced academic and research environment. The *Qatar National Research Strategy*, which was launched in 2012, outlines an extensive framework of goals and objectives under five priority themes that reflect local needs (The Qatar National Research Strategy (QNRS), Qatar Foundation, 2012). The government has signalled the importance of these initiatives with commitments to allocate 2.8 per cent of total government revenue to finance the development of facilities and research. The Qatar Foundation, in particular, has played a critical role in funding research and also by developing leading centres for research in medicine, science, and technology. Evidently, policies were generated and resources were allocated, but moving towards a knowledge-based future requires a social and cultural revolution, and radical changes towards positively acknowledging the unique human mix living and working in Qatar. The state changed the sponsorship laws and now punishes business owners for keeping the passports of their employees. This law is appreciated and needed, but it is up to the expectations of the society for cultural and social revolution that would create a different bond between people and place, and facilitate individual or collective decision-making by expatriates to settle freely and proudly in Qatar and consider it home.

The Transformation of Doha into a Knowledge City

In the last decade, Qatar has transformed itself into a major hub for numerous economic and cultural activities. Whether to counter regional economic competitors or to further ties with the economies of the world's leading countries, this brand is designed innovatively to counter a range of security concerns; in short, Qatar is diversifying its dependencies (Roberts, 2017; Alraouf, 2016). Furthermore, Qatar has become attractive as a place for foreign knowledge workers and the creative class – the class of people who are moving around the world and are attracted to the quality of urban environments that maintain their creative and intellectual outputs (Florida, 2002, 2005). Qatar's national vision for the year 2030 consists of basic foundations focused on the necessity for continuous social development in order to achieve a fair and safe society based on upholding human values and social welfare. It also aims to maintain and improve its economic standards in order to further strengthen its national economy and remain competitive, while continuing to secure and satisfy the needs of its citizens (QSDP, 2009). Maintaining the current growth of its urban population and fostering quality of life is seen as critical to the future development of the country, as indicated in the *National Development Strategy 2011–2016* (QSDP, 2011). Such vision is supporting the way in which the new generation of knowledge workers decide where to live, as Florida argues (Florida, 2008).

In 2005, the Qatar Investment Authority (QIA) was established with a vision to reinvest oil and gas revenues and build a diversified international asset portfolio. According to financial analysis done by RGE Monitor New York, Qatar has around US$75 billion worth of investments outside the country. Strategically, Qatar has been on a multibillion dollar spending spree to acquire assets across the globe. Yet, the country's leaders fully acknowledge the importance of development from within. So, while Qatar is spending a fortune on foreign shores, it has not forgotten to invest at home. As part of this development, the face of Doha will change immeasurably over the coming years. So far, Doha is a more successful example of incorporating knowledge within the city. Undoubtedly, architecture and urbanism are excellent tools that help cities create their niche in the global competition. Doha, while investing in positioning itself on the map of world emerging economies, was alert to the use of architecture and urbanism as a manifestation of a new era of planning and urban development (Jodidio, 2015; Alraouf, 2012, 2016). The shift occurs and differentiates Doha from other Gulf cities because of the move towards the KBUD paradigm. Within the boundaries of such a paradigm, the notion of spectacle was revisited to allow transformation from a focus on vertical development, skyscrapers, and iconic real estate to an alternative spectacle constructed around the pillars of KBUD, such as museums, universities, research centres, and a stimulating public realm.

Starting from 2008, Qatar adopted a new vision towards achieving a holistic development that was crystallized in the doctrinal document *Qatar National Vision 2030* (QSDP, 2009). It is structured around huge investments in education, science, and research. In other words, the knowledge economy was explicitly declared to be the selected economic platform for the country's future. While Doha's position is radically different from cities like Manama and Dubai when it comes to oil and gas reserves, Qatar leaders were convinced that the post-oil paradigm is becoming a reality. Qatar's situation is different because of the availability of oil and its position as the third country in the world in terms of natural gas reserves. Hence, moving from a resource economy to a knowledge-based economy is a global and inevitable transformation that requires understanding and better engagement. To pave the way for this process to be implemented, main steps were taken. In 1995, Sheikh Hamad Al Thani authorized the establishment of the Qatar Foundation, a comprehensive and dynamic knowledge structure that includes all levels of educational services from basic to university education.

The Alternative Spectacle: Doha's Knowledge-Based Urbanity

The paradigm shift from resource to knowledge economy requires courageous decisions and radical transformations. One of the most clearly manifested aspects of such transformations is the newly introduced mechanism for creating the city spectacle. The real estate industry still represents a sign of development, but it has moved from speculative process to the actual needs of the society. Alternatively, the city leaders and planners invested in two essential dimensions: first, establishing a fiscal and social momentum, which sees Doha as a resilient and thriving city, not a place for real estate adventures; and second, restructuring the architectural and urban image of the city to resonate with its newly assembled identity as a knowledge and creative city. It is a city that is not fundamentally concerned with the glossy image of its cloud-piercing towers and luxurious mega shopping malls but, rather, a city that celebrates social and urban diversity and invests in projects that facilitate integration and knowledge sharing and dissemination – a city with places for people.

In terms of architecture and urbanism, these two main categories can be observed within the boundaries of Doha as the main channels for articulating the new urban brand. KBUD is the first category. The balanced combination between local and global urbanism is the second. Qatar underwent a radical transformation to go beyond the typical image of a Gulf city relying on presumably endless assets of oil and gas. Significant investment has been made in knowledge-based urban development in the country during the last decade. Architectural and urban evidence of the new trend towards knowledge-based urbanism can be observed around Doha, including iconic projects like Education City, Qatar Science and Technology Park, National Library, Qatar National Museum (QNM), and the Museum of Islamic Art (MIA). In the Middle East, museums were traditionally geared towards the elite and well-educated minority, as well as towards foreigners and tourists (Alraouf, 2016). However, museums are now using a different approach to blend into the cities where they are located, expanding their target audience by engaging all segments of the local community (Anderson, 2004; Black, 2005). MIA in Doha is an interesting example that shows how museums are moving from independent and isolated buildings to a vibrant urban entity where exhibition spaces, public places, educational facilities, and entertainment venues are blended harmoniously (Fairs, 2008). MIA situated Qatar on a global stage, connected it to regional and local architectural trends, and enabled it to display its adherence to the creation of KBUD (Alraouf, 2008, 2012). More importantly, the Qatar Foundation accommodates creativity and innovation forums, a leadership academy, a sports academy, research centres, intellectual debates, and state-of-the-art conference facilities. For the sake of this chapter, a focus on some specific projects from within the Qatar Foundation is provided. Such projects are used to evaluate Qatar's effort to

Figure 3.12. The new Qatar National Museum (QNM), a major contribution to the city's new identity as a knowledge and creative city characterized by cultural and knowledge buildings, not by skyscrapers. Source: Author.

construct its identity as a knowledge and creative city within the Gulf's emerging urbanism. The analysis suggests that Qatar is using this new paradigm to create an identity for its capital city that is more hybrid and balanced.

Another keystone in the vision of Qatar as a platform for KBUD is manifested in projects related to the culture of education, research, and knowledge dissemination. Education City (EC) is creating a culture of research and knowledge that is located in a unique campus on the outskirts of Doha. EC hosts branch campuses of some of the world's leading universities, as well as numerous other educational and research institutions. EC is envisioned as a hub for the generation of new knowledge: a place that provides researchers with world-class facilities, a pool of well-trained graduates, the chance to collaborate with like-minded people, and the opportunity to transfer ideas into real-world applications. To be confident that EC is playing its social role within Doha, a deliberate effort is geared towards the internal and external integration of EC with greater Doha. To achieve this goal, some strategies were suggested, including the borderless campus, inviting local communities to use the city's facilities, and providing new amenities that speak to the needs of the surrounding community and the residents of Qatar

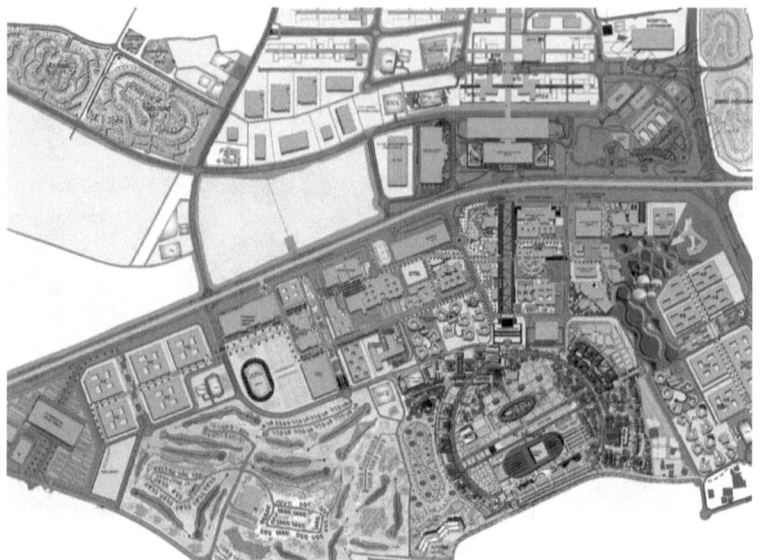

Figure 3.13. Smart KBUD: The case of Education City in Doha. Source: Courtesy of the Qatar Foundation.

as a whole. On the same path, Qatar's Science and Technology Park (QSTP) aims at turning Doha into a vibrant science and technology hub and attracting and retaining highly skilled employees, as outlined in the *Qatar National Vision 2030*. QSTP was established to provide the ideal environment to develop and market hi-tech intensive innovations and products, and to provide services and locations with international standards for global companies to incubate new technological projects. The fact that QSTP is located close to EC's top universities adds a positive element, particularly when it comes to research collaboration, innovation, and creativity.

The different strategies Doha adopts to go beyond its regional and global weight causes major problems and has escalated conflicts with its neighbours, particularly the UAE. As explained in Alraouf (2017), Doha acted as a conflict moderator to emphasize local stability and to gain regional and global credibility. Evidence, particularly after the blockade imposed on Qatar, suggests that Doha is a more "successful" example of moving towards an alternative mode of development in the post-oil future. Yet, there are a number of critical aspects to be considered if the case of Doha is to be seen as an interesting model for the new paradigm of Gulf cities' development. In some cases, predominantly

Figures 3.14–3.18. (previous page and above) The architectural and urban components of Education City in Doha are contributing to constructing an alternative spectacle that is founded on knowledge-based urban development. Source: Author.

the aftermath of the Arab Spring, Doha's position in supporting democratic changes in the Middle East annoyed its close neighbours who felt radically and existentially threatened during the saga of the Arab Spring. Doha's position was also criticized in terms of being one of the Gulf monarchies and a solid case of ruling families controlling "rentier states."[6] The state is still facing the challenges and contestations, and what remains to be achieved in its current development process.

Conclusion

The two Gulf cities Dubai and Doha have been perceived chronologically as two major success stories in the evolution of contemporary Middle Eastern cities during the last decade. The main objective of this chapter is to provide an alternative analysis suggesting that, with all the similarities between the two cities – since both shared humble beginnings and underwent swift modernization due to oil and gas revenues – their approach to the role of real estate, the construction of the city's spectacle, and the speculation about its future are radically different. The narrative recited in this chapter suggests that, for a fair and just analysis of the Gulf cities' evolution, it is essential to examine the different approaches independently and refrain from grouping all the Gulf cities into one homogenous group, as all the different layers and aspects of analysis suggest the heterogeneous nature of contemporary Gulf cities. More significantly, the juxtapositioning of the two narratives of Dubai and Doha illustrates a number of crucial issues, particularly in the shadow of one of the most alarming and unprecedented crises in the modern history of Gulf states: the blockade. A prime issue is related to the collective identity of this geographical context as it was swiftly fractured. It was realized that the only working model of unity and solidarity in the Middle East is on the verge of collapse. More significantly, most of the promises that came with the spectacle construction approach in developing Gulf cities were diminished.

Clearly, preparing for the post-carbon paradigm was not perceived as an inevitable destiny for Gulf states. Rather, the same strategy of shallow representation of knowledge-based urban development (KBUD) was implemented without making the radical changes and essential transformations at every level needed to cope with the

---

6 Rentier state theory (RST) is a political economy theory that seeks to explain state-society relations in states that generate a large proportion of their income from rents, or externally derived, unproductively earned payments.

challenges of the new paradigm. Hence, in some locations within the Gulf, and particularly in Dubai, KBUD is limited, as it is relying only on the construction of the physical environment, not on the creation of the just, free, and authentically tolerant one. The current Gulf crisis shows that the image of any city results not only from its architectural and urban spectacle but rather from a holistic assessment of the political, economic, and cultural context. The acknowledgment of a new concept of citizenship is fundamentally and direly needed in Gulf states. As a result of the current Gulf crisis, Qatar decided to consider a new law of residency that allows selected expatriates to gain full residency, but not nationality. The UAE, on the other hand, still deals with expatriates as foreigners working on a contractual basis related to a specific time frame.

Doha has gained global significance through the growth of knowledge economy–related projects. The city's new urban development and its spatial qualities contribute to the global attractiveness of Doha for knowledge economy investments, firms, and people. Such urbanism fulfils the requirements of knowledge workers coming to the city from literally every part of the globe, anticipating an attractive, smooth quality of life that would foster their creativity and innovation. While Dubai's model was based on glittering façades, high-end hotels, artificial islands, huge shopping malls, and the tallest constructions in the world, Doha strategically decided to move to another development model, a model that would better prepare the city to go beyond oil and attract people from all over the world to settle in Doha as a new centre for education, research, and culture (Alraouf, 2012, 2016, 2018). Therefore, Doha's regional and global importance has been amplified significantly over the last decade. While the only constant component in the matrix of contemporary Gulf states' development is the unprecedented rapid development, the current crisis alludes to the shifting sands that they sit upon. Urban development is not only in a constant state of flux in the region, but the adopted strategies differ in terms of the post-oil future. Much of the continuing urban development of the Gulf region rests on the oil economy. But it seems that the typical threat of what will happen when the oil runs out is not the prime concern. More critically, the need for oil will slow down in the near future with the outcomes of extensive research in alternative sources of energy that promise cleaner, more reliable, and cheaper sources. The new urban development strategies for Gulf states should highlight how architecture and urbanism might be developed to generate new urban settings that are economically viable, socially inclusive, and environmentally sustainable.

REFERENCES

Al Hathloul, S. (2004). Planning in the Middle East, moving toward the future. *Habitat International*, 18(5), 641–3. https://doi.org/10.1016/j.habitatint.2004.04.004

Al-Nakib, F. (2016). *Kuwait transformed: A history of oil and urban life*. Stanford University Press.

Al Qassemi, S. (2013, 8 October). Thriving Gulf cities emerge as new centers of Arab world. *Al-Monitor: The pulse of the Middle East*. http://www.al-monitor.com/pulse/originals/2013/10/abu-dhabi-dubai-doha-arab-centers.html#ixzz4sLNSlI3A

Alraouf, A.A. (2008). Emerging Middle Eastern knowledge cities: The unfolding story. In T. Yigitcanlar, K. Velibeyoglu, & S. Baum (Eds.), *Knowledge-based urban development: Planning and applications in the information era* (pp. 240–59). IGI Global Publishing.

Alraouf, A.A. (2010, 3–6 January). Critical paradigms in analyzing contemporary Gulf cities. In *Proceedings of the Conference on Technology & Sustainability in the Built Environment* (pp. 581–602). Organized by the College of Architecture and Planning at King Saud University, Riyadh, Saudi Arabia. https://cap.ksu.edu.sa/en/TSBE

Alraouf, A.A. (2012). A tale of two souqs. In or out of place: The paradox of Gulf urban diversity. *Open House International Journal*, 37(2), 72–81. https://doi.org/10.1108/OHI-02-2012-B0009

Alraouf, A.A. (2016). "Dohaization": An emerging interface between knowledge, creativity, and gulf urbanity. In G. Katodrytis & S. Syed (Eds.), *Gulf cities as interfaces* (pp. 47–67). Gulf Research Centre Cambridge.

Alraouf, A.A. (2017). Interrogating Qatar's urbanity as a catalyst for building knowledge-based societies and economies. In R.G. Bertelsen, N. Noori, & J.-M. Rickli (Eds.), *Strategies of knowledge transfer for economic diversification in the Arab states of the Gulf* (pp. 53–66). Gerlach Press.

Alraouf, A.A. (Ed.). (2018). *Knowledge-based urban development in the Middle East*. IGI Global Publishing.

Anderson, G. (2004). *Reinventing the museum: Historical and contemporary perspectives on the paradigm shift*. AltaMira Press.

BBC News. (2018, 26 November). Matthew Hedges: British academic pardoned by UAE. *BBC News*. https://www.bbc.com/news/uk-46341310

Black, G. (2005). *The engaging museum: Developing museums for visitor involvement*. Routledge.

Carrillo, F.J., Yigitcanlar, T., García, B., & Lönnqvist, A. (2014). *Knowledge and the city: Concepts, applications and trends of knowledge-based urban development*. Routledge.

Cooke, M. (2014). *Tribal modern: Branding new nations in the Arab Gulf*. University of California Press.

Davidson, C.M. (2008). *Dubai: The vulnerability of success*. Hurst.

Davidson, C.M. (2009). *Abu Dhabi: Oil and beyond*. Columbia University Press.

Dubai strategic plan 2015: Dubai... where the future begins. (2007). Emirate of Dubai, UAE. http://www.dsg.gov.ae/SiteCollectionImages/Content/pubdocs/Dubai_Strategic_Plan_2015.pdf

Dudley, D. (2019, 29 January). Dubai has become a "money laundering paradise," says anti-corruption group. *Forbes*. https://www.forbes.com/sites/dominicdudley/2019/01/29/dubai-has-become-a-money-laundering-paradise-says-anti-corruption-group/

Elsheshtawy, Y. (2010). *Dubai: Behind an urban spectacle*. Routledge.

Elsheshtawy, Y. (2015, 6–7 March). *Speculation, excess and urban growth: The case of Dubai* [Paper presentation]. The Speculative City Emergent Forms and Norms of the Built Environment, The University of Hong Kong, Hong Kong.

Elsheshtawy, Y. (2019). Real estate speculation and transnational development in Dubai. In H. Molotch & D. Ponzini (Eds.), *The new Arab urban: Gulf cities of wealth, ambition, and distress* (pp. 235–55). New York University Press.

Ergazakis, K., Metaxiotis, K., & Psarras, J. (2006). Knowledge cities: The answer to the needs of knowledge-based development. *Journal of Information and Knowledge Management Systems*, 36(1), 67–81. https://doi.org/10.1108/03055720610667381

Fairs, M. (2008, 2 December). Museum of Islamic Art by IM Pei. *de zeen*. https://www.dezeen.com/2008/12/02/museum-of-islamic-art-by-im-pei/

Florida, R. (2002). *The rise of the creative class*. Basic Books.

Florida, R. (2005). *Cities and the creative class*. Routledge.

Florida, R. (2008). *Who's your city?* Basic Books.

Frey, W.H. (2010). *Investigating change in American society*. Wadsworth.

Fromherz, A.J. (2012). *Qatar: A modern history*. Georgetown University Press.

Gambrell, J. (2018, 12 June). Report describes Dubai real estate as money-laundering haven. *Financial Post*. https://financialpost.com/pmn/business-pmn/report-describes-dubai-real-estate-as-money-laundering-haven

Gray, M. (2013). *Qatar: Politics and the challenges of development*. Lynne Rienner Publishers.

Hertog, S. (2017). *A quest for significance: Gulf oil monarchies' international "soft power" strategies and their local urban dimensions*. London School of Economics and Political Science, LSE Kuwait Program, Paper Series, 42. http://eprints.lse.ac.uk/69883/1/Hertog_42_2017.pdf

ISOCARP (The International Society of City and Regional Planners). (2016). *Urban development and planning in the age of megacities: An overview of global trends and current practices*. ISOCARP Publications.

Jodidio, P. (2015). *The new architecture of Qatar*. Skira Rizzoli Publications.

Kamrava, M. (2013). *Qatar: Small state, big politics*. Cornell University Press.
Kanna, A. (2011). *Dubai, the city as corporation*. University of Minnesota Press.
Kanna, A. (Ed.). (2013). *The superlative city: Dubai and the urban condition in the early twenty-first century*. Harvard University Press.
Keshavarzian, A. (2016). From port cities to cities with ports: Towards a multiscalar history of Persian Gulf urbanism in the twentieth century. In M. Kamrava (Ed.), *Gateways to the world: Port cities in the Gulf* (pp. 19–41). Oxford University Press.
Knight, R. (2008). Foreword: Knowledge based development: The challenge for cities. In T. Yigitcanlar, K. Velibeyoglu, & S. Baum, (Eds.), *Knowledge-based urban development: Planning and applications in the information era* (pp. xiv–xix). IGI-Global.
Kunzmann, K. (2008). Afterword: Spatial dimensions of knowledge production. In T. Yigitcanlar, K. Velibeyoglu, & S. Baum, (Eds.), *Knowledge-based urban development: Planning and applications in the information era* (pp. 296–300). IGI-Global.
McGinley, A. (2015, 30 September). Revealed: Top 12 Dubai Expo 2020 projects. *Arabian Business*. https://www.arabianbusiness.com/revealed-top-12-dubai-expo-2020-projects-607516.html
Miller, R. (2016). *Desert kingdoms to global powers: The rise of the Arab Gulf*. Yale University Press.
Ministry of Municipality and Environment. (2016). *Qatar National Development Framework 2032*. https://www.mme.gov.qa/QatarMasterplan/Downloads-qnmp/QNDF/English/English_QNDF.pdf
Molotch, H., & Ponzini, D. (Eds.). (2019). *The new Arab urban: Gulf cities of wealth, ambition, and distress*. New York University Press.
Municipality of Dubai. (2014). *Dubai 2020 urban masterplan*. Mimeo. https://www.dm.gov.ae/wp-content/uploads/2020/08/Dubai-2020-Master-Plan-ENG.pdf
Qatar Foundation. (2012). *Qatar national research strategy 2012*. https://www.qnrf.org/Portals/0/QNRS_2012.pdf
QSDP (Qatar General Secretariat of Development Planning). (2009). *Qatar national vision 2030: Advancing sustainable development, Qatar's second human development report*. Gulf Publishing and Printing Company.
QSDP (Qatar General Secretariat of Development Planning). (2011). *National development strategy 2011–2016*. Gulf Publishing and Printing Company.
Ouroussoff, N. (2008, 14 December). For I.M. Pei and the Museum of Islamic Art, history is still happening. *New York Times*. https://www.nytimes.com/2008/12/14/arts/design/14ouro.html
Reuters. (2014, 15 June). Is another property bubble looming over Dubai? *Gulf Business*. https://gulfbusiness.com/another-property-bubble-looming-dubai/

Roberts, D.B. (2017). *Qatar: Securing the global ambitions of a city-state.* Hurst
Sassen, S. (1991). *The global city, New York, London, Tokyo.* Princeton University Press.
Sassen, S. (2002). *Global networks, linked cities: Urban connections in a globalizing world.* Routledge.
The National. (2016, 9 February). New UAE Cabinet announced. *The National.* https://www.thenationalnews.com/uae/government/new-uae-cabinet-announced-1.224699
Transparency International. (2018a). Corruption perceptions index, 2018. https://www.transparency.org/en/cpi/2018/index/are
Transparency International. (2018b, 12 June). Dirty-money hub Dubai must clean up its real estate section. *Transparency International.* https://www.transparency.org/en/press/dirty-money-hub-dubai-must-clean-up-its-real-estate-sector
Ulrichsen, K.C. (2011). *Insecure Gulf: The end of certainty and the transition to the post-oil era.* Oxford University Press.
Wainwright, O. (2018, 1 January). Dubai frame: UAE's latest surreal landmark frames a controversy. *The Guardian.* https://www.theguardian.com/world/2018/jan/01/dubai-frame-uaes-latest-surreal-landmark-frames-a-controversy
White, A. (2010, 11 July). Qatar Inc.: How Doha's dollars are changing the world. *Arabian Business, 11*(28), 26–34. https://www.arabianbusiness.com/qatar-inc-how-doha-s-dollars-are-changing-world-305571.html
Wiedmann, F. (2010). *Post-oil urbanism in the Gulf.* Städtebau Institut, FG SIAAL der Universität Stuttgart.
Wippel, S. (Ed.). (2014). *Under construction: Logics of urbanism in the Gulf region.* Ashgate.
Woodman, E. (2008). I.M. Pei's MIA opens in Doha. Review. Retrieved on 28 March 2014 from http://www.bdonline.co.uk/story.asp?storycode=3129204
Yigitcanlar, T. (2011). Redefining knowledge-based urban development. *International Journal of Knowledge Based Development, 2*(4), 340–56. https://eprints.qut.edu.au/47809/2/47809.pdf

SECTION II

Reconfiguring the State: The Politics and Pragmatics of Speculation

4 Mega-Event Urbanism and the Politics of Speculative Urban Development in Shanghai

YUNPENG ZHANG AND SHENJING HE

Introduction

In 2017, Budapest, following Hamburg and Rome, formally dropped the race against Paris and Los Angeles for hosting the 2024 Summer Olympics. With only two cities left in the bidding game, the International Olympics Committee decided to revise the procedures and awarded the 2024 Summer Olympics to Paris and the 2028 Summer Olympics to Los Angeles, finding some breathing time to sustain the invented tradition of the Olympics. The declining interest of many cities in hosting global events like the Olympics is largely related to the fiscal and political challenges such as cost overruns, underutilized facilities, short-term boostering effects, and public absorption of risks (Horne, 2007; Müller, 2015). These adverse effects upon the hosting cities, regions, and nations were never absent in the past but only marginalized or repressed by the event-media-corporate complex (Horne, 2007; Hall, 2006). As many advanced economies are still recovering from the global financial crisis, these negative effects are brought to the fore. Unless cures to the "mega-event syndrome" (Müller, 2015) are found, it is likely that the interest of cities in hosting these once enthusiastically sought-after mega-events is bound to further decline, except maybe in Asia, and in particular China, where several megacities – Shanghai, Chengdu, and Guangzhou – are exploring the possibilities of hosting the Olympics in 2032 or later.

The fetishism of Chinese cities for global events is the subject of this chapter. Specifically, we focus on the political economy and the politics of hosting the 2010 World Expo in Shanghai. Born in the context of state and nation building in the nineteenth century, the cultural institution of World Expo was prescribed with important functions of commercial exchange, technological and cultural display, as well as ideological indoctrination (Roche, 2003). With the popularization of digital mass communication, the world fair, unlike the sporting event, has long lost its glory. It can no longer compete against global sporting events in attracting millions of visitors and television viewers. Nevertheless, it remains an important temporal marker, registering the technological and cultural progress of humanity in different epochs (Roche, 2003). Lasting for six months, a much longer period than the Olympics and other sporting events, the World Expo brings a different rhythm to the spatial organization of the flows of capital, people, and goods. The empirical ambition of this chapter is to flesh out the dynamics and consequences of hosting the World Expo. We shall address a key question raised by this book: what is speculative about the World Expo as an urban development strategy?

Our main conceptual reference point is David Harvey's theorization of the geographies of capitalism. Specifically, we engage with his often-cited notions of spatial fix and capital switching (Harvey, 1985, 2001), which explain the spatial mechanisms that enable a capitalist system to expand and reproduce. Instead of reducing the state to an instrument of capital switching or spatial fix as in Harvey's theorization, we take a further step to unravel the crucial and complex roles of the state. The state serves as more than a regulator; it is the very agent that switches capital between circuits. Our contribution in this regard draws upon much wider literature on state restructuring and the land-centred regime of accumulation in late socialist China, which has compellingly demonstrated the tensions within the bureaucratic field regarding land uses and land development (Hsing, 2010; Lin, 2009). Our purpose in situating our analysis of mega-events in this literature is to provide a grounded understanding of the political economy of mega-events as an urban development strategy in a broader context, since they are often part or a catalyst of spatial restructuring of the host cities and regions of different scales.

Our key argument is that the World Expo – especially the globality attendant to it – created a common vision that not only temporarily suspended the tension between state units but also united them to work together towards the common goal. This alliance within the state – albeit contentious and unstable – preconditions the economic project of capital accumulation through land recommodification and capital switching. Through hosting the World Expo, the Shanghai municipal government expanded territorial control and rationalized territorial organization. Speculation on land values was built into this Expo-induced spatial restructuring strategy.

The empirics of this chapter are derived from a larger research project on the socio-spatial impacts of the World Expo 2010, which relied on various sources of data, including policy and planning documents, newspaper articles, semi-structured interviews, and participant observation. For this chapter, we draw on a narrower set of data, mainly including official documents, reports from real estate consultancy firms, and interviews with four planning professionals and three Shanghai-based artists.

In the rest of this chapter, we first review Harvey's thesis on capital switching and spatial fix. We respond to the critique of Harvey's theorization for reducing the state to an instrument of capital by underscoring its agency in switching capital. Centring on the state, our discussion proceeds to chart out the conflicts and synergies between state units involved in land development in post-reform China. We then embed our examination of the World Expo within its own development trajectory in order to flesh out the connection of this strategy with Shanghai's overall socio-spatial restructuring. Against this conceptual and empirical background, we move to examine the transformations caused by hosting the World Expo 2010, which has redeveloped the waterfront area from a place of heavy industrial manufacturing to one of high-end cultural consumption and service industry.

Capital Switching, the State, and Mega-Event Urbanism

The primary inspiration for our conceptual understanding comes from Harvey's insight on urban processes under capitalism, particularly the geographical mechanisms that reproduce capitalism along with its crisis tendencies and apparent inequalities (Harvey, 1985, 2001). In Harvey's view, an inherent contradiction of capitalist accumulation is the tendency to over-accumulate, which reduces profitability and induces accumulation crisis (Harvey, 2001). Temporal-spatial fixes are therefore necessary to overcome the crisis of over-accumulation and enable capitalism to survive and expand. Harvey's idea of temporal-spatial fix is closely related to his other notion of capital switching (Harvey, 1985). He analytically distinguished three circuits of capital, namely the primary circuit of commodity production, the secondary circuit of the built environment production, and the tertiary circuit of investments in research, technology, and labour power reproduction (Harvey, 1985). In times of falling profitability rates and over-accumulation crises, Harvey (1985) argued, surplus capital can be directed to other circuits, such as building infrastructure networks, constructing social housing, or funding basic research. Such switches can occur within or beyond a given territory, thereby expanding the reach of capitalist relations, geographically and societally (Harvey, 2001). They can absorb the surplus labour and capital, and in turn can potentially improve productivity and surplus value extraction in the primary circuit, thereby fixing the crisis of over-accumulation. The secondary circuit is particularly important to the spatial forms of cities. Harvey pointed out that switching capital to this secondary circuit has its limits due to the immobility and durability of the built structure, meaning long turnover time and hence frictions for capital accumulation (Harvey, 1985). Therefore, switching capital to the built environment as a solution to the crisis of over-accumulation can only temporarily defer and spatially displace it. The built environment itself is also subject to the contested process of periodic and cyclic restructuring.

Although Harvey's theorization offers a useful lens to understand the spatiality of capitalist accumulation, his underestimation of the power of financial actors and the state has attracted some valid critiques. For Harvey, "a general condition for the flow of capital into the secondary circuit is ... the existence of a functioning capital market, and, perhaps, a state willing to finance and guarantee long-term, large-scale projects with respect to the creation of the built environment" (1985, p. 7). Financial institutions are conceived to provide credits and essential financial services, while the state is to assume the responsibility of creating an enabling regulatory environment or ensuring the development of projects that individual capitalists are unwilling or unable to carry out on their own, for instance, when directing capital to the tertiary circuit. This view reduces agents of financial capital and the state to instruments in the process of switching capital, devoid of their own agency (Gottdiener, 1985).

In fairness, this situation might have been the case at the time when Harvey developed his theorization. However, considerable update is required in order to capture the changing dynamics brought by the ascendency of the financial sector under neoliberal capitalism. The fast expansion of the financial sector and the proliferation of financial products have enabled the penetration of financial logics and narratives in economic management, political governance, and everyday life (Langley, 2008; Soederberg, 2014). An important effect is seen in the financialization of the built environment (Aalbers & Christophers, 2014; Li, 2014; van Loon & Aalbers, 2017). This development not only overcomes the contradiction between fixity and motion inhering in capital switching to the secondary circuit (Gotham, 2009) but also makes accumulation through the secondary circuit increasingly independent of that through industrial production. Moreover, in a finance-dominated regime of accumulation, as in the United States (Krippner, 2005) or Hong Kong (Smart & Lee, 2003), profits are mostly procured through investments in the capital market. Financial products unrelated to the built environment offer additional outlets for surplus capital. Aalbers (2008) thus proposed to add a quaternary circuit to highlight the relative autonomy of the capital market, accumulation within which relates to the other three circuits but also occurs in its own right.

The state, on the other hand, is also not passive in the process. It operates more than a regulatory agency that lays out rules for urban builders, industrial capitalists, and financial institutions. It has also become an important enterprising actor that proactively engages with the capital market and deploys financial tools to deliver public goods (Weber, 2010; Weber & O'Neill-Kohl, 2013). Many activities and services (for example, education, social housing, public security, and so on) that are traditionally coordinated and provided by the state to ensure the reproduction of labour power have been transferred to the private domain (Soederberg, 2014). This recent development entails profound reconfiguration of the state and renegotiation of state responsibilities (Pacewicz, 2013; Hackworth, 2007). Herein lies the second critique of Harvey's account of capital switching. It appears that Harvey's thesis privileges a centralized state, which mediates inter-class struggles and coordinates social activities for the interests of capital. Agendas of the central state are translated straightforwardly into local policies. This view overlooks conflicts between state units and struggles among the political elites resulting from varying political configurations at both vertical and horizontal levels.

Taking stock of Harvey's work and the critique of it, we situate this conceptualization in China's peculiar socioeconomic contexts. While acknowledging the changing dynamics brought by the expansion of the financial sphere, we centre our analysis on the role of the Chinese state and statecraft. We do so for three reasons. First, we recognize the significant progress of marketization and modernization of the financial sector as part of the overall economic structuring in China. We also acknowledge the ever closer links between financial capital and other circuits of capital accumulation. But our observation suggests that state dominance is clearly evident in economic and financial management in spite of these changes. This dominance is manifested in many ways, including state ownership of dominant banks and financial institutions (including those publicly listed banks within and outside China), strong control of credit allocation, and the licensing mechanism for financial institutions (Stent, 2017; Heilmann, 2005). Even in the fast expanding shadow banking sector – a main contributor to speculative real estate development and public debt bubbles – both state banks and state-controlled firms are heavily involved through taking advantage of their mastery of regulatory landscapes and their easier access to cheap credit (Tsai, 2015). To finance local development, many local governments have become the vanguard of financialization and mobilized public assets – land in particular – to raise funds from the capital market through the mediation of special purpose vehicles (Wang, 2015). In short, while the Chinese state has conceded and perhaps will further concede power to the market, it still has a firm grip on economic management through a variety of socialist or capitalist means.

Second, the Chinese state dominates land tenure and land use planning. In legal texts, China has a dualistic land ownership. Land in cities is owned by the state, whereas land in the countryside is owned by rural collectives. Rural land can only be converted for urban use through state-led land appropriation. Furthermore, as a result of several rounds of land enclosures since the reform, the central government has established a rigid land use planning system so as to limit the expansionary impulse of subnational authorities (Lin, 2009). Switching capital and accommodating resultant changes in the built environment will inevitably bring about changes in land use patterns, which must comply with existing regulations. As elsewhere, this is a contested process. One important source of contention comes from within the state, resulting from competing claims for authority over land ownership and land uses (Hsing, 2010).

Third, although the state economy has shrunk considerably as a result of massive privatization and corporatization since the late 1990s, state-controlled firms remain important actors in the primary circuit, and in fact they dominate several strategic sectors such as energy, steel production, oil refinery, and telecommunications (Lin & Milhaupt, 2013). They are also heavily involved in land and real estate development (Hsing, 2010). Moreover, as a result of the socialist land use legacies, these manufacturing corporations often occupy large parcels of land in central locations and act as *de facto* public landlords. Therefore, in discussing the dynamics of capital switching, the Chinese state does more than enable the flows of capital between circuits. In many cases, it is the very agent that switches capital. In doing so, it adjusts the relations not only between the state and different species of capital but also between different state segments. This state-market problematic differs from that in Harvey's theorization, partly because capitalism is created from the foundations of a socialist planned economy in the Chinese context. It aligns more to Jessop's (1990) theorization of the state, especially the conflicts and contradictions within the state itself.

While taking a state-centric view, we reject a coherent and monolithic view of the Chinese state. Following established literature on state restructuring in reform China (Lieberthal, 1995; Hsing, 2010), we take seriously the nested structure of the Chinese state and fragmented authority within the state, which make political bargaining central to decision-making and policy implementation (He et al., 2018). As Hsing (2010) astutely observed, the incentive structure resulting from the reforms in public administration, land, housing, and public finance has made land an important object of political bargaining. Here, we are interested in the tensions between state units along both vertical and horizontal lines in switching capital and landing the spatial fix. Vertically, we consider the relations between the central and local authorities regarding the competing imperatives of legitimation and accumulation. While the Chinese state agencies at different levels place great emphasis on rapid economic growth, the central government focuses on legitimation more than lower-level authorities for the durable dominance of the Communist Party. Facing the pressure of party discipline, local state agents often base their decisions and pursue accumulation strategies that are in line with, or do not compromise too much, the integrity of the hegemonic project of the central government. Horizontally, we refer to the conflicts between the territorial coordinating states (that is, local government at different levels: municipal, district-level, and sub-district-level governments) and the functional state agencies (for example, the military, state-owned firms, educational establishments, and others) regarding land uses. As stated earlier, many functional states are *de facto* landlords. Although we agree with Hsing's (2010) observation that territorial states, the *de jure* landlords, have consolidated their power through their command of regulatory and administrative resources (for example, zoning control and monopoly of the primary land market), our contribution in this chapter adds nuances and illustrates that they do not necessarily do so through undercutting functional states, but also seek to reconcile the interests of functional states with their own agenda of recommodifying valuable land in prime locations and rationalizing urban land uses. In other words, the tensions between horizontal state units do not always lead to a zero-sum land battle in which one wins over the other. They can also be resolved through win-win tactics, such as pursuing common interests or sharing the benefits from land development or the costs of industrial relocation.

Worlding Shanghai: From a City of Industrial Production to the City of Design

The World Expo is an important milestone in Shanghai's re-emergence as a global metropolis. It is integrated with Shanghai's long-term strategies of industrial development and territorial organization that seek to move Shanghai further up the global value chain and turn it into an international centre of finance, logistics, and trade. To understand the conditions and dynamics of capital switching enabled by the World Expo, it is necessary to situate it within Shanghai's development trajectory, especially the property-led development strategy since the 1990s (He & Wu, 2005), which drastically transformed Shanghai's landscape.

In this process, the political and economic elites have demonstrated considerable craft in creatively destructing and reconstructing existing institutions. For example, in the development of Pudong, local states in Shanghai pioneered the land financing model, using state-controlled land as collateral to raise funds to assemble land and speculate on land value increase. To pacify social conflicts and persuade local households to give up their land, the governments also introduced the land for social security scheme and granted land-losing farmers access to social security, albeit substandard at that time. Both schemes have now travelled well beyond the boundaries of Shanghai. They are also the essential ingredients of the land-based speculative urbanization since the 2000s. While underscoring the agency of the local governments, we nonetheless share the view of Wu (2016) that we cannot overlook the power of the central state in clearing the political obstacles for policies of an experimental nature and setting up the parameters for boundary-expanding policies. This is a critical condition for local states to bend the rules, because the benefits of doing so would transcend the political risks of demotion or possible prosecution (see Lin, 2017).

These central-local state dynamics clearly shaped the development path of Shanghai and the formation of its social space. Both the fall and the ascendency of Shanghai are closely related to such state politics. After 1949, Shanghai – the economic and financial centre in the Asia-Pacific region in the 1920s and 1930s – quickly lost its development momentum. Its tertiary industry (for example, finance and real estate) shrank considerably, while the manufacturing industry (particularly in the sectors of metallurgy, chemicals, machinery, and textiles) fast expanded. There were several reasons for this change. First, one exceptional condition for Shanghai's rapid development in the first three decades of the twentieth century was the occurrence of domestic and international wars, the military demands from which contributed to industrial production operated by international and Chinese domestic capitalists. Second, as the Communist Party came into power, fear of the communist regime and imminent socialist transformations led to the outmigration of financial elites and industrial capitalists. Third, the prevailing rationality to eliminate capitalist forces and build a socialist city of production resulted in an adjustment of the industrial mix. Fourth, the national development strategy prioritized inland regions and suppressed new investments in coastal regions for fear of the outbreak of another war. The governing elites therefore took advantage of Shanghai's industrial base and developed Shanghai to support the national economy.

This position of Shanghai in the national political economy had several noteworthy consequences. To begin with, Shanghai had a high concentration of state economy sectors. Industrial operations were controlled by various state agencies at different levels. Owing to socialist planning rationality, these industrial firms were allocated land at prime locations in close proximity to residential compounds in order to reduce commuting hours and better organize labour reproduction. In 1985, for instance, slightly more than half of all industrial companies (n = 5,397) were operating in the city centre, occupying nearly one-fourth of land (Zhang & Du, 2001). Although these industrial complexes offered employment for urban populations and provided some facilities of collective consumption for neighbouring communities, their manufacturing activities added considerable constraints on neighbourhood resources and the environment. As the industrial base, Shanghai provided a crucial source of fiscal revenues for the central government. Between 1949 and 1990, the Shanghai government collected 398.5 billion RMB in total, nearly 85 per cent of which was submitted to Beijing to support national development (Editorial Committee of Shanghai Local History, n.d.). However, during the same period, only 7.38 per cent was transferred back to Shanghai for local development (Cui, 2008). This disparity resulted in significant underinvestment in collective consumption, especially housing. Between 1950 and 1978, average living space per capita increased extremely slowly and was only 4.5 square metres before the market-oriented reform (Editorial Committee of Shanghai Local History, n.d.).

These socio-spatial conditions limited Shanghai's opportunities in the first decade of China's reform. Shanghai was not placed at the forefront of China's sequential reforms of marketization due to its strategic import to the national economy, the experimental nature of many initiatives, and the strong presence of a state economy sector. After the rural economy and Southern China took off, many industrial firms in Shanghai experienced greater financial difficulty due to increased competition and the loss of protected markets. The turning point for Shanghai came after Deng Xiaoping's southern tour, during which he endorsed the development of Shanghai and thus cleared the political obstacles for putting Shanghai at the front of institutional experiments. As the party elites shifted the focus towards restructuring the state economy and creating a hybrid economy in the second decade of the reform,

Shanghai's high concentration of state-controlled firms also made it a logical candidate for the coming reforms. With the blessing of the central leadership, Shanghai once again became the top destination for inward investments. In 1990, Shanghai attracted only 0.2 billion USD foreign investment, but at the turn of the century it managed to attract investment of 6.4 billion USD (Shanghai Bureau of Statistics, 2004).

The development of Pudong and other suburban areas opened up new spaces to absorb inward investments. The Shanghai government encouraged lower-level authorities in suburban areas to establish development zones as main destinations for foreign investments. Pudong was chosen as a main destination, hosting three major development zones. Development of these zones served the interests of Shanghai well in pursuing property-led development and rationalizing urban land uses. These zones became the host for industrial companies relocated from the urban core. Land in the urban core was then released for more profitable uses, which partially financed the relocation of industrial firms. However, industrial relocation was not a non-discriminatory process. The Shanghai government was strategic about the desired industrial mix. It facilitated technology upgrading of existing industries and prioritized technology-advanced and export-oriented companies, while those less suitable ones were either closed down or pushed out of the city. This spatial redistribution of industrial capital was institutionalized in the Shanghai masterplan 1999–2000. Land in the inner ring was reserved for the tertiary industry and modern manufacturing industry that was more environmentally friendly and technology intensive. Between the inner ring and the outer ring, industrial land was restricted for high-tech, high-value-added industries with less or no pollution. Industrial development outside the outer ring was encouraged to align with new town development in suburbia.

This spatial reconfiguration of industrial landscape went hand in hand with housing stock renewal in the inner city and real estate development in the suburbs. In 1991, the Shanghai government identified housing of 365 hectares as dangerous and disordered simple shacks to be demolished, although some housing stock under this classification was in fact of decent quality (Ren, 2014). By 2000, more than 670,000 registered households were displaced, involving nearly 2 million residents (Shanghai Bureau of Statistics, 2004; Editorial Committee of Shanghai Housing Construction Chronicles, 1998). This housing stock renewal created a dual housing market – newly built apartment buildings on demolished sites targeting emerging middle and upper class residents and a resettlement housing market in urban fringes for both the displaced and migrant workers due to the cheap rent. The development of Pudong again was critical, not only serving as the new central business district but also forming a main resettlement site in the outer suburbs. It is a public secret that this dual housing market lies behind Shanghai's breath-taking spatial transformation. By displacing denizens from prime locations cheaply and leasing land for profitable real estate development, the government has been able to recover the costs of resettlement and gain a significant profit.

Seen from Harvey's perspective, Shanghai's socio-spatial restructuring shapes, and is shaped by, capital switching. At a global level, international value chain restructuring and Shanghai's emergence as a premium destination for investing in a marketizing China effectively absorbs surplus capital from outside China. At the metropolitan level, Shanghai's suburbia and Pudong provided the outlet for industrial capital. Yet, as Shen and Wu (2017) argued, capital accumulates simultaneously through industrial production (the primary circuit) and the built environment production (the secondary circuit). It is also partially directed towards the tertiary circuit (for example, expanding the coverage of social welfare or supporting technological innovation and research). On the one hand, geographical switching of industrial capital from the urban core to these peripheral regions frees up land for more profitable development, while its concentration in these regions not only attracts industrial workers but also boosts land values in surrounding areas. On the other hand, such geographical and sectoral switching of capital is enabled, and partially financed, by speculative real estate development.

The property-led development strategy has worked well for two important reasons. First, weakly protected land tenure and relatively decentralized, relaxed land governance in the 1990s made it easy to acquire land of a large scale. Resettlement housing that was offered to displaced households as part of their compensation improved the housing conditions of many poor residents caught up in an increasingly marketized housing system, thus creating an illusion of upward social mobility. This situation made it possible to bulldoze and gentrify the city without much resistance. Second, many industrial firms suffered great financial loss due to competition from an emerging private sector and the restructuring of the state economy. Using revenues from land capitalization and land development provided a way to fund their relocation, settle outstanding debts, and eventually restore their profitability.

While it might be relatively easier for the Shanghai government to mobilize industrial companies under its control, it is a categorically different matter when it comes to industrial companies that administratively outrank the Shanghai government. Adjusting their locations or business operations would require approvals from the central government. Moreover, relocation of these industrial operations entails more than valuing their assets, land included, and finding land to accommodate their activities. It also needs to make arrangements for the welfare of their workers. Furthermore, as the ruling elites become increasingly concerned about land enclosures and resultant social unrest, they have centralized and restricted land uses through a host of administrative and regulatory tools. These conditions set limits to property-led (re)development.

To further rationalize territorial organization, the Shanghai government has promoted the development of the cultural and creative industry since the 2000s, echoing the practices of creative cities elsewhere (Florida, 2005). This strategy aligned well with the central government's interest in reorienting the Chinese economy towards domestic consumption, finding new growth engines, and improving China's soft power (Ren & Sun, 2012; Keane, 2007). In 2005, the Shanghai government established the first batch of fifteen cultural and creative zones, exceptional spaces of accumulation through cultural and creative activities. Sporadic at the beginning, the cultural and creative industry quickly took off. It should be pointed out that the cultural and creative industry is rather expansively defined, including business activities ranging from fashion shops, tourism, and catering (cafes, tea houses, and bars) to industrial design and software development. Capitalizing on the growth of this industrial sector, the Shanghai government in 2010, the year when the World Expo was hosted, joined the UNESCO Creative Cities Network. Shanghai was branded as a City of Design, further consolidating its expertise on design activities in areas such as architecture, fashion, software, and industrial manufacturing.

Facilitating the cultural and creative industry also provided another way to put industrial land into higher and better use. In this regard, the Shanghai government sought to build alliances with industrial landlords by encouraging the development of creative and cultural activities on their premises – on condition that such development did not change land use attributes, property rights, and physical structure (He, 2019). In this way, it found an alternative way for industrial landlords to extract rent while at the same time respecting the authority of the central government in land uses (He, 2019). In appearance, this approach seems to have undermined the interest of the government in land revenues. But, as He (2019) astutely pointed out, the government can expect increased taxes and revenues from new business activities and an inflated property market in surrounding areas. This strategy also catered to the growing demand of the middle and upper class by promising improvements in cultural diversity, environment sustainability, and overall quality of life. Seen in this light, similar to Peck's (2005) observation, the creative city strategy thus consolidates rather than disrupts existing class structure and prevailing rationality in the production of urban space. Land's exchange value determines the allocation of land uses. The upshot, as Harvey (1973) warned, is speculation. In his words, when value determines uses, "the allocation can take place under the auspices of rampant speculation, its artificially induced scarcities, and the like, and it loses any pretence of having anything at all to do with the efficient organization of production and distribution" (p. 190).

The State-Led Mega-Event Fix

The World Expo demonstrates continuity in Shanghai's development strategy and offers an excellent case to illustrate the politics of capital switching in making a creative Shanghai. It unravels the tensions as well as alliances between different state units in configuring Shanghai's social space. To host this global event, the Shanghai government cleared land of 5.28 square kilometres along the waterfront in the city centre for the construction of exhibition halls and event venues in the Expo Park. This area has been integral to Shanghai's overall waterfront redevelopment plan since the 2000s. The waterfront area of more than 20 square kilometres, dominated by industrial landscapes, was envisioned to serve the functions of tourism, entertainment, and green space. However, socio-spatial restructuring directly and indirectly induced by the World Expo went much beyond the Expo Park. Adjacent to this park, the planners demarcated an area of 1.4 square kilometres as the coordinated planning zone. The goal was to selectively demolish or upgrade buildings of poor conditions or illegal status and relocate industrial operations so that the façade of this area was aesthetically compatible with that inside the Expo Park. At the metropolitan level, rapid transformation was brought about by the expansion of infrastructure networks, city beautification projects, and land development for hosting relocated industries.

Such drastic transformation depended on, and triggered, a geographical and sectoral switch of capital. However, it was not an easy task, not least because of the fragmented property relations (see Figure 4.1). Before the wholesale demolition and redevelopment, the Expo Park was used mostly for industrial manufacturing and logistical purposes, including industrial premises of 3.92 square kilometres, warehouses of 0.21 square kilometres, and construction sites of 0.14 kilometres (Cui, 2008; Editorial Committee of Shanghai Expo Planning, 2010). Within

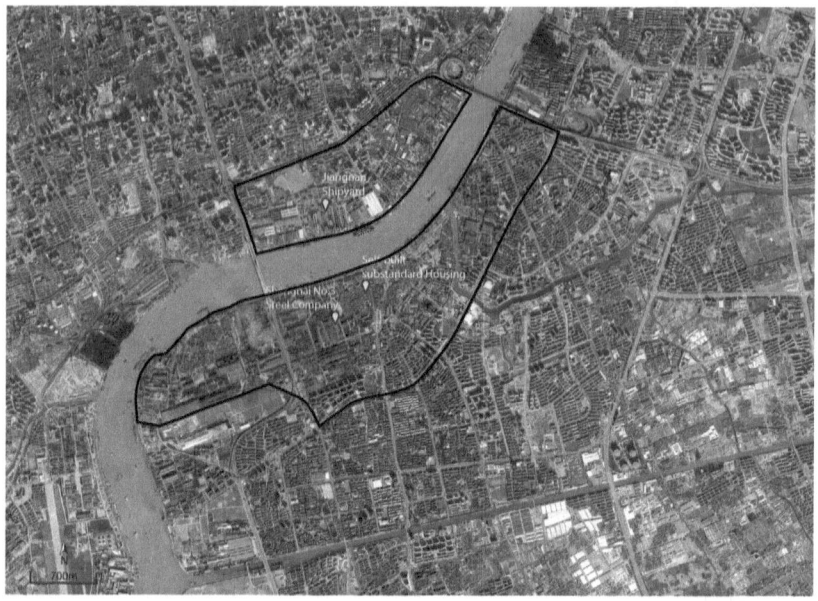

Figure 4.1. The planned area of the Expo Park before demolition. Source: Based on Google Earth, 2 February 2004.

them, 23 industrial businesses were owned by various ministries of the national government, occupying nearly 60 per cent of land on the Expo site. The municipal government, on the other hand, controlled 54 enterprises, whereas district authorities owned 114 businesses, which altogether used 17 per cent of land on the Expo site. A direct consequence of this layered ownership of industrial operations meant fragmented authority over land. It might have been easier for the Shanghai government to force out companies under its own control. It would require more political manoeuvre and incur more costs for the national government to negotiate with industrial landlords and reclaim land under their control. What makes it even more complicated is that some industrial companies were in decent financial shape, which raised the bar for a compelling relocation offer. Furthermore, a few buildings were listed as industrial heritage entitled to protection, such as the dockyard of the Jiangnan Shipyard. In addition to these industrial operations, this area was also densely populated. Within a residential area of 1.75 square kilometres surrounded by factories and workshops, there was a registered population of 47,900 residents, excluding migrants-cum-renters who were invisible in official statistical accounts. Nearly 60 per cent of households lived in housing that fell under the official category of simple shacks, whereas 35 per cent lived in planned multistorey apartment buildings with mixed tenures. The complexity of land, property, and housing relations posed significant challenges to land clearance and redevelopment. In fact, it was a crucial reason that property-led development left this area largely intact. It was also the reason that the Shanghai World Expo Bidding Committee set their eyes on land in Shanghai's urban fringes in their initial bidding plans for the World Expo.

Invoking state power proved critical to overcoming the barriers to land the tempo-spatial fix of the global spectacle. The unswerving support from the central government realigned power relations between state units and elevated the position of the Shanghai government vis-à-vis other state units. Instead of pursuing piecemeal reutilization of exiting industrial premises (He, 2019), the Expo-led redevelopment opted for wholesale demolition, which released large-scale industrial land in prime locations for constructing cultural facilities during the global event. To clear land, the municipal government joined forces with relevant district governments, which was unprecedented in the history of land and property dispossession in Shanghai. It also negotiated with state units in Beijing that owned enterprises on the Expo site.

Compensation to the industrial enterprises was differentiated, dependent upon the bargaining power of the enterprises as well as their alignment with Shanghai's overall industrial development strategies. In most cases, monetary compensation was offered. Those companies that met the requirement of Shanghai's industrial development strategy were directed to the industrial parks in rural fringes (Chan & Li, 2017). Industrial operations that required high energy input and produced heavy pollution were forced to upgrade their technology or change their business operations, or simply move outside the city. Workers were either made redundant or had no choice but to commute to work. Residents similarly were forced out of their homes, the majority of whom chose to move into two planned resettlement sites, while some found new homes from the commercial housing market.

The support from the central government also mattered a great deal for the financing of the event. Viewing the World Expo as a showcase of China's re-emergence as a global power, the Chinese central government openly pledged to the selection committee to deliver a best Expo at any costs during the bidding process. According to the bidding report, land clearance and resettlement alone required an investment of nearly 30 billion RMB (Expo 2010 Shanghai China State Bidding Commission of the People's Republic of China, 2002). The actual cost of land clearance was not disclosed in the final audit report, but it more than likely exceeded this number considerably, given that indirect costs related to the construction of resettlement apartments were excluded.

Displacement and resettlement cost, however, was only a tiny fraction of capital investments that flowed to wider spatial restructuring in order to make Shanghai presentable to the global audience in time. The Shanghai government spent 19.3 billion RMB on the construction of event venues and major supportive networks (Shanghai Municipal Audit Bureau, 2011). In addition, it dedicated 500 billion RMB to building and upgrading infrastructure networks before the global financial meltdown in 2008 and injected another 150 billion RMB into infrastructure development as part of China's 4 trillion RMB investment package to compensate the slowing down of China's export and rescue the Chinese economy (Jones Lang Lasalle, 2010, p. 2). One noticeable project is the fast extension of Shanghai's underground rail networks. Between 2005 and 2010, Shanghai added nine new metro lines, with total network length reaching 420 kilometres. The other major project is the Hongqiao transportation hub, which consists of a coach terminal, a public bus station, a high-speed railway station, an airport terminal, and an interchange station for a few metro lines. Although these infrastructures have a planned lifespan beyond the World Expo, they were constructed within a short period of time to cope with large inflows of visitors (70 million in six months according to the official estimate).

The commitment of the central government provided the last resort of financial bailout in the event of a deficit in addition to the guarantee of the Shanghai government, instilling confidence in investors worldwide concerning the financial health of the Expo and associated development. The central government's blessing also encouraged regulatory leniency and exceptions to enable the Shanghai government to find money from alternative sources. Through the Shanghai World Expo Group, a state-owned investment company, the government issued corporate bonds of 11 billion RMB, the first of their kind in financing the organization of mega-events in China (Lin & Xu, 2019). Land clearance and preparation, on the other hand, was financed through the Expo Land Bank, another state institution. With a registered capital of 10 billion RMB, coming from municipal budgets and two state-controlled corporations, the government borrowed substantially from commercial banks and the policy bank of the National Development Bank by collateralizing its only asset – land. Risks of these financial institutions were further passed on to retail investors through wealth management products.

This financing strategy brings land speculation and the temporality of the spatial fix through a mega-event to the fore. While the central government provided some financial support, the financial health of the World Expo project – and by extension the public finance – critically hinged upon a continuously inflating land and real estate market on and surrounding the Expo Park and related facilities. Speculation was built into the planning of the Expo site. It was normalized as a good practice and explicitly communicated to the international selection committee. According to the bidding report, the bidding committee estimated that the Expo could boost the property values in surrounding areas by 300 per cent through the improved provision of public goods (Expo 2010 Shanghai China State Bidding Commission of the People's Republic of China, 2002). There was indeed good reason to expect so. According to the plan, most event venues would be demolished to give way to a second-round land development after the Expo, where real profits could be made. Redevelopment plans aimed to turn this Expo site into a new mixed-use central business area to complement the Lujiazui financial district, which was only a few kilometres away upriver. As per redevelopment plans unveiled in 2011 (see Figure 4.2), the redeveloped area would mainly consist of cultural centres, tourism complexes, high-grade official blocks, and an upper class residential area. Exhibition venues such as the Chinese National Pavilion and the Mercedes-Benz Arena were planned to host cultural events and commercial performances. The vision for the museum district was to attract global museums, galleries, and designing studios, the arrival of which was expected to boost the needs for fine catering, tourism facilities, and high-end products. One large retailing complex in the business district had already opened for business. This complex had been transformed from the formerly known Expo axis, with a floor area of 13,000 square kilometres and total investment amounting to 150 million RMB (Xu et al., 2011). These new developments were situated in close proximity to new office towers. With a total floor area of nearly 600,000 square kilometres, the office district became the headquarters of many state-owned enterprises and began to compete for the hosting of transnational corporations (Xu et al., 2011).

By geographically switching industrial capital and deploying a huge amount of economic and cultural capital in this area, the phased development of the World Expo integrated well with, and boosted, the real estate market. According to a report by Jones Lang Lasalle (2010, p. 9), housing prices in one housing project within an area less than a kilometre from the Expo site grew more than ten times between 2002 and 2010. Even in Sanlin, which was a few kilometres further away from the Expo Park in Pudong, the average price of an apartment rose to 25,000 RMB per square metre in 2010, higher than the average in the

Figure 4.2. Redevelopment of the Expo site. Source: Based on Google Earth, 27 May 2017.

rest of Shanghai (Jones Lang Lasalle, 2010, p. 10). Of course, we must treat these numbers with caution, considering that the real estate market experienced wild inflation in that decade. However, it would be a mistake to simply treat it as an effect instead of the very intention of the state-led growth machine. Important to recognize here is that land acquired on the Expo site and for hosting relocated industrial firms was allocated to Shanghai by the central government on top of its annual land use quotas, which was, in fact, a special deal for the city against the backdrop of much tightened land supply since early 2000s.

With speculative land development at heart, the state-led event urbanism is bound to benefit more developers, financiers, politicians, cultural elites, and citizens on the upper rung of society. In fact, these were also the groups that dominated in the debates about the necessity of hosting the World Expo in the first place. Shortly after Shanghai won the bid, the city government organized a public debate on the significance of the Expo and the challenges ahead in order to manufacture societal consensus and further rationalize the decision to host the Expo project (Contemporary Shanghai Institute, 2003). Think tanks and commissioned academics readily contributed to journalistic pieces and research papers justifying the World Expo project. Although the slogan of the Expo – Better City, Better Life – sought to invoke hope, an important theme of these debates, however, triggered fear and manufactured a sense of urgency. In an editorial piece in the *Jiefang Daily*, it was argued that Shanghai had reached a critical juncture where its GDP per capita was between 5,000 USD and 7,500 USD and that the city could easily stagnate or sink down if it did not adapt to changed circumstances and take advantage of the global and national capital switching (Jiefang Daily, 2003). The World Expo, catalyzing a culture-oriented urban function upgrading, was thus celebrated as the logical path to rationalize industrial mix and put different industrial activities in their right places.

However, the creative and cultural industry–oriented urban development is premised upon a hierarchization of creative labour. While most human actions involve creativity to some extent, creativity is hierarchized according to the utility for accumulation. Artistic activities and technological innovation that can yield maximum value extraction are deemed more important in creative cities (Krätke, 2011). In this logic, despite the fact that residents had demonstrated considerable creativity in coping with housing distress and making ends meet, the priority to create labour for cultural commercialization and economic growth in this Expo-led development foreclosed the possibility for them to stay put and forced them to make other living and working arrangements. Similarly, the creative labour of industrial workers was also depreciated. Although their interests were directly at stake when their plants were closed or relocated, they had to accept the terms imposed by their employers, even though these terms might aggravate their conditions in the long run because neither the cultural and creative industry nor land development could effectively absorb their labour.

Although industrial landlords also had little choice but to move away, they were not entirely victims of the process. Some enterprises displaced from the Expo site insisted on sharing land revenues from post-Expo land redevelopment (Interview with planner, June 2012). Whether or not they were successful in doing so remained unclear, given the secrecy surrounding compensation. Yet, the huge investments in upgrading infrastructure and land clearance meant that the Shanghai government would take the lion's share from speculative land redevelopment. But industrial landlords were handsomely compensated anyway. On average, they were given 133,333 to 200,000 RMB per hectare of land, in addition to compensation for losses of business operations incurred in the process (Cui, 2008). This amount was nearly three to four times the rent in industrial parks. Moreover, as land was more accessible in rural fringes, industrial firms would no longer be limited by the planning control and restrictive land supply that existed in the city centre. With the compensation, many industrial companies acquired larger areas of land for their production, expanded their production capacity, and/or upgraded their means of production. For instance, the Shanghai Port Machinery Plant expanded the scale of its operations more than four times after relocation (Cui, 2008). Similarly, the Jiangnan Shipyard, a dominant factory with military background on the west side of the Expo Park, enlarged its premises eight times after relocating to Chongming Island, occupying nearly 600 hectares (Cui, 2008). No longer limited by the hydrological conditions of the Huangpu River, the factory's production capacity was increased ninefold. Therefore, while there were indeed tensions between industrial landlords and territorial states on valuing and capitalizing land (see Hsing, 2010), there was also a shared interest between them in accommodating the Expo on this site and switching capital geographically. Sectoral and geographical switching temporarily contributes to surplus value extraction and restores profitability for them.

Conclusion

Extending Harvey's notions of capital switching and spatial fix, we examined Shanghai's socio-spatial reconfigurations since the 1990s as a state-dominated process of geographical and sectoral switch of industrial capital, which coordinates different urban territorial organizations based on land's exchange value. Emphasizing the fragmented nature of the state, we paid attention to the conflicts as well as alliances between different public landlords in choreographing capital flows and urban space production. Geographical and sectoral switching of economic capital from the primary circuit is partially financed by, and leads to, capital accumulation through land and real estate development.

We illustrated our arguments further through the case of the World Expo and situated our analysis in Shanghai's property-led redevelopment, including the recent edition of territorial rationalization triggered by the creative city movement. Unlike earlier development of the cultural and creative zones, the Expo-led development did not pursue a piecemeal approach and swiftly demolished industrial complexes and residential settlements all at once. Inflating the property market was not only explicitly stated as a main rationale for hosting the World Expo in the waterfront but also acted as a crucial way to finance it.

However, industrial landlords did not completely lose out in the process. Cheap land from the outer suburbs enabled many of them to expand production capacity. The workers, on the other hand, were less fortunate. They barely had any control over the process, even though their livelihood was at stake. Similarly caught up in the process were residents surrounding the industrial land. While the event may have left behind a few cultural venues, it seems unlikely that grassroots and independent artists/creative workers could take advantage of them, given the post-Expo's plan for commercialized culture production and consumption. The temporality of the Expo and its financing bring the dubious nature of the Expo into question. It is indeed possible to argue that the World Expo is a project of public interest for the educational opportunity it brings, the cross-cultural understanding it contributes, the short-term economic benefits it boosts, and the cultural legacies it leaves behind. The post-Expo real estate development nevertheless challenges the public interest test of the Expo project. It also raises the valid question as to a fairer distribution of land revenues from post-Expo redevelopment.

In post-Expo Shanghai, the creative and cultural industry is expected to play a greater role in territorial rationalization. In 2017, the Shanghai government announced a new plan for the creative and cultural industry under the thirteenth five-year plan (Shanghai Municipal Commission of Economy and Informatization, 2017). In this plan, Shanghai was envisioned to capitalize on its recent recognition by UNESCO as a City of Design and to expand its global influence as a centre of innovation and technology. The city also announced an aggressive plan to attract talent globally, although most of this targeted talent will need to have a background in science and technology. The primary concern still remained the use of such labour for improving efficiency and profitability in production. The sustained interest of the government in this creative city strategy will inevitably accelerate reutilization of existing industrial land. This acceleration is due to Shanghai's ambitious plan to accommodate continuous population growth and urban economy development on the one hand, while controlling the expansion of the urban built area and containing the footprint of Shanghai on the other. This agenda rules out the possibility of further appropriation of farmland or green space for construction. In doing so, it puts pressure on existing built structures, particularly industrial operations and "obsolete" housing stock, in order to find land for emerging needs. Therefore, the pursuit of the creative city strategy will trigger new rounds of gentrification and consolidate social inequalities.

REFERENCES

Aalbers, M.B. (2008). The financialization of home and the mortgage market crisis. *Competition & Change*, 12(2), 148–66. https://doi.org/10.1179/102452908X289802

Aalbers, M.B., & Christophers, B. (2014). Centring housing in political economy. *Housing Theory & Society*, 31(4), 373–94. https://doi.org/10.1080/14036096.2014.947082

Chan, R.C.K., & Li, L.Y. (2017). Entrepreneurial city and the restructuring of urban space in Shanghai Expo. *Urban geography*, 38(5), 666–86. https://doi.org/10.1080/02723638.2016.1139909

Contemporary Shanghai Institute. (2003). *Shibohui yu shanghai xinyilun fazhan dataolun jishi* [Expo and the new round of development of Shanghai]. Shanghai People's Press.

Cui, N. (2008). *Mega-event led urban spatial reconstructuring* [in Chinese]. Southeast China University Press.

Editorial Committee of Shanghai Expo Planning (2010). *Planning of Expo 2010, Shanghai, China*. Shanghai Press of Science and Technology.

Editorial Committee of Shanghai Housing Construction Chronicles. (1998). Shanghai zhuzhai jianshe zhi [Shanghai housing construction chronicles]. Shanghai Academy of Social Sciences Press. http://www.shtong.gov.cn/Newsite/node2/node2245/node75091/index.html

Editorial Committee of Shanghai Local History. (n.d.) *Shanghai difang tongzhi* [*Shanghai local history*]. http://www.shtong.gov.cn/Newsite/node2/node2247/index.html

Expo 2010 Shanghai China State Bidding Commission of the People's Republic of China. (2002). Expo 2010 Shanghai China bid documents. Shanghai.

Florida, R.L. (2005). *Cities and the creative class*. Routledge.

Gotham, K.F. (2009). Creating liquidity out of spatial fixity: The secondary circuit of capital and the subprime mortgage crisis. *International Journal of Urban and Regional Research*, 33(2), 355–71. https://doi.org/10.1111/j.1468-2427.2009.00874.x

Gottdiener, M. (1985). *The social production of urban space*. University of Texas Press.

Hackworth, J.R. (2007). *The neoliberal city: Governance, ideology, and development in American urbanism*. Cornell University Press.

Hall, C.M. (2006). Urban entrepreneurship, corporate interests and sports mega-events: The thin policies of competitiveness within the hard outcomes of neoliberalism. *The Sociological Review*, 54(2), 59–70. https://doi.org/10.1111/j.1467-954X.2006.00653.x

Harvey, D. (1973). *Social justice and the city*. Edward Arnold.

Harvey, D. (1985). *The urbanization of capital*. Blackwell.

Harvey, D. (2001). Globalization and "spatial fix." *Geographische Revue*, 2, 23–30. https://publishup.uni-potsdam.de/opus4-ubp/frontdoor/deliver/index/docId/2251/file/gr2_01_Ess02.pdf

He, S. (2019). The creative spatio-temporal fix: Creative and cultural industries development in Shanghai, China. *Geoforum*, *106*, 310–19. https://doi.org/10.1016/j.geoforum.2017.07.017

He, S., Li, L., Zhang, Y., & Wang, J. (2018). A small entrepreneurial city in action: Policy mobility, urban entrepreneurialism, and politics of scale in Jiyuan, China. *International Journal of Urban and Regional Research*, *42*(4), 684–702. https://doi.org/10.1111/1468-2427.12631

He, S., & Wu, F. (2005). Property-led redevelopment in post-reform China: A case study of Xintiandi redevelopment project in Shanghai. *Journal of Urban Affairs*, *27*(1), 1–23. https://doi.org/10.1111/j.0735-2166.2005.00222.x

Heilmann, S. (2005). Regulatory innovation by Leninist means: Communist Party supervision in China's financial industry. *China Quarterly*, *181*, 1–21. https://www.jstor.org/stable/20192441

Horne, J. (2007). The four "knowns" of sports mega-events. *Leisure Studies*, *26*(1), 81–96. https://doi.org/10.1080/02614360500504628

Hsing, Y.T. (2010). *The great urban transformation: Politics of land and property in China*. Oxford University Press.

Jessop, B. (1990). *State theory: Putting the capitalist state in its place*. Penn State Press.

Jiefang Daily. (2003, 18 March). Jinkou zhuti, bawo zhongdian – ertan shibohui yu shanghai xinyilun fazhan da taolun [Second commentary on the World Expo and Shanghai]. *Jiefang Daily*.

Jones Lang Lasalle. (2010) Shibohui – wei shanghai weilai fazhan dianding jichu [The World Expo: Laying solid foundations for Shanghai's future development]. Jones Lang Lasalle.

Keane, M. (2007). *Created in China: The great new leap forward*. Routledge.

Krätke, S. (2011). *The creative capital of cities: Interactive knowledge creation and the urbanization economies of innovation*. Wiley-Blackwell.

Krippner, G.R. (2005). The financialization of the American economy. *Socio-Economic Review*, *3*(2), 173–208. https://doi.org/10.1093/SER/mwi008

Langley, P. (2008). *The everyday life of global finance: Saving and borrowing in Anglo-America*. Oxford University Press.

Li, T.M. (2014). What is land? Assembling a resource for global investment. *Transactions of the Institute of British Geographers*, *39*(4), 589–602. https://doi.org/10.1111/tran.12065

Lieberthal, K. (1995). *Governing China: From revolution through reform*. W.W. Norton.

Lin, G.C.S. (2009). *Developing China: Land, politics and social conditions*. Routledge.

Lin, G.C S., & Xu, Z. (2019). Remaking China's urban space of the spectacle: Mega-events, temporary growth, and uneven spatial transformation in

Shanghai. *Geoforum, 102*, 126–36. https://doi.org/10.1016/j.geoforum.2019.03.013

Lin, L.-W., & Milhaupt, C.J. (2013). We are the (national) champions: Understanding the mechanisms of state capitalism in China. *Stanford Law Review, 65*(4), 697–759. https://www.jstor.org/stable/23530170

Lin, Y.-M. (2017). *Dancing with the devil: The political economy of privatization in China.* Oxford University Press.

Müller, M. (2015). The mega-event syndrome: Why so much goes wrong in mega-event planning and what to do about it. *Journal of the American Planning Association, 81*(1), 6–17. https://doi.org/10.1080/01944363.2015.1038292

Pacewicz, J. (2013). Tax increment financing, economic development professionals and the financialization of urban politics. *Socio-Economic Review, 11*(3), 413–40. https://doi.org/10.1093/ser/mws019

Peck, J. (2005). Struggling with the creative class. *International Journal of Urban and Regional Research, 29*(4), 740–70. https://doi.org/10.1111/j.1468-2427.2005.00620.x

Ren, X. (2014). The political economy of urban ruins: Redeveloping Shanghai. *International Journal of Urban and Regional Research, 38*(3), 1081–91. https://doi.org/10.1111/1468-2427.12119

Ren, X., & Sun, M. (2012). Artistic urbanization: Creative industries and creative control in Beijing. *International Journal of Urban and Regional Research, 36*(3), 504–21. https://doi.org/10.1111/j.1468-2427.2011.01078.x

Roche, M. (2003). Mega-events, time and modernity: On time structures in global society. *Time & Society, 12*(1), 99–126. https://doi.org/10.1177/0961463X03012001370

Shanghai Bureau of Statistics. (2004). *Shanghai statistics yearbook 2004.* China Statistics Press. http://tjj.sh.gov.cn/tjnj/20170629/0014-1000190.html

Shanghai Municipal Audit Bureau. (2011). Zhongguo 2010 nian shanghai shibohui genzong shenji jieguo gonggao [Follow-up audit report of the World Expo 2010, Shanghai, China]. http://sjj.sh.gov.cn/node379/20110929/0029-16090.html

Shanghai Municipal Commission of Economy and Informatization. (2017). Shanghai chuangyi yu sheji chanye fazhan shisanwu guihua [Planning for the creative and design industries under the 13th five-year plan]. Shanghai. http://sheitc.sh.gov.cn/sswgh/20170119/0020-672902.html

Shen, J., & Wu, F. (2017). The suburb as a space of capital accumulation: The development of new towns in Shanghai, China. *Antipode, 49*(3), 761–80. https://doi.org/10.1111/anti.12302

Smart, A., & Lee, J. (2003). Financialization and the role of real estate in Hong Kong's regime of accumulation. *Economic Geography, 79*(2), 153–71. https://doi.org/10.1111/j.1944-8287.2003.tb00206.x

Soederberg, S.A. (2014). *Debtfare states and the poverty industry: Money, discipline and the surplus population*. Routledge.

Stent, J.A. (2017). *China's banking transformation: The untold story*. Oxford University Press.

Tsai, K.S. (2015). The political economy of state capitalism and shadow banking in China. *Issues & Studies*, *51*(1), 55–97. https://doi.org/10.2139/ssrn.2607793

Van Loon, J., & Aalbers, M.B. (2017). How real estate became "just another asset class": The financialization of the investment strategies of Dutch institutional investors. *European Planning Studies*, *25*(2), 221–40. https://doi.org/10.1080/09654313.2016.1277693

Wang, Y. (2015). The rise of the "shareholding state": Financialization of economic management in China. *Socio-Economic Review*, *13*(3), 603–25. https://doi.org/10.1093/ser/mwv016

Weber, R. (2010). Selling city futures: The financialization of urban redevelopment policy. *Economic Geography*, *86*(3), 251–74. https://doi.org/10.1111/j.1944-8287.2010.01077.x

Weber, R., & O'Neill-Kohl, S. (2013). The historical roots of tax increment financing, or how real estate consultants kept urban renewal alive. *Economic Development Quarterly*, *27*(3), 193–207. https://doi.org/10.1177/0891242413487018

Wu, F.L. (2016). Emerging Chinese cities: Implications for global urban studies. *Professional Geographer*, *68*(2), 338–48. https://doi.org/10.1080/00330124.2015.1099189

Xu, X., Zhou, R., & Ji, M. (2011). *Shanghai 'hou shibo' kaifa lantu fuchu shuimian* [The blueprint for redeveloping the expo park unveiled]. https://www.163.com/money/article/7B6OCO8400253B0H.html

Zhang, S., & Du, D. (2001). The functional transferring and spatial restructuring in the central urban area in Shanghai. *City Planning Review*, *25*(12), 16–21. http://www.planning.com.cn/WKE/WebPublication/paperDigest.aspx?paperID=7f30c36c-166f-426a-8fe7-e58924d172b0#

5 Urbanization as Mass Speculative Event: Informal Finance and City-Making in Ordos, Inner Mongolia

MAX D. WOODWORTH

Introduction

Over the past two decades, there has been growing awareness of the rising share of national economies commanded by the financial sector and of their central role in speculating on the built environment in cities around the world (Foster, 2007; Brenner et al., 2009; Sawyer, 2014; Christophers, 2015; Lin, 2017). This awareness has fueled debates in critical urban studies around the topic of "financialization," understood as the ascending importance of financial institutions, actors, and practices to contemporary economies at the micro and macro scales (see Aalbers, 2017). Where financialization intersects with the urban process specifically, it is understood as a process that transforms land and real estate into liquid assets that are then speculated upon far and wide (Fainstein, 2016). Put simply, finance and its manifold practices and institutions become dominant in the urban process. Given the depth and breadth of the global financial crisis that erupted in 2008 and its connections to the securitization of mortgages by major transnational financial entities based mostly in the United States, it is little wonder that financialization has become a hot topic in the years since. Scholars have tended to link financialization to globalization and neoliberalization, seeing the ascendance of the financial sector as the result of successive crises in the productive economies of the advanced industrialized countries and the accompanying rollback of social protections and public ownership of housing and other social goods (Fainstein, 2016). In this literature, financialization advances hand in hand with financial deregulation, innovation, and global integration (see Fainstein and Novy, Chapter 1, this volume).

If this summary describes, in broad terms, the extant literature on financialization, China has largely fallen outside the scope of the discourse. While foreign investment in real estate is not trivial in China's major cities (He et al., 2011), it is dwarfed by domestic investment in the sector. Despite China's deepening integration with the global economy, land and property markets have not been targets of "hot money" flowing around the world. Moreover, the state at various levels, but especially at the municipal level, is a key shaper and participant in land and property markets, and the financial sector has not been significantly liberalized during this period, reflecting China's peculiar post-socialist "neoliberal urbanism" in which the state maintains a fairly strong interventionist role in many spheres of the economy (He & Wu, 2009). In short, China and its cities have not followed a path that corresponds to the typical pattern of neoliberal globalization.

Yet, China's land and real estate markets have clearly been objects of rampant financial speculation. Rapidly urbanizing localities, for instance, have devised innovative schemes to circumvent the Chinese central government's strict quotas on arable land preservation by "creating" arable land in other regions and trading the resulting surplus arable land for local urban construction land (Wang et al., 2009; Ong, 2014). In so doing, land is effectively rendered a liquid asset traded across provincial boundaries. Recent work has also shed light on China's system of "land finance" (*tudi caizheng*) whereby municipalities, as monopoly *de jure* owners of urban land under the People's Republic of China (PRC) Constitution, became increasingly reliant on income from land transactions (Ding & Lichtenberg, 2011; Lin & Yi, 2011). Moreover, reliance on land-based income (chiefly from rents and conveyance fees) has established structural incentives favouring the perpetual expansion of debt-driven land development. The astonishing rise of the real estate sector in the Chinese economy since the 1990s was thus enabled by massive-scale commodification of land brought about through state-led modes of "accumulation by dispossession" and matched in scale and intensity by surging consumer demand (Hsing, 2010; Ong, 2014). In consequence, the built environment has been a key motor of city-regional economic growth and a major arena of speculation by the local state, developers, homebuyers, and of course financial operators. Further, as recent work has sought to show (Ong, 2011; Woodworth, 2018; Zhang and He, Chapter 4, this volume), speculation in China's urban development transcends the quest for profit in a purely pecuniary sense; construction of spectacular new cityscapes also has political and cultural objectives, as transformations of city spaces are broadly understood to stimulate deeper social and political transformations. Studies on speculative city development, therefore, have come to embrace speculation, understood as a future-oriented vision of growth and change, and exemplified by the chapters of this volume as a deeply penetrating economic, political, and social phenomenon.

But, as Theurillat (2017) has noted, critical urban studies on China's urbanization have largely sidestepped the problem of how urban projects are actually funded. Amid the frenetic growth of urban land and property development, the simple question remains: where does the money come from? While considerable attention in the urban literature has focused on policies supporting land and property development, and the roles of private home purchases and mortgage markets in support of rapid urban growth (see Song & Ding, 2007; Wu et al., 2015), the actual financing of urban projects in China remains remarkably opaque.

This chapter responds simultaneously to Theurillat's provocative entreaty to more deeply explore the "'actually existing ways' in which the development industry finances its operations" in China (2017, p. 839) and to this volume's examinations of how financial speculation is reshaping cities in diverse geographical settings. Rather than focus on developers and their relations with financial institutions and the state, however, I focus here on informal financial mechanisms and their role in driving urban expansion. Specifically, this chapter explores informal financial networks that mobilized capital to developers and homebuyers in the 2000s in Ordos Municipality, a resource-abundant prefecture-level territory located in central Inner Mongolia Autonomous Region. It assesses the nature of informal financial networks and practices as well as their implications for city growth and residents. In so doing, this chapter contributes to the literature on China's urban expansion by shedding light on the important, but overlooked, role that non-bank financial networks play in funding urban growth and the ways that speculation in urban development became a pervasive practice. In the context of this volume's focus on speculative activities, I am also keen to illustrate how state-led urban development schemes stimulate widespread informal financial practices, exemplifying the interwoven qualities of state and non-state realms as well as that of the formal and informal. In particular, I draw attention to quotidian and non-elite forms of speculation, and in so doing, I emphasize the pervasive character of speculation in China's everyday urban process. To approach these issues, I set forth a number of questions: Who is engaged in financial speculation in urban growth? How does ubiquitous participation in informal lending circuits shape the nature and pace of urbanization? And what sorts of built environments emerge through such speculative forms of economy?

To answer these questions, this chapter draws upon fieldwork conducted between 2011 and 2014 among participants in informal financial circuits in Ordos, as well as follow-up visits to the city during the following two years. During my research, I lived for a period of four months with an executive of a coal-mining equipment supplier who was deeply engaged in borrowing and lending activities as a side business. This experience allowed for gradual revelations of new details pertaining to the operations of informal finance in Ordos and its impressive scope. Informal investment geared towards urban growth in Ordos was nothing short of a mass speculative event in Ordos. The ethnographic portions of this chapter draw upon twenty-five interviews arranged through a snowball method originating with my host in Ordos. The interviewees were operators of underground banks, lenders in these types of illegal schemes, managers of micro-lending firms, and pawnshops, as well as middle-level managers and executives in property development firms and coal-mining companies. Additional interviews were conducted with bilked lenders to ascertain how conflicts in informal finance are handled. I supplement this work with a range of primary and secondary materials.

Informal Finance: Mobilizing Capital, Cementing Social Relations

Beginning with Hart's (1970, 1973) pioneering studies of the "informal economy," scholars have argued that so-called informal activities enable large segments of society, particularly in developing-world settings, to survive and sometimes even to thrive. Because the original conception of the informal sector challenged the economic and social marginality frequently ascribed to the poor, it stimulated a vigorous debate on relations between capital and labour, and between development and market regulation, as well as on the role of policy in managing housing, employment, and much else. Awareness of informal economies also brought into question bedrock assumptions in political economy regarding the necessity of clear property rights and labour contracts, while simultaneously underscoring the social embeddedness of economies. Given how informality cuts to the core of long-standing political-economic debates, it has inspired vociferous reactions from many angles (Portes & Haller, 2005). For some, informality is seen as a means to justify the flexibilization of poor-country labour forces (Peattie, 1980), while for others it provides evidence of a laudable entrepreneurial verve with the potential to ignite economic development (De Soto, 1989). Additional studies of informal finance have focused on the relative merits and risks of non-bank lending and usury in places underserved by formal financial institutions (see Adams & Fitchett, 1992). Striking a middle ground, Castells and Portes argue that the informal economy "encompasses flexibility and exploitation, productivity and abuse, aggressive entrepreneurs and defenseless workers, libertarianism and greediness" (1989, p. 12).

In China, informal finance has recently garnered considerable attention from scholars and policymakers. The new attention paid to informal finance is rooted in the vital role it has played in supplying capital to the private sector since the outset of market reforms in 1978 and in recognition of its significant scale, estimated at around 7 per cent of total outstanding domestic bank loans, or 3.8 trillion yuan, in 2011 (Mao & Luo, 2011). The vibrancy of informal financial markets in China coexists uneasily, however, with the central government's strong desire for macro-economic control and social stability. Consequently, governments at various levels have exhibited inconsistent approaches to usurious lending practices. Local governments directly charged with overseeing finance as well as economic development have been especially erratic in their approach to informal financing activities: supportive to the extent that it provides capital for growth, and antagonistic during the inevitable episodic crisis moments.

Under current law, individuals, groups, and firms are forbidden from accepting deposits from the public, while loans between individuals and firms are legal, as are "mutual assistance associations" (*huzu hui*), sometimes known as rotating credit and savings associations (ROSCAs). Article 28 of the "Provisional Regulations of the PRC on Bank Oversight" states: "Local governments are not permitted to establish banks. Individuals are not allowed to establish banks or other financial institutions, nor to conduct financial business." In practice, grey areas abound within the legal framework and regulations governing non-bank finance; ROSCAs sometimes evolve into underground banks, bank loans are sometimes diverted into informal lending circuits, and so forth. Separation of the formal and informal is far from complete and permanent. In addition, oversight and enforcement of extra-institutional lending practices are notoriously inconsistent and prone to erratic swings in response to collapses of local lending networks or policy changes issued from the central or provincial governments. This irregularity makes it especially difficult to generalize the Chinese state's stance towards informal finance. Still, for analytical purposes, a distinction is sometimes made between the formal banking system and the broad range of non-bank sources of finance, where interest rates can range much higher than the People's Bank of China's base lending rate (Tsai, 2002; Allen et al., 2005; Ayyagari et al., 2010). A recent volume by Chinese and American experts on the topic, for example, defines informal finance to include all "nonbank financing activities, whether conducted through family and friends, local money houses, or other types of financial associations" (Hsu, 2009, p. 3). In short, dualities between legal and illegal, state and non-state, or private and public are poor guides to informal finance in China. Following Hsu (2009), my use of the term "informal" here is intended to denote non-bank finance of all sorts. Hence, an incomplete typology of informal finance in China includes ROSCAs, personal loans among acquaintances, inter-firm credit, pawnshop lenders, micro-lending enterprises, money houses, chain lending, pyramid schemes, and Ponzi schemes. These were all present in Ordos in the 2000s amid a spectacular building boom and a burst of extraction-driven economic growth that I have described elsewhere (Woodworth, 2015).

Much of the scholarly literature on informal finance in China examines the apparent paradox of the private sector's exclusion from formal bank loans and its dynamism when compared with the state sector, which has historically enjoyed favourable access to credit while also being the least dynamic segment of the national economy. As of 2010, private-sector firms comprised 70 per cent of the total number of firms and provided 85 per cent of new urban jobs, yet received less than 1 per cent of total bank loan capital (Wang, 2011). Non-bank lending is thus found to arise both as a supplement to bank loans and as a necessary source of capital due to private-sector exclusion (Li & Hsu, 2009; Pairault, 2012). Non-bank finance plays a critical role in supplying capital to capital-scarce smaller-sized firms in particular, precisely the type of firms that are the lifeblood of the reform-era economy. The prevalence of informal finance in China today is also attributed to the imperative for growth faced by local-level officials (Li & Hsu, 2009). Officials are prepared to turn a blind eye to illegal, usurious, or risky non-bank lending practices if they provide needed capital to local firms. Indeed, lending of all types is generally accepted until it triggers a crisis and prompts enforcement of rules that earlier were openly flouted. Local non-enforcement of financial regulations thus represents a major schism in central-local governance. In spite of regulations issued from Beijing proscribing certain lending activities, especially those that take deposits from the public, such rules are routinely ignored lower on the administrative ladder, either because local authorities do not have the capacity to enforce rules or are unwilling to do so for fear of depressing local economic growth, the key metric of local leaders' career-defining performance assessments. Moreover, informal finance's demonstrated positive impacts on economic growth further help to explain the inconsistent approach adopted by different levels of the state towards regulation in this arena. In Ordos, non-bank financial activities were pervasive, as I detail further below, and even municipal officials and city government agencies were directly engaged in informal lending practices. This not only underscored the permissive milieu of financing that one finds on the ground in Chinese rural and urban areas, but also illustrates the interpenetration of the formal and informal sectors in China.

Two threads running through work on informal finance in China are, first, a focus on firms and, second, an examination of the implications of informal finance for understandings of Chinese political economy. Connections between informal finance and urbanization have been quite neglected. But precisely these aspects were inescapable in Ordos, where informal finance was tied to the local property bubble in multiple ways and became a major source of income for regular citizens. In this sense, what many scholars have described as the state-led process of urbanization became entwined with the bandwagon effects that drive classic speculative manias (see Kindleberger & Aliber, 2011, especially chap. 4). The Ordos experience suggests that economic growth driven by urbanization was intimately connected to informal financial speculation in the areas that fed into urban expansion, such as land acquisition, construction, architecture and landscape design, and property management, not to mention speculative purchases of finished homes. The entwinements connecting informal finance and urban development have important implications for the kind of urbanization that unfolds, for while informal finance performs the vital productive function of supplying capital, it can also quickly turn a well-intentioned developer or amateur investor into a huckster or cast an unfortunate depositor or lender into the class of dispossessed urban poor with little legal recourse. The interest rates and repayment schemes on which informal finance operates are notably volatile. Moreover, the lack of oversight and institutional protections introduces risks in borrowing and lending that affect participants and non-participants alike.

The next two sections of this chapter present the following: first, I sketch out the different kinds of informal finance in Ordos and offer a view (inevitably incomplete) upon its scale, scope, and connections with urban growth; and second, I discuss some of the social impacts brought about by the mania in informal lending in Ordos as a way to underscore financialization's implications for actual people and places.

Informal Lending in Ordos

In Ordos, the most common types of informal finance were interpersonal loans, underground banks, also known as money houses (*qianku, qianzhuang,* or *yinbei*), pawn broking, and microfinance. These four types of informal finance varied in the number of participants/depositors, interest rates, and time frames for repayment. A number of pyramid and Ponzi schemes were also revealed in 2010 and 2011, when informal lending, which burgeoned during the first decade of the 2000s, suddenly faced a crisis triggered by a drop in the price of coal (Qin, 2011). The drop in coal prices rippled through the local economy, undercutting lending schemes and halting urban construction projects. Mutually reinforcing growth in the resource sector, the finance sector, and the urban construction sector ground to a virtual halt in mid-2011 and exposed a number of dubious financial schemes. It also imperiled many legal informal financial networks. Thousands of depositors involved in various informal mechanisms lost private savings.[1]

Interpersonal loans and underground banks were especially common. Reflecting the pervasive nature of the phenomenon, deposits into Ordos's underground banks were sometimes as low as 10,000 RMB, indicating participation from even low-income residents (Feng, 2012; Zhang, 2011). The terms of interpersonal loans were negotiable and remarkably lax when compared with requirements for loans at formal banks. Based on interviews with borrowers and lenders, it was common, for example, for loans between close acquaintances to not require collateral or demand interest. Repayment terms were similarly permissive, and written contracts were the exception. Personal ties through relatives, friends, and even distant acquaintances facilitated lending. Moreover, social norms made lenders highly uneasy about setting down rigid loan terms or chasing down payment. In the tight social circles of a relatively small city, such behaviours were described in interviews as unseemly, even when outstanding debts were large (debts amounting to over 100,000 RMB were commonplace).

Underground banks also became widespread in Ordos amid its urbanizing boom for two main reasons. For depositors, underground banks offered interest rates multiple times those offered in formal bank savings accounts. Creditors received monthly dividends between 2 and 5 per cent of their deposit, meaning annual interest rates ranged from 24 to 60 per cent. For borrowers, money houses offered flexibility and speed. Interest rates and dividend payment schedules were negotiable and were usually tied to the amount of collateral offered up front. In Ordos, underground banks could lend up to 100 million RMB within days and, given the high interest rates, were willing to lend to

---

1 Many informants attributed Ordos's informal financial crisis in 2011 to news reports that the local government had commenced a crackdown on underground banks. Others within and outside the local government accused the municipality of spooking depositors, undermining local financial networks, and cutting short the city's remarkable streak of economic growth.

businesses and individuals that would likely not have been deemed creditworthy by a formal bank.

Money houses were typically founded by a core group, sometimes business associates and other times family members, who enjoyed strong reputations in their communities based on success in business, high social standing, and/or connections with powerful people, including government officials or local crime syndicates. Underground bank operations tended to be formed through strands of personal relations that stretched out from the founders through lieutenants who functioned as intermediaries between the money house and depositors. Because underground banks were illegal in a strict sense and thus carried higher degrees of risk for all involved, introduction into a lending operation was almost always done through at least one direct acquaintance, though depositors were not always mutual acquaintances. Indeed, investigations carried out by local regulatory officials following the collapse of schemes in 2011 found that depositors sometimes numbered in the hundreds, which meant that, in large operations, relations among depositors were diffuse and impersonal, much like a bank. But, without depository insurance, news and rumours of failed schemes that began to circulate in 2010 triggered panic among depositors and accelerated what Kindleberger and Aliber (2011) call the "panic phase" of the bubble. The extra-institutional (and illegal) character of underground banks only intensified the sense of panic.

Micro-lending firms and pawnbrokers also emerged in Ordos as important financial intermediaries in the 2000s. Pawnbrokers were eradicated during the socialist period (1949–78) but have seen a remarkable comeback since the first reform-era establishment was opened in Chengdu, Sichuan Province, in 1987. According to regulations, pawnbrokers are permitted to charge up to seven times the official lending rate set by the People's Bank of China (PBoC, 2006). By contrast, micro-lending is a new concept in China, having been introduced on an experimental basis in Shanxi, Shaanxi, Guizhou, and Sichuan in 2005 and then in Inner Mongolia in 2008. Micro-lending was originally devised as a means to open capital markets and reintroduce formalized and regulated lending mechanisms in rural areas underserviced by the banking sector (Jiang, 2009). Indeed, a study by the China Banking Regulatory Commission found that 2,945 towns, mostly in the country's western regions, had no banking outlets in 2009, forcing people in these areas to either store savings in their homes or find alternative means of safely depositing accumulated savings (Wang, 2011). Micro-lending firms are forbidden to accept deposits from the public and can only lend up to 5 per cent of the firm's founding capital for any single loan at interest rates not to exceed four times the centrally set baseline rate (PBoC, 2006). Though micro-credit was conceived as a transitional service for farmers by issuing small loans of 5,000 RMB or less, microfinance in Ordos serviced nearly exclusively urban clients and advanced loans worth tens of millions of RMB. As microfinance grew into a high-profit industry, the number of such firms grew from zero in 2007 to over 100 four years later. Local mining and property development firms, such as Yitai, Elon, Vanzip, and Vibor, all established microfinance subsidiaries. According to informants, loans at microfinance or pawnbroker firms in Ordos were rarely less than 200,000 RMB. As one loan officer explained, "micro-lending firms in Ordos have few staff. We can't waste time reviewing applications for loans smaller than that amount."

Financial mediation was also rife through legally registered shell companies that would draw depositors calling themselves "investors" and promise regular dividends labelled as "profits." In addition, bank loans intended for one purpose were also directed instead towards money houses and other high-risk lending schemes. Loan officers at formal banks in Ordos spent much of their time following up on loans they had issued for fear they had been misdirected into informal lending schemes.

What is also remarkable is the estimated volume of capital circulating through informal lending networks and the widespread nature of local participation in Ordos. Rapid economic growth fueled by a resource boom generated significant private savings, while mass relocations of rural residents to the city, coupled with urban redevelopment, spurred demand for housing and space for retail and commercial development. The ascendance of Ordos's city-making agenda went hand in hand with the growth of informal lending.

Definitive measures of the volume and velocity of informal financial capital circulating in Ordos during the boom have proved elusive. Nonetheless, studies conducted by the Ministry of Housing and Urban-Rural Development estimate the private capital circulating through *gaolidai* circuits in Ordos in 2011 at roughly 200 billion RMB, or about 83 per cent of local GDP in 2010 (Qin, 2011). By 2011, the formal banking sector had outstanding loans in property development totalling 5.97 billion yuan, or about 16.5 per cent of the 36.57 billion yuan invested in the property sector in 2010 alone. The ministerial reports just mentioned also found that local networks extended into nearby mining cities and towns across the Shanxi and Shaanxi provincial borders. These reports also concluded that money circulating in these underground networks flowed into retail and small-scale industry, but was especially prevalent in the real estate sector and its associated industries due to the huge number of new development projects, rising land and property values, high rates of return for lenders, and a relative openness of the sector (Tian, 2012). According to one report, 80 per cent of capital invested in local property development originated in informal financial networks (Li, 2011). Informal financial networks supplied abundant opportunities to amateur investors and professional operators alike for lucrative speculation.

The flood of capital into property development set in motion an escalating speculative dynamic. As long as a high volume of home sales was maintained, developers were willing to shoulder high financing costs under the assumption that loans would be easily repaid. Interest as high as 60 per cent per annum only attracted more creditors, thus further stimulating new and larger schemes and pushing the pace and scale of local construction to staggering levels. As the round of speculation in property gathered pace, the number of private property development firms in Ordos rose: from 7 in 2001 to over 400 by 2011 (Li, 2011). In practice, however, the number of firms was unclear, as many were unregistered. As an informant in Dongsheng who worked as a real estate agent explained, almost all were small family operations in which family members assumed management titles and subcontracted design, engineering, accounting, construction, marketing, advertising, and sales to other specialized firms that were also drawing on informal finance. As the local economic boom gathered steam by 2005, urban construction and its informal financing were sustained by the chase for capital gains; use value of purchased homes seemed to be superseded by their exchange value, as households and investors accumulated multiple properties. Across all types of urban real estate, nearly 22 million square metres of new property were built between 2007 and 2016.

Amid this spectacular boom, participation in informal financial schemes was extraordinarily high. The local branch of the People's Bank of China found that 62.43 per cent of respondents to a survey had either borrowed or loaned money in informal circuits in 2008 (Li, 2011). The popular perception during the boom was that "everyone" was engaged in informal finance in one way or another, even if the sums deposited or borrowed were small. Creditors included members of the local stratum of wealthy industrialists and professional class, bureaucrats and high-level officials, and farmers. There was no typical profile of a creditor in schemes beyond their possession of some amount of idle savings that could be mobilized with the right connections and opportunities, of which there was no shortage. As a local saying went, everyone was "eating interest" (*chi lixi*) (Zhu, 2011).

Also critical to making informal finance a mass speculative event in Ordos's urbanization were private accumulations generated through urban development programs. Between 2006 and 2010, 7.65 million square metres of floor space were demolished in old sections of the main city, Dongsheng, forcing the relocation of 51,772 households. Similarly massive urban redevelopment campaigns were undertaken in other urban centres in the municipality; in the town of Ejin Horo, for instance, virtually the entire town was demolished and rebuilt between 2009 and 2011. In rural areas too, whole villages were relocated to make way for the expansion of mining operations or as part of grassland restoration programs. To facilitate the relocation process, free or heavily subsidized new urban housing was provided, as well as cash compensation, often as high as 8,000 yuan per square metre for demolished homes (Yu, 2012). Compensation in excess of 1 million yuan was not uncommon, particularly for rural residents whose homes tend to be larger and whose cultivated plots also qualified for compensation. In urban areas, given the pace and scale of demolition in the 2000s, it was not uncommon for households to undergo two rounds of compensated relocation within a few years. Depending on the size of relocation sums, households frequently ended up, after purchasing a new home and other necessities, with several hundred thousand RMB in idle windfall savings. These savings, along with accumulated business profits and capital from outside Ordos arriving through investor groups, were channeled into informal financial circuits, finding their way as loans invested in the city's urban expansion.

An important outlet for such savings was the municipality's new town project, named the Kangbashi New District. Begun in 2004, the new town's first-phase construction featured a planned area of 32 square kilometers, with a 2020 population target of 300,000 residents. Soon after inaugurating the new town with great fanfare in 2006, residential and office construction proceeded at breakneck pace, driving prices upward and attracting further investments. The municipal government's heavy promotion of the new town project included discounted home prices for civil servants, whose offices were relocated en masse to Kangbashi, and low land prices on massive development parcels. Informal financial networks mobilized rapidly to invest in the development of Kangbashi, according to interviewees. Underground banks supplied capital to establish construction firms, landscaping companies, and other services essential to the development of the new town. Networks were also engaged in providing capital to individuals and groups for speculative property purchases. The arrangements achieved dizzying complexity. An example described to me by officials of the local financial bureau is illustrative of the entangled relations between the state's building projects, formal banks, and informal investment schemes: an informal consortium of local investors drew upon loans through underground banks to purchase an office building, which then served as collateral for a bank loan to establish a property development firm that constructed a residential project in the new town. Arrangements of this sort were far from uncommon in Ordos and typify the blurred boundaries between state and market, legal and illegal, and formal and informal operations at the heart of urban development.

The direct consequence of this frenzy of construction was massive overbuilding. By 2010, international and domestic media began to take notice of Kangbashi's fevered construction and labelled the site a "ghost town" (see Woodworth & Wallace, 2017). Built through intricate combinations of formal and informal economies, Kangbashi came to exemplify, for many, the perils of China's state-led urban development push in the 2000s. Largely ignored in the global hype about Kangbashi as a "ghost town," however, was the degree to which the project's completion contributed to astonishing wealth gains for many investors in informal schemes and the acquisition of multiple properties by residents of this formerly impoverished municipality. These varied household and personal outcomes have contributed to the ambivalence many local residents express retrospectively towards the speculative mania of the 2000s, as discussed further below.

Society of the Speculation

How can we explain the mass appeal for informal finance in Ordos? And how did the sudden unwinding of loan networks impact the process of city-making to which people had contributed so enthusiastically? While there surely can be no single overarching answer to these questions, certain motivations became clear during fieldwork. In conversation after conversation, respondents noted the extreme speed of urban transformation and economic growth as processes that commanded a giant share of people's attention. They observed that excessive optimism seemed to infect everyday discussions about urban growth and that the city's belated and spectacular urban growth was a historic – and exciting – transformation.

Participation in informal finance, either as creditors or lenders or both, was ubiquitous. Rural migrants to the city relied on informal finance for dividend income and to start small businesses. Urban office workers were also eager to supplement their incomes in this fashion. Rather than merely surviving on a few thousand RMB per month, as is typical for salaried workers in Ordos, by putting savings into underground banks or lending at high interest rates to entrepreneurs, one could rapidly multiply one's income. Although rules prohibit civil servants from participating in lending schemes or holding sideline businesses, their access to privileged information was a spur to lending and borrowing. It was an open secret that high-level officials were deeply involved as well, trading on connections and access to information.

Real estate was a logical outlet for amateur investors. Massive-scale redevelopment in Dongsheng stimulated demand for new housing, as discussed above. At the same time, the municipal government initiated the new town project, Kangbashi, while also massively expanding infrastructure and opening numerous industrial parks and development zones throughout the vast municipality. The city's expansion of the urban land supply vastly exceeded its allotted quotas.[2] The takeoff in property prices beginning around 2005 amplified the euphoria in the real estate sector: prices in popular housing projects in Dongsheng and Kangbashi rose from around 2,000 RMB per metre square to 8,000 RMB within three years (Sheng, 2012). With prices rising at such rates, informal capital found its way into every corner of the development industry, from developers, to decorators, to marketing and advertising firms, to speculative purchases of multiple homes. Moreover, property speculation in Ordos became even more profitable than in higher-end property markets in Beijing and Shanghai, where Ordos's new wealthy were also well-known buyers (Qin, 2011; Yu, 2012). It thus became difficult to distinguish cautious purchases of multiple homes as a means to safely stash accumulated savings, as purchases are often characterized in China (Chovanec, 2011), from speculative purchases in pursuit of short-term profits. In conversations with informants, the impression provided was that such purchases could serve both ends simultaneously. The emphasis placed locally on the combined use and exchange values of property made ownership of multiple homes standard practice for urban residents. It was not uncommon during research for informants to possess several dozen homes in Ordos, only some of which were used on a regular basis and none of which were intended as rental properties. First and foremost, they were speculative investments.

Rapid economic growth in Ordos fostered a high acceptance of financial risk. Borrowing from informal networks was a daring proposition, as repayment typically began after the first month of obtaining a loan. One needed to be confident of rapid profits (or of access to fresh liquidity) to risk ventures on the terms standard in informal finance networks. For a few, work as an intermediary between underground banks and borrowers and lenders became a new occupation, with intermediaries taking a cut of borrowed and lent money. Perhaps not surprisingly, successful intermediaries held sanguine views of informal finance.

---

2 Interview with urban planning official, Ordos, September 2011.

A twenty-seven-year-old CEO of a local financial services firm and son of a wealthy retired local official explained that informal finance was a proto form of finance, a stage in the city's movement towards a more "mature" economy.[3] "This kind of lending lacks professionalism and so it has many problems. But the formal finance sector here is very underdeveloped, which produces both the demand and supply for such lending. It is normal that it sees ups and downs." Numerous reports and widespread rumours of suicides by borrowers and lenders in networks that collapsed around 2011 suggest, however, that the downsides of informal finance could exert themselves with surprising speed and intensity, causing economic crisis and threatening social stability.

The manias in informal finance and real estate clearly also thrived in Ordos's anything-goes atmosphere. In the interest of maintaining rapid economic growth and keeping informal lending networks afloat, regulatory violations were legion. The city was awash in rumours of backroom deals between government officials, developers, and operators of different financial schemes. As the crisis of 2011 later revealed, the lure of easy money facilitated all manner of foul play in informal finance and helped make the city a beacon for charlatans. There was a palpable sense among informants that the local government exercised little consistent regulatory authority. Yet, distinctions between corruption, incompetence, and incapacity were unclear. The local bureau of finance, for example, was only established in 2009 and had fewer than ten full-time staff whose main tasks were oversight of the formal banking institutions in the municipality and who, only secondarily, were charged with keeping an eye on informal finance as well as possible.

However deep was local corruption during the boom years, it was rarely remarked upon during interviews before the bust. Indeed, Ordos's reputation for permissiveness was known far and wide, and was stressed approvingly by many informants as a positive regional cultural trait and a sign of local people's "pioneer spirit" (*kaituo jingshen*).[4] It was in the context of the lending crisis in 2011, however, that recriminations and the search for culprits began. Investigations launched in 2011 by the Autonomous Region Government and Municipal Government into the entangled networks of non-bank lending, land deals, public works contracts, and real estate developments revealed a slew of violations. Disciplinary measures were meted out in 2012 to the Dongsheng District commissioner, the vice commissioner

---

3 Interview with CEO of financial services firm, Ordos, December 2011.
4 Group interview, Ordos, August 2012.

and his predecessor, the director of the local land bank, the director and vice director of the land and resources bureau, the director of the district urban construction bureau, the director of the planning bureau, and the vice director of the development and reform bureau. A vice president for the Guangzhou-based Star River property development group was jailed for offering bribes (Xinhua, 2012).

Once the foundations of the informal financial system began to evaporate, panic ensued in which creditors at once all sought to reclaim their principal from their borrowers. But, having changed hands through sometimes multiple intermediaries in the process of being extended as credit, many individuals' claims gained little traction. Anxiety and desperation became topics of daily conversation in Ordos during fieldwork stints from 2011 to 2014. At the outset of the financial meltdown, in the autumn of 2011, everyday talk in Dongsheng was of suicides and murders related to failed informal financial schemes. Borrowers and creditors short on cash discovered they were either destitute or owed sums they had no hope of repaying. News in October of that year that a prominent local judge had hanged himself due to his inability to make good on loans seemed only to confirm the severity of the crisis.

Informal finance functioned not just in a legal grey zone but in a sphere of institutional inconsistency and opacity that the powerful could employ against the weak. Sharp information asymmetries are a key element in informal finance, as the organizers of schemes maintain exclusive control over information on the number of depositors and the structure of investments. When coupled with the minimal legal protections afforded creditors in informal schemes, opportunities for abuse are rife. Depositors are cognizant of this asymmetry, yet lend all the same into the networks based on assurances whose credibility was measured along understandings of trust and kinship. Emulation was also essential grease in the system, compelling people to join networks based on the sudden enrichment of acquaintances. One interviewee said: "When you see other people doing it, it puts your mind at ease."[5] Another remarked: "When the system works, it is easy to trust that it will continue to work without problems."[6] But anxiety rooted in the relative lack of information was also a frequently voiced concern and ultimately was an accelerant to the implosion of networks, as shaky trust between creditors and lenders in various schemes broke down in 2011. The bubbles in finance and urban construction had made the euphoric moment of sudden and

---

5 Interview, Ordos, August 2012.
6 Interview, Ordos, August 2012.

rapid urbanization in Ordos into a casino-like environment of high-risk business dealings and related social disruptions. In the wake of the informal finance bubble, Ordos was left with enormous landscapes of sparsely occupied built space, reflecting the production of what He et al. (2016) call "wasted cities." Now, a decade after the collapse of lending circuits, Ordos's urban areas remain littered with halted construction projects serving as ubiquitous reminders of the boom period.

Conclusion

This chapter addresses the productive role of informal finance in supplying capital for urbanization and its centrality to broad social transformations. In this sense, financialization of the urban process in Ordos reflected the ways that financial activities have potential to reshape spaces and social life at once. The kinds of financing mechanisms evidenced in Ordos are largely neglected in the study of China's recent urban expansion. Yet, the florescence of informal lending mechanisms demonstrated how everyday people, not normally associated with driving the urban growth process in China, were actually deeply and directly engaged in it. People became creditors in schemes advancing finance to developers; they established their own small networks to fund real estate projects (among other investments); and they used informal credit to purchase homes as speculative investments, turning profits on the quick resale of properties. Amid this sort of vibrant speculative realm, people earned incomes, grew businesses, and expanded the city. Yet it also entailed a high degree of risk, given the unreliability of institutional protections afforded such activities.

Taking stock of this milieu for urban expansion alerts us to a number of important themes that contribute to the extant literature on Chinese urbanization. First, the scope and scale of informal finance in urban growth suggests the notion that state-led urbanization is incomplete. Informal finance and its ties to small-scale developers play important roles in shaping urban growth. Second, profits from speculating on the built environment are not commanded exclusively by elite coalitions. Rather, a broad set of people also gains materially from urban growth through participation in financial schemes. Finally, profits derived from speculation in city-building arguably contribute to broad popular support for highly disruptive modes of urban expansion – as long as profits are forthcoming. With informal finance transforming the urbanization process into a mass speculative event, significant numbers of people are drawn into the city's growth for personal pecuniary gain and become invested in the fortunes of the local state's urbanization agenda.

Given the ubiquity of informal finance in China that has long been observed, the Ordos case should not be taken as an anomaly. Rather, further research is needed to explore the connections of similar informal mechanisms with urbanization in other regions. In doing so, such studies promise to challenge the preoccupation with the state and elite actors shown in much of the literature in Chinese urban studies. The state, of course, remains a dominant force in shaping urban expansions. But, based on the evidence in Ordos, additional attention should be paid to the more diverse economies and modes of speculation driving expansion than have heretofore been acknowledged.

The Ordos case also resonates with key themes of financialization in different parts of the world as examined in this volume. We see in this rather remote corner of China the incursion of the unmistakable logics of finance into the urban process – the founding of growth on speculative activity and the chase for capital gains, the speeding up of growth, the uncertainty and volatility at the heart of expansion, and new expressions of power tied to financial wealth. Also evident is the enmeshment of the state with the activities of finance, including its actors, institutions, and practices. Amid these new relations, the state and society undergo fundamental reorientations not just to money and capital but also to time and space, as the latter two figure into the currency of speculation.

REFERENCES

Aalbers, M.B. (2017). Corporate financialization. In D. Richardson (Ed.), *The international encyclopedia of geography: People, the earth, environment, and technology*. https://onlinelibrary.wiley.com/doi/10.1002/9781118786352.wbieg0598

Adams, D.W., & Fitchett, D.A. (1992). *Informal finance in low-income countries*. Westview Press.

Allen, F., Qian, M., & Qian, J. (2005). Law, finance, and economic growth in China. *Journal of Financial Economics*, 77(1), 57–116. https://doi.org/10.1016/j.jfineco.2004.06.010

Ayyagari, M., Demirgüç-Kunt, A., & Maksimovic, V. (2010). Formal versus informal finance: Evidence from China. *The Review of Financial Studies*, 23(8), 3048–97. https://doi.org/10.1093/rfs/hhq030

Brenner, N., Marcuse, P., & Mayer, M. (2009). Cities for people, not for profit. *City*, 13(2–3), 176–84. https://doi.org/10.1080/13604810903020548

Castells, M., & Portes, A. (1989). World underneath: The origins, dynamics, and effects of the informal economy. In A. Portes, M. Castells, & L.A. Benton (Eds.), *The informal economy: Studies in advanced and less developed countries* (pp. 11–40). Johns Hopkins University Press.

Chovanec, P. (2011, 18 December). China's real estate bubble may have just popped. *Foreign Affairs*. http://www.foreignaffairs.com/articles/136963/patrick-chovanec/chinas-real-estate-bubble-may-have-just-popped

Christophers, B. (2015). The limits to financialization. *Dialogues in Human Geography*, 5(2), 183–200. https://doi.org/10.1177/2043820615588153

De Soto, H. (1989). *The other path*. Harper & Row.

Ding, C., & Lichtenberg, E. (2011). Land and urban economic growth in China. *Journal of Regional Science*, 51(2), 299–317. https://doi.org/10.1111/j.1467-9787.2010.00686.x

Fainstein, S. (2016). Financialisation and justice in the city: A commentary. *Urban Studies*, 53(7), 1503–8. https://doi.org/10.1177/0042098016630488

Feng, J. (2012, 7 April). Chuan E'erduosi minjianjJiedai "Heimingdan" yi duanxin xingshi xielou (Ordos informal finance "black list" reportedly leaked by text message). *Economic Observer*. http://business.sohu.com/20120407/n339971780.shtml

Foster, J.B. (2007). The financialization of capitalism. *Monthly Review*, 58(11), 1–12. https://doi.org/10.14452/MR-058-11-2007-04_1

Hart, K. (1970). Small-scale entrepreneurs in Ghana and development planning. *Journal of Development Studies*, 6(4), 104–20. https://doi.org/10.1080/00220387008421338

Hart, K. (1973). Informal income opportunities and urban employment in Ghana. *The Journal of Modern African Studies*, 11(1), 61–89. https://doi.org/10.1017/S0022278X00008089

He, C., Wang, J., & Cheng, S. (2011). What attracts foreign direct investment in China's real estate development? *The Annals of Regional Science*, 46(2), 267–93. https://doi.org/10.1007/s00168-009-0341-4

He, G., Mol, A.P.J., & Lu, Y. (2016). Wasted cities in urbanizing China. *Environmental Development*, 18, 2–13. https://doi.org/10.1016/j.envdev.2015.12.003

He, S., & Wu, F. (2009). China's emerging neoliberal urbanism: Perspectives from urban redevelopment. *Antipode*, 41(2), 282–304. https://doi.org/10.1111/j.1467-8330.2009.00673.x

Hsing, Y.T. (2010). *The great urban transformation: Politics of land and property in China*. Oxford University Press.

Hsu, S. (2009). Introduction. In J. Li & S. Hsu (Eds.), *Informal finance in China: American and Chinese perspectives* (pp. 3–11). Oxford University Press.

Jiang, S. (2009). The evolution of informal finance in China and its prospects. In J. Li & S. Hsu (Eds.), *Informal finance in China: American and Chinese perspectives* (pp. 12–38). Oxford University Press.

Kindleberger, C., & Aliber, R. (2011). *Manias, panics, and crashes: A history of financial crises* (6th ed.). Palgrave.

Li, J., & Hsu, S. (Eds.). (2009). *Informal finance in China: American and Chinese perspectives*. Oxford University Press.

Li, X. (2011, 4 August). E'erduosi minjian jiedai: Yonggan zhe de youxi [Ordos informal finance: A game for the brave]. *First Economic Daily*. http://finance.sina.com.cn/leadership/20110804/013710257216.shtml

Lin, G.C.S. (2017). Making sense of the uneven geography of urban and regional growth in the era of financialization: Financial intermediation, institutions, and markets. *Area Development and Policy*, 2(3), 245–50. https://doi.org/10.1080/23792949.2017.1347049

Lin, G.C.S., & Yi, F. (2011). Urbanization of capital or capitalization on urban land? Land development and local public finance in urbanizing China. *Urban Geography*, 32(1), 50–79. https://doi.org/10.2747/0272-3638.32.1.50

Mao, J., & Luo, J. (2011). Zhongguo minjian jiedai fenxi [Analysis of informal finance in China]. China International Capital Corporation.

Ong, A. (2011). Hyperbuilding: Spectacle, speculation, and the hyperspace of sovereignty. In A. Roy & A. Ong (Eds.), *Worlding cities: Asian experiments and the art of being global* (pp. 205–26). Wiley-Blackwell.

Ong, L.H. (2014). State-led urbanization in China: Skyscrapers, land revenue and "concentrated villages." *The China Quarterly*, 217, 162–79. https://doi.org/10.1017/S0305741014000010

Pairault, T. (2012). Pratiques microfinancières: Les nouveaux habits du gouvernement chinois. In F. Leloup, J. Brot, & H. Gérardin, (Eds.), *L'état, acteur du développement* (pp. 103–22). Karthala Editions.

Peattie, L.R. (1980). Anthropological perspectives on the concepts of dualism, the informal sector, and marginality in developing urban economies. *International Regional Science Review*, 5(1), 1–31. https://doi.org/10.1177/016001768000500101

People's Bank of China (PBoC), (Ed.). (2006). *Xiao'e daikuan gongsi zhidao shouce* [Microfinance company manual]. China Finance Publishing House.

Portes, A., & Haller, W. (2005). The informal economy. In N.J. Smelser & R. Swedberg (Eds.), *The handbook of economic sociology* (2nd ed., pp. 403–36). Princeton University Press.

Qin, H. (2011). Shoufa: Zhongguo minjian ziben touzi diaoyan baogao E'erduosi bian (First draft: China private finance research report, Ordos edition). Ministry of Housing and Urban-Rural Development.

Sawyer, M. (2014). What is financialization? *International Journal of Political Economy* 42(4), 5–18. https://doi.org/10.2753/IJP0891-1916420401

Sheng, Y. (2012). Gemi E'erduosi zhi "guai" xianxiang [Exposing the "strange" phenomenon of Ordos]. *Chengshi Zhongguo*, 53, 69–71.

Song, Y., & Ding, C. (2007). *Urbanization in China: Critical issues in an era of rapid growth*. Lincoln Institute of Land Policy.

Theurillat, T. (2017). The role of money in China's urban production: The local property industry in Qujing, a fourth-tier city. *Urban Geography*, 38(6), 834–60. https://doi.org/10.1080/02723638.2016.1184859

Tian, Y. (2012, 17 January). Fang qi 7 cheng zijin laizi gaolidai: 400 yi minjian jiedai taolao loushi [70 percent of capital for property firms comes from informal finance: 40 billion tied up in the property market]. *Commercial Times*. http://dg.focus.cn/news/2012-01-17/1726181.html

Tsai, K. (2002). *Back-alley banking: Private entrepreneurs in China*. Cornell University Press.

Wang, H., Tao, R., & Tong, J. (2009). Trading land development rights under a planned land use system: The "Zhejiang Model." *China & World Economy*, 17(1), 66–82. https://doi.org/10.1111/j.1749-124X.2009.01131.x

Wang, Y. (2011). Financial sector and development of private capital. In Q. Ma (Ed.), *Private capital and the road to developed economy* (pp. 60–78). Economic Science Press.

Woodworth, M.D. (2015). Ordos Municipality: A market-era resource boomtown. *Cities*, 43, 115–32. https://doi.org/10.1016/j.cities.2014.11.017

Woodworth, M.D. (2018). Landscape and the cultural politics of China's anticipatory urbanism. *Landscape Research*, 43(7), 891–905. https://doi.org/10.1080/01426397.2017.1404020

Woodworth, M.D., & Wallace, J.L. (2017). Seeing ghosts: Parsing China's "ghost city" controversy. *Urban Geography*, 38(8), 1270–81. https://doi.org/10.1080/02723638.2017.1288009

Wu, J., Gyourko, J., & Deng, Y. (2015). Evaluating the risk of Chinese housing markets: What we know and what we need to know. [Working paper 21346]. National Bureau of Economic Research. https://www.nber.org/papers/w21346

Xinhua (2012, 25 July). E'erduosi weifa zhandi an duo guanyuan shou chufen xinghewan gaoguan she an [Multiple officials disciplined in Ordos for illegal land expropriation in Ordos. Star River project officials involved]. *Xinhua*. http://finance.sina.com.cn/china/dfjj/20120725/180012668879.shtml

Yu, G. (2012). E'reduosi jingji tengfei beihou de luoji [The logic behind Ordos's economic take-off]. *Chengshi Zhongguo*, 53, 66–7.

Zhang, L. (2011, 22 October). Su Yenü an: E'erduosi gaolidai zuihou kuanghuan [Su Yenü Case: The last hoorah for Ordos's informal finance mania]. *China Business Journal*. http://finance.sina.com.cn/china/jrxw/20111022/024410668994.shtml

Zhu, R. (2011, 5 April). E'erduosi: "Da jia dou lai chi gaolidai" de houguo [The aftermath of "everyone eat interest" in Ordos]. *Investment and Management*. https://finance.qq.com/a/20140529/006110.htm

6 El Quiñón: Corruption and Speculative Development in the Spanish Financial Crisis

MARTA CATALÁN ERASO AND CECILIA L. CHU

I am building flats for 33–34 millions [of pesetas] for you, the young people ... We are constructing a model for this country. It will be the pride of all Spaniards.
– Francisco Hernando, developer of El Quiñón[1]

Seseña is the symbol of the real estate bubble, also of the downfall for housing prices of the unpaid mortgages, of the massive evictions, of the accumulation of toxic loans in the banks, of the private Spanish debt that cannot be refinanced.
– *El País*, 2010[2]

Around 2007, maybe this was a ghost city, as there were very few residents. But in 2014, 80 per cent [of El Quiñón] is occupied. There is enough commerce, so I am very, very happy. I have been living there a year and half, and I am happy.
– Lola Pérez, resident in El Quiñón[3]

To many passers-by, El Quiñón, the mega residential development located in Seseña, a small town about half an hour's drive from Madrid, appeared to be a blot on the dusty Castilian plateau. The huge housing project, which was originally conceived by its developer to offer affordable apartments for 40,000 residents, became a symbol of the reckless speculation and malpractices associated with Spain's housing bubble leading up to the 2008 financial crisis. Like many thousands of property projects built in the 1990s and 2000s, El Quiñón was a consequence of macro-economics and micro-politics (Paumgarten, 2013).

---

1 Hernando's press release (our translation). For more details see Bécares & Mengual (2006).
2 See Bassets (2010) for the quotation (our translation).
3 Quoted on the television program *En Profundidad* (2014, 1 February; our translation).

Figure 6.1. View of El Quiñón. Source: Photo by authors, 2017.

During the boom years, Spanish cities and towns rezoned surrounding agricultural land and transformed them into speculative financial products (Alexandri & Janoschka, 2018). Although such fast-tracked urbanization followed similar projects in other cities in Europe and elsewhere in this period, Spanish patterns of development were also significantly shaped by the nation's specific economic and institutional histories. These include the long-standing dependence of the national economy on the construction sector, the lack of effective administrative and legal frameworks in urban planning, and the decentralization of administrative power in the post-Franco era that encouraged rampant corruption in real estate dealings. To more fully explain the unfolding phenomenon, it is also crucial to take into account the broad support for property ownership among the Spanish population, inculcated by state policies since the post-war period, as well as the widespread tolerance for irregular practices in urban development over the past decades (Nieto, 2008; Romero et al., 2012; Fernández & Collado, 2017).

This chapter attempts to connect the dynamics behind the Spanish financial crisis with popular discourses about housing by tracing the development of El Quiñón. In the years following the collapse of the real estate market in 2008, the incomplete project was transformed into a toxic asset, with its developer forced to hand over the properties to the banks, which subsequently sold the housing units at hugely reduced prices to would-be homeowners.[4] Despite its negative image and ongoing legal challenges, El Quiñón has gradually become occupied, and as the economy began to recover and property prices started to rise once again in the Madrid region over the last few years, the project seems to have finally begun to fulfil the developer's proclaimed vision

---

4 See note 16 for more details on the banking operations in El Quiñón.

of providing dream homes for the Spanish working class. By examining the perspectives and sentiments of different agents involved in the scheme, including government officials and architects employed by the developer and homeowners, we seek to provide a more nuanced understanding of the cultural and political rationalities behind the making of El Quiñón and, more generally, the meanings of property ownership to citizens in neoliberal Spain.

To approach these issues, we draw upon fieldwork carried out over several months in 2017 that includes first-hand interviews with key stakeholders of the project. The study also involves analysing a substantial number of news reports, social commentaries, and secondary sources on the housing crisis. It is worth noting that, compared with other property schemes that defaulted, El Quiñón has attracted comparatively more public attention largely due to the celebrity status and strong media presence of its developer, Francisco Hernando, whose rags-to-riches story has long captured the imagination of a large number of the Spanish working class.[5] Ultimately, this chapter illustrates a need to understand financial processes on the ground by taking into account the multiple and sometimes conflicting perspectives of people with stakes in real estate and the ways that the economic, political, and cultural rationalities behind housing development are divergent yet intertwined.

Constructing the Spanish Homeownership Discourse

Since the financial crisis in 2008, there has been a growing number of critical writings on the expansion of financial capital around the world and how states have rebuilt mortgage markets for enabling securitization and predatory lending (Brenner, 2009; Gotham, 2009). Other commentators have focused their critiques on the negative impacts of financialization in perpetuating unsustainable consumption (Lapavitsas, 2009). However, as pointed out by Jaime Palomera (2013), while these critiques offer important insights from macro-economic perspectives, few have engaged with the mechanisms that allow financial processes to take hold in everyday discourse or determined how they shape the politics of collective identity among the working class. In a similar vein, Sophie Gonick (2015) argues for an urgent need to understand the role of property in fostering a particular political subjectivity that resonates with the demands of capitalist expansion, as well as making

---

5 For a discussion on Hernando's story, see Urreiztieta (2006), Hidalgo (2006b), and Daniels (2009).

that expansion possible. The work of Palomera, Gonick, and others underscore the importance of connecting the penetration of financial logics among the wider citizenry in contemporary Spain with the country's institutional and spatial histories (García, 2010; Maldonado, 2017). Their arguments challenge the prevalent assumption that the high rate of homeownership in Spain is "cultural"; that is, its tradition of valuing private property is similar to those of other southern European nations such as Portugal and Greece. In fact, up until the 1960s, more than half of the total Spanish population were still renters (Alberdi, 2014). A closer look at demographics suggests that the rapid growth of homeownership is not so much the result of tradition but a product of social and economic changes that took place over the past six decades. At the same time, these changes parallel the emergence of a homeownership discourse that played a role in shaping dispositions of Spanish citizens towards property investment and speculative urbanization.

Housing historians have pointed out that the Spanish economic model originated in the modernization program of the Franco dictatorship in the late 1950s, predicated on the radical expansion of homeownership (Llordén, 2003; López & Rodríguez, 2011). A key policy behind this development was the 1959 National Stabilization Plan, which was introduced to loosen economic barriers and increase market efficiency (Tamames, 2005; Marcinkowski, 2015; Fernández, 2015). In consultation with international organizations, including the International Monetary Fund, the Franco government made homeownership a top priority in its national policies. The belief was that property could be a key "stabilizing force" that would not only help expand the economy but also foster social harmony by incorporating a large part of the population into the capitalist system as property owners. The move, which was famously represented by the claim to "transform a country of proletarians into a country of homeowners," was underpinned by the regime's anxiety to stave off the growth of communism perceived to be associated with working class renters (Naredo, 2010).[6] To this end, a host of policies were implemented with the aim to discourage renting, promote real estate development, and encourage the purchase of private homes. Among these was the Housing Plan 1961–76, which provided state subsidies for building new privately owned residential flats for the working class (Sánchez-Martínez, 2002), and the 1996 state decision to fiscally reward homeowners as opposed to those renting (Leal, 2005;

---

6 In 1957, Falangist leader José Luis Arrese, then the Spanish housing minister, said: "Queremos un país de propietarios, no de proletarios."

García-Montalvo, 2008). These arrangements, which favoured the incorporation of state-subsidized housing into the private market, have remained a key feature of Spanish housing policies that differentiate it from those in many other European nations in the post-war years, where the terms "social," "public," or "state-subsidized" are mostly associated with rental housing (Palomera, 2013). Remarkably, by the time of Spain's inclusion in the European Union, the rate of homeownership of the nation had reached 80 per cent (Instituto Nacional de Estadística [INE], 2016), while in the United States and Britain it never rose above 70 per cent.[7]

Over time, these state policies have effectively made the purchase of private property the only way to acquire a decent shelter for a majority of the working population (Rodríguez, 2009; Pareja-Eastaway & Sánchez-Martínez, 2017). They have also contributed to a collective consensus that renting is a waste of money, while purchasing a property is a logical and indeed necessary lifetime investment. Furthermore, such dispositions have created expectations that the state would continue to help facilitate the expansion of the private housing market while protecting the property value of homeowners. This mind-set partially explains why Spanish citizens have been generally resistant to fiscal measures aimed at providing universal welfare and other policy measures that they saw would negatively affect their own assets. Likewise, the redistributive function of the state and its ability to address social inequality have been substantially weakened. Despite the embrace of democracy and the advent of progressive politics in the post-Franco era, the macro-economic model, which was arguably the first attempt in Europe to provide economic growth through a financial and asset-price bubble, remains unchanged (López & Rodríguez, 2011). Meanwhile, the lack of support for equalitarian provision of welfare prevails even under the left-leaning Socialist Workers' Party (*Partido Obrero Socialista Español*, PSOE) government.

Urban Planning and the Propensity for Corruption

The economic boom that lasted throughout the 1960s facilitated the rapid growth of the construction industry, which received generous loans from the state for building private housing with a low interest rate (Keogh, 1994). However, despite accelerated economic development,

---

7 In 2016, Spain had a population of 46.5 million and 25.6 million housing units, of which 77 per cent were owned (INE, 2016).

other industrial sectors in the period remained largely undeveloped. After the recession of the 1970s, the Spanish government continued to rely on internal housing bubbles to sustain the growth of capital. As pointed out by López and Rodríguez (2011), the state's economic strategy in deepening its existing "specializations" in property development and construction adapted advantageously to the emerging global economy in the 1980s (that is, high capital mobility and growing competition to capture financial incomes). Following the inclusion of Spain in the European Union, the government issued a series of liberalizing measures, including the Boyer Decree, that aimed to propel the construction sector by unfreezing and therefore increasing rental prices. To pave the way for the expansion of the financial sector, the state undertook gradual deregulation that allowed commercial banks to grant mortgages and extend the length and amount of loans, as well as enable mortgages to be turned into marketable securities (Palomera & Vetta, 2016). It was with these deregulatory policies, along with a general easing of credit in the global market and a decrease in social housing provision, that the Spanish housing bubble rapidly took hold, with the scale and intensity of speculative development reaching its peak between the late 1990s and early 2000s (Alberdi, 2014; Fernández & Collado, 2017).

To explain the specific forms of these developments in this period, it is important to contextualize them against the existing planning framework and readjustment of the Spanish land law. Up until 1998, the regulation of urban development in Spain was based on the Francoist 1956 Urban Land Law, which classified land into developed, developable, and non-developable land. While rural land was regarded mostly as unsuitable for development and had little or no value, the land classified as "fit for development" was valued highly, as if it were already fully developed (Romero et al., 2012; Ponce, 2012; González, 2007; Jiménez, 2009). Under such an arrangement, the municipal plan became a powerful tool for increasing the value of land and thus also a source for political corruption (García et al., 2013). As Romero and colleagues (2012) explain, this planning model led to significant land speculation on the one hand and irrational development of towns on the other.

In 1998, the government introduced the Land Act, which provided the legal basis to transform more land into developable land. The law reduced land categories into developable and non-developable. Under this arrangement, non-developable land was no longer a residual category, and any piece of land could now be developed unless it possessed a particular preservation value or carried risks. Although the 1998 Land

Act was formulated with the intention to limit speculation, and as some commentators have argued, the curb of land stock shortage would be sufficient to control it (Soriano, 1995; Orgaz, 1995), the disconnection between planning expectations and actual demand ended up creating a highly speculative virtual market of real estate assets (Roca & Burns, 2000).

Another key feature associated with planning practices since the 1980s was the decentralization of administrative control over development. Following some of the "bottom-up" trends in land development that were taking place in Europe, the Spanish Autonomous Communities through General Plans (*Planes Generales*) shifted urban planning competencies from an administrative centralism to a regional and municipal urban legislation. From the mid-1980s, a number of major cities began to sign urban planning agreements with developers who would then promise to fulfil more commitments to the town council in exchange for amendments on the plan. The 1998 Land Act accelerated these processes by separating the right to ownership and the right to build, thus affecting the rights and responsibilities of landowners.[8] The law implemented the right to urban development, no longer tied to a series of planning obligations (González, 2007) but as the result of an approved plan, with full autonomy over the urban process once it was approved. Although the intentions of such arrangements were to improve regional economic performance, they have been criticized for their opacity and for leading to widespread corruption. Overall, the reclassification of land, the empowerment of the local administration, and the autonomy of the plan contributed to suburbanization and peri-urbanization through the uncontrolled emergence of urban developments in the Spanish landscape.

The Inception of El Quiñón and the Developer's Battle

The consequences of these shifts in land regulation and planning frameworks can be seen in the course of development of El Quiñón, a huge housing complex situated 5 kilometres away from the compact township of Seseña with 6,000 inhabitants (INE, 2003).[9] In 2003, the mayor

---

8 Roca and Burns (2000) define the "ladder" of obligations and rights as follows: the right to land development incurred the obligation to develop land/ cede and distribute equally; the right to development return incurred the obligation to apply for building permission; and the right to build incurred the obligation to build within a fixed period.
9 The population of Seseña in 2003 was 6,424 inhabitants (data from INE).

granted approval for the project, which sought to bring a tenfold increase to Seseña's population. As in other less populated localities, Seseña lacked a General Plan. The planning was regulated through loose subsidiary norms, with an average population density of thirty dwellings per hectare, a maximum height of two floors, and a buildable area of 0.5 square metres. In El Quiñón, the population density would be raised to seventy-four dwellings per hectare, with a maximum height of ten floors and a buildable area of 0.99 square metres (Boletín Oficial del Estado [BOE], 2011). These changes were made possible under the land law's Program of Urban Actuation (PAU),[10] which allowed the new planning figure to override the existing standard norms once the project was approved by the municipality.

The inception of El Quiñón was not dissimilar to many other speculative schemes that were approved through shady dealings with local town councils during the boom years. It was also caught up with the competing social goals of different political parties that came to power over the span of its construction. The scheme was the brainchild of Francisco Hernando, a notorious developer with the nickname "el Pocero" (the sewer man), which serves as a reminder of his humble origins unclogging drains (Paumgarten, 2013). In the 1990s, Hernando began to develop a series of urban complexes in the region and, in 2003, proposed an ambitious plan to build El Quiñón, which he envisaged would become a small city for the Spanish working class with 13,500 units. The scheme was approved by the mayor of Seseña, José Luis Martín, under the PSOE government, which had embraced liberal economic policies since the political transition (Magone, 2004). The project soon encountered numerous challenges after the United Left (*Izquierda Unida*, IU) won the local election. Formed as an excision of the Communist Party, the IU's agenda was to advocate social justice and empower civil society in decision-making processes (Ramiro & Verge, 2013). After a series of setbacks imposed by the new mayor to stop the project, it was unblocked under the new government of the right-wing People's Party (*Partido Popular*, PP) in 2011.

The first critique of El Quiñón by the IU related to whether there was a need for such a large housing complex for a small township, as the projected population growth of El Quiñón was much higher than that of Seseña. Using irregularities in its infrastructure provision and other malpractices as reasons, the IU denied approval for the first occupation licences for El Quiñón. The developer, left with empty apartments that he was unable to sell, put pressure on the local government

---

10 In Spanish, Programa de Actuación Urbana.

by getting his workers to protest against the decision and filed several lawsuits against the mayor, Manuel Fuentes, for illegally stopping the project.[11] The development became so contested that, in 2011, the Court of Audits published a report on the irregularities of the municipality of Seseña and urged the central government of Spain to intervene (BOE, 2011). After numerous trials, however, none of the agents involved in El Quiñón's development were formally charged. Indeed, similar situations could be seen in many other cases of housing speculation, where malpractices had been widely condemned in the media but continued to be legally tolerated.[12]

The inability of the IU to stop the project was partly due to the fact that it was already approved by the former authority. Nonetheless, the party tried to advocate its agenda by calling for a sustainable urban growth for Seseña that respected demographics and followed the concept of a compact city.[13] To do so, the IU ordered the publication of several reports that criticized El Quiñón as a commuter town with a high probability of social exclusion due to the lack of a civic centre, which left it with "no places to cohabitate or to raise awareness of our society."[14] The IU went further by hiring a renowned Madrilenian urban planner, José María Ezquiaga, to develop a unitary territorial model for Seseña. It even went as far as to create an online platform that encouraged residents to share their collective future visions for their town. However, these well-intended planning initiatives, which aligned with the oft-reiterated claims of community empowerment and democratic development in the post-Franco era, did not seem to have much influence on shaping popular perceptions. Ironically, many residents of Seseña shared the view that the developer had been unfairly treated by the mayor and blamed the latter for delaying the completion of the project.[15]

By the time the housing bubble burst in 2008, only one-third of the proposed flats were completed. As Hernando was unable to sell his

---

11   Amid numerous quarrels, Francisco Hernando decided to launch his own newspaper, *La Voz de la Sagra*, to control some of the media attention. See Duva (2007).
12   El Quiñón is not an isolated case of corrupt practices in Spanish land development. Elsewhere in Spain, intertwined relationships between local politicians, financial stakeholders, and developers contributed to economic neglect that peaked before the financial collapse. Many cases were disclosed during and after the economic crisis. Among the most heated ones, we find the development in Las Teresitas (Santa Cruz de Tenerife) or the scandal to build a Palace of Congress in Palazuelos de Eresma (Segovia). For more details of these cases, see García et al. (2013).
13   Manuel Fuentes, personal interview, 21 March 2017.
14   Ibid.
15   For more on these contestations see Los obreros (2006) and El Pocero (2006).

properties, the banks reclassified his debt as "toxic assets." The project entered a new phase in 2011 after the IU lost the election. The incoming PP mayor soon unblocked the occupation licences. Many of the flats were put on sale with a substantial price reduction and were swiftly acquired.[16]

El Quiñón and the Pride of Place

Although El Quiñón has been widely described as a speculative project in local and international media, it should be noted that many agents involved in its development strongly disagreed with the notion. The developer himself, for one, has stressed repeatedly that the project was intended to be his crowning achievement in providing dream homes for the Spanish working class.[17] Despite being criticized for its monotonous design – the outward appearance was not dissimilar to many fast-tracked speculative schemes in Spain – Hernando was proud of the design of El Quiñón. His pride was exemplified by his decision to both name the project after himself and also dedicate various icons within the complex to his family.[18] Juanjo Cortés, head of the Architecture Department at the developer's company ONDE2000, shared his satisfaction with Hernando concerning the good quality of the project and challenged the idea that it was a mere speculative scheme. Cortés also defended Hernando, saying that he was not a speculator. A speculator, he pointed out, rezones the land and then moves on, always with the aim of maximizing profitability. Hernando, however, stayed in Seseña and until today has been in charge of some of its maintenance.

Cortés and his colleagues further explained that El Quiñón should be commended for being a pioneer in high-rise housing construction.[19] The scale and speed of the construction and its overall quality were

---

16 The price reduction was possible following the change of ownership of the flats between various savings banks after the financial crisis. El Quiñón was originally funded by CAM (Caja del Mediterráneo), Caja Duero, Banco de Galicia, Banco Popular, Caja Cantabria, Ibercaja, and Caja España. After the bubble burst, Sabadell Bank, Santander Bank, Banco Popular, and Abanca were the institutions owning the flats. The most powerful financial entities, Sabadell and Santander, were able to dispose of units at a very reduced value, whereas the two other banks, unable to compete financially, still retain some of them. For more on this transition, see International Monetary Fund (2012).
17 Hernando shared his views in a public press release on 13 November 2006. For more details, see Bécares & Mengual (2006).
18 These included placing a sculpture of his parents in a roundabout and naming the largest park in the complex after his wife, María Audena.
19 Juanjo Cortés and colleagues, personal interviews, 16 March 2017 and 25 March 2017.

Figure 6.2. Entrance to the public park María Audena, named after Hernando's wife. Source: Photo by authors, 2017.

Figure 6.3. Amenities in the buildings of El Quiñón include swimming pools, paddle courts, children's playgrounds, and gardens. Source: Photo by Andrea Ramos Arias.

hard to match in nearby housing complexes. Its building materials were sourced locally to save transportation time, including the ceramic bricks for the façade. Most importantly, the project offered residents a high-value product that was comparative to those offered in Madrid, with all buildings equipped with amenities such as swimming pools and paddle courts as well as 1.5 parking lots per apartment. Likewise, each unit was designed with cross ventilation that improved passive indoor climate control. Each unit also had a large terrace and top-quality interior finishes.

Isidoro González, a civil engineer in ONDE2000, agreed with Cortés that El Quiñón was a distinctive housing project especially built with a focus on efficiency – an opinion that contradicted many outside critics who associated such fast-tracked construction negatively with speculation (Rodríguez, 2009; Romero et al., 2012; Naredo, 2015). To accomplish such a large construction in a short time span, González explained, ONDE2000 employed a huge work force, at one point reaching 10,000 workers, including those of the outsourced companies. It also built its own concrete production plant and even a water treatment plant. Acknowledging the water scarcity in the region, it purchased materials for water tanks, even though they were never built. That said, González agreed that the project also faced numerous challenges in infrastructure provision that were beyond the company's control. A case in point was the high voltage line that crossed the development, which was expected

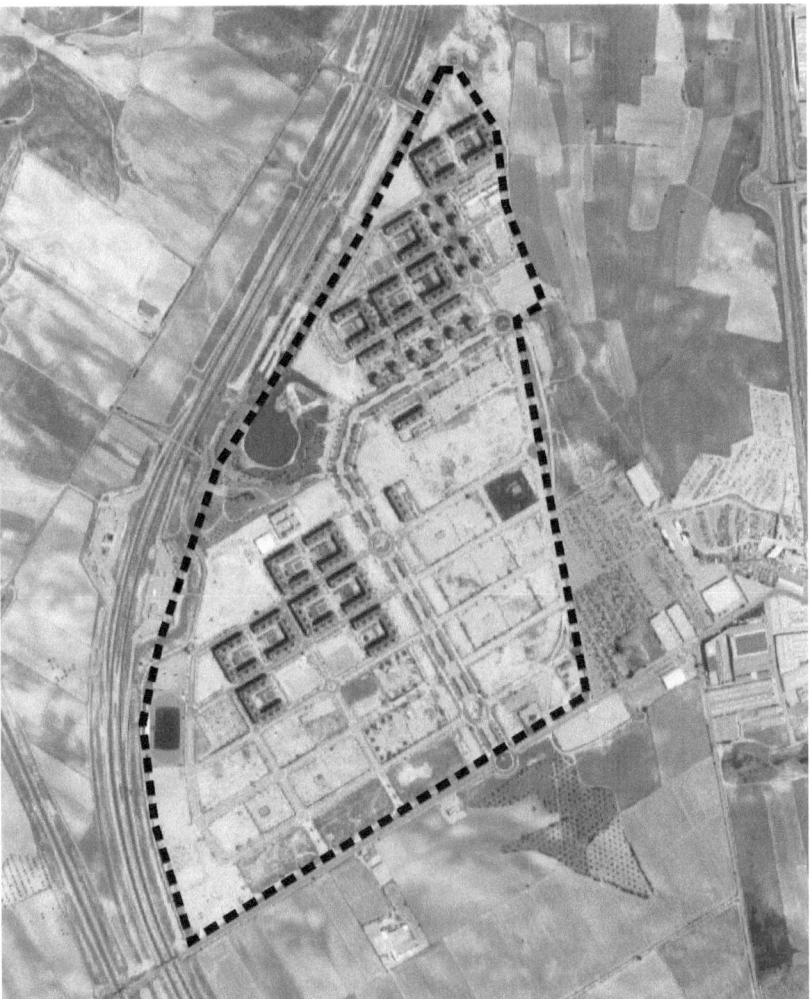

Figure 6.4. Aerial view of El Quiñón that shows the undeveloped southern part. Source: Photo from Google Maps.

to be buried underground. Due to the refusal of the electric company to issue a permit on the grounds that it would be unsafe, the area close to the main entrance of the complex remains unbuilt until today.

To some critics, such a situation reinforced the negative image of El Quiñón as an incomplete project that exemplified the extent of speculative urbanization in Spain, where so many extravagant housing schemes were abandoned after the financial crisis, leading to what has been referred to as a "crisis landscape" with devastating environmental consequences (Marcinkowski, 2015). Up until today, El Quiñón still lacks certain basic infrastructures, including medical services. The branch connecting to the A4, the main highway that goes to Madrid, is still an unsafe local road. As one resident contended, the public transport to Madrid is not very frequent, and there is only a bus every half an hour going to Seseña.[20]

Although the absence of basic infrastructure led to much frustration among the residents, most of them nevertheless have not regretted their decision to buy homes in El Quiñón. But rather than being resigned to the adverse conditions, many residents have become active in fighting for their right to better infrastructure and urban services. This activism was reflected, for example, in the aftermath of a severe fire that destroyed thousands of abandoned tires in a nearby plot in 2016.[21] The dumping site had been denounced several times in the last decade, but the authorities had given little response to these petitions. To capture public attention, the residents have demonstrated numerous times, calling for the government to address this and other problems, including road access and the urgent need for more educational facilities.

In our interviews with the residents, it became clear that there is a largely shared, dignified sentiment associated with being part of El Quiñón.[22] "The best is our neighbours," said one resident, "mostly young people with kids that enjoy the tranquility of the place." Another interviewee expressed a similar opinion. She arrived five years ago and has apparently been very satisfied with her purchased apartment, especially its interior quality and amenities. "We have an almost Olympic-sized swimming pool," she proclaimed. She also challenged the negative image in the media of El Quiñón as a ghost town and defined the population growth as "vertiginous."[23] She even added that, because of this population increase, a second school was built in 2020 and it has become harder to find a parking spot in the street.

Another interviewee, a woman in her fifties, proudly invited us to tour her flat.[24] We passed the security doorman, and she walked us through the common area where her granddaughter, still an infant, was playing. "It is a safe place," she proclaimed as we began the visit. She

---

20 From personal interviews with residents, 19 March 2017.
21 See more details in España: Miles de personas (2016) and Barroso (2016).
22 From personal interviews with residents, 19 March 2017.
23 For a media articles depicting Seseña as a ghost town, see Hidalgo (2006a) and McGovern (2008).
24 From personal interviews with residents, 19 March 2017.

also praised the finishes of the interiors and the spaciousness of her apartment, including an ample terrace facing the Castilian landscape. As we took the elevator and visited the parking and storage rooms, she reminded us how spotless and bright these areas were. She then told us that, although she purchased the apartment before the price reduction and did not move in right away, she is now very satisfied with her investment. When she became divorced, she moved to El Quiñón and found that it was the ideal place to take care of her granddaughter, who frequently stayed with her. When we left her and her family, they joined a group of neighbours looking after their kids in the playground.

Despite the numerous media critiques of corruption in El Quiñón, recent articles have begun to describe the project in a more positive light, increasingly centring the discussion on the contentment of the current residents. "Seseña, the Brick's Pride" and "The Awakening of Seseña" were two such articles published in the newspaper *El País* (Domínguez, 2016; Sánchez, 2016). These articles no longer focus so much on the irregularities of the development but instead portray a pleasant image of a vibrant neighbourhood. Furthermore, despite inadequate infrastructure, the attractive price reductions offered by the banks involved after the financial crisis enticed new buyers and contributed to the more socially diverse community that today occupies El Quiñón. The development was initially targeted at middle-income working families and approved just a few months before the 2003 modification of the Law of Territorial Ordinance and Urban Activity (LOTAU), which required a minimum quota for social housing. Yet, at least one-fifth of the homeowners purchased the apartments after the financial crisis at a much reduced rate, contributing to the creation of a more heterogeneous neighbourhood than its initial conception.

This unexpected change in the social profile of El Quiñón has also led to tensions. In several conversations, our interviewees differentiated the social status of residents between two distinct areas of the development: the northern area with owners who had purchased the units before the financial crisis, and therefore had more economic means, and the southern area with owners who had acquired the units after the crisis, often implying a lesser financial capacity.[25] Some residents of the northern area contended that they considered the newcomers in the south to be potentially damaging to the well-being of the development. Some of them further complained about the sight of "not-so-desirables" occupying the newest area of El Quiñón near the entrance. They referred to

---

25 From personal interviews with residents, 19 March 2017.

these people as *"chonis"* (which can loosely be translated as "trash"). The interviewees acknowledged that they feel uncomfortable about the social disparity between themselves and the "lower-class" people associated with the more economical housing price range.

And yet, despite threads of social disapproval and class tensions, those who live in the new area expressed satisfaction with their decision to move there. In interviews, they often underscored their contentment with having acquired an apartment at such an affordable rate.[26] As an example, one of the interviewees was walking with his father, who had just come to visit. He mentioned that he mostly used his flat to sleep as he was a truck driver and spent most of the time away. But still he was very happy with the property and enjoyed his time there. "I could have never afforded something like this in Madrid," he said.[27]

Conclusion

Although many social commentators have condemned the pervasive corruption associated with speculative urbanization in Spain, particularly in the years leading up to and since the financial crisis, it is important to note that these processes took place within a backdrop of broad-based support for property ownership (Allon, 2010). The personal stories of the inhabitants in El Quiñón show how financial risks were deeply intertwined in everyday spaces, and although the crisis disrupted long-standing narratives of individual wealth growth – by citizens, media, or politicians – housing continued to be a site of accumulation that homeowners needed to protect. The complex entanglement of vested interests in housing investment involved not only developers, architects, and local officials but also homeowners, who often willingly tied their fortunes through lifelong mortgages with the trajectory of their property assets.

As discussed earlier, the high homeownership rate in Spain was a result of deliberate state policies that channelled state subsidies into the construction of private housing. Over time, these policies gave rise to a housing discourse in which property ownership has been seen as a logical, lifetime investment. This widely shared social sentiment was a key factor supporting the property bubble, as housing moved from satisfying real demand to speculative investment in the era of financialization. The pervasiveness of this view also helps to explain why, even after the bubble burst, it has not significantly affected the idea of

---

26 From personal interviews with residents, 19 March 2017.
27 From personal interviews with residents, 19 March 2017.

homeownership and of welfare, the role of the state, and ways of providing housing. The protest against social inequality, as seen in the El Quiñón case, was not so much always about helping the disadvantaged but rather about residents asserting their rights as property owners. In this process, malpractices in the planning of the development were generally tolerated, except in those cases where they had a direct negative impact on the residents themselves. Despite the tangled history of the project, it has in time fulfilled much of its implicit promise, at least in terms of the propertied imaginary of those living there. For now, it seems doubtful that El Quiñón will ever be complete in terms of infrastructures and urban provisions. However, this unfinished condition is contributing to the shaping of a civic consciousness by reuniting the inhabitants and strengthening the sense of belonging through their fights for neighbourhood betterment. As one interviewee exclaimed, when all is said and done, if everything that was on the project was finished "it would be the perfect place to live."[28]

REFERENCES

Alberdi, B. (2014). Social housing in Spain. In K. Scanlon, C. Whitehead, & M. Fernández Arrigoitia (Eds.), *Social Housing in Europe* (pp. 223–37). Wiley.

Alexandri, G., & Janoschka, M. (2018). Who loses and who wins in a housing crisis? Lessons from Spain and Greece for a nuanced understanding of dispossession. *Housing Policy Debate*, 28(1), 117–34. https://doi.org/10.1080/10511482.2017.1324891

Allon, F. (2010). Speculating on everyday life: The cultural economy of the quotidian. *Journal of Communication Enquiry*, 34(4), 366–81. https://doi.org/10.1177/0196859910383015

Barroso, J. (2016, 14 May). Un gran incendio en Seseña arrasa el mayor cementerio de neumáticos de España. *El País*. https://elpais.com/ccaa/2016/05/13/madrid/1463120336_194139.html

Bassets, L. (2010, 22 February). Entre Seseña y Barcelona. *El País*. https://elpais.com/diario/2010/02/22/catalunya/1266804442_850215.html

Bécares, R., & Mengual, E. (2006, 14 November). "El Pocero" ante los medios: "Cuando yo llegué a Seseña sólo había un señor con un burro. " *El Mundo*. https://www.elmundo.es/elmundo/2006/11/14/espana/1163501935.html

Boletín Oficial del Estado (BOE). (2011, 28 October). No. 260. https://www.boe.es/boe/dias/2011/10/28/

---

28 From personal interviews with residents, 19 March 2017.

Brenner, R. (2009). What is good for Goldman Sachs is good for America: The origins of the present crisis. *UCLA: Center for Social Theory and Comparative History.* https://escholarship.org/uc/item/0sg0782h

Daniels, A. (2009, 19 February). Property in Spain: Castles in the sand. *The Telegraph.* https://www.telegraph.co.uk/finance/property/international/4640857/Property-in-Spain-Castles-in-the-sand.html

Domínguez, I. (2016, 2 March). Seseña, orgullo del ladrillo. *El País.* https://elpais.com/elpais/2016/02/29/eps/1456761278_486731.html

Duva, J. (2007, 17 May). La sombra de El Pocero domina Seseña. *El País.* https://elpais.com/diario/2007/05/18/espana/1179439212_850215.html

El Pocero moviliza a sus obreros para exigir al alcalde de Seseña más licencias de construcción. (2006, 13 November). *El País.* https://elpais.com/elpais/2006/11/13/actualidad/1163409422_850215.html

En Profundidad [Television broadcast]. (2014, 1 February). Castilla-La Mancha Televisión.

España: Miles de personas evacuadas por incendio en el mayor vertedero de neumáticos de Europa. (2016, 13 May). *BBC World.* https://www.bbc.com/mundo/noticias/2016/05/160513_espana_incendio_en_vertedero_neumaticos_ap

Fernández, J. (2015, 14–15 December). Políticas de vivienda y modelo residencial: Características del parquet inmobiliario infrautilizado como producto de las medidas legislativas desarrolladas en España durante la segunda mitad del siglo XX [Paper presentation]. Conference Obsolescence and Renovation: 20th Century Housing in the New Millennium, Seville, Spain.

Fernández, S., & Collado, L. (2017). What has happened in Spain? The real estate bubble, corruption and housing development: A view from the local level. *Geoforum, 85*, 206–13. https://doi.org/10.1016/j.geoforum.2017.08.002

García, M. (2010). The breakdown of the Spanish urban growth model: Social and territorial effects of the global crisis. *International Journal of Urban and Regional Research, 34*(4), 978–80. https://doi.org/10.1111/j.1468-2427.2010.01015.x

García, M., Jiménez-Sánchez, F., & Villoria, M. (2013). Building local integrity systems in Southern Europe: The case of urban local corruption in Spain. *International Review of Administrative Sciences, 79*(4), 618–37. https://doi.org/10.1177/0020852313501125

García-Montalvo, J. (2008). *De la quimera inmobiliaria al colapso financiero. Crónica de un desenlace anunciado.* Antoni Bosch Editor.

Gonick, S. (2015). *At the margins of Europe: Homeownership, inclusion, and protest in contemporary Madrid.* (Doctoral dissertation, University of California, Berkeley). https://escholarship.org/uc/item/4wp1q3kb

González, J. (2007). Urban planning system in contemporary Spain. *European Planning Studies, 15*(1), 29–50. https://doi.org/10.1080/09654310601016481

Gotham, K. (2009). Creating liquidity out of spatial fixity: The secondary circuit of capital and the subprime mortgage crisis. *International Journal of Urban and Regional Research*, 33(2), 355–71. https://doi.org/10.1111/j.1468-2427.2009.00874.x

Hidalgo, C. (2006a, 18 June). Seseña: Una ciudad fantasma en el secarral. *ABC*. https://www.abc.es/espana/abci-sesena-ciudad-fantasma-secarral-200606180300-1422062757959_noticia.html

Hidalgo, C. (2006b, 2 July). "El Pocero" de los 1.000 millones de euros. *ABC*. https://www.abc.es/espana/abci-pocero-millones-euros-200607020300-1422272608575_noticia.html

Instituto Nacional de Estadística (INE). (2003). Toledo, población por municipios y sexo. https://www.ine.es/jaxiT3/Tabla.htm?t=2902&L=0

Instituto Nacional de Estadística (INE). (2016). Hogares por régimen de tenencia de la vivienda y CCAA. https://www.ine.es/jaxiT3/Tabla.htm?t=4566&L=0

International Monetary Fund (IMF). (2012). *Spain: The reform of Spanish savings banks technical notes*. [IMF Country Report no. 12/141]. https://www.imf.org/external/pubs/ft/scr/2012/cr12141.pdf

Jiménez, F. (2009). Building boom and political corruption in Spain. *South European Society and Politics*, 14(3), 255–72. https://doi.org/10.1080/13608740903356541

Keogh, G. (1994). Land law and urban planning in Spain: An economic perspective. *European Planning Studies*, 2(4), 485–98. https://doi.org/10.1080/09654319408720282

Lapavitsas, C. (2009). Financialised capitalism: Crisis and financial expropriation. *Historical Materialism*, 17(2), 114–48. https://doi.org/10.1163/156920609X436153

Leal, J. (2005). La política de vivienda en España. *Documentación Social*, 138, 63–80. https://dialnet.unirioja.es/servlet/articulo?codigo=1373178

Llordén, M. (2003). La política de vivienda del régimen franquista. In G. Sánchez & J. Tascón (Eds.), *Los empresarios de Franco: Política y economía en España, 1936–1957* (pp. 145–70). Crítica

López, I., & Rodríguez, E. (2011). The Spanish model. *New Left Review*, 69, 5–29. https://newleftreview.org/issues/ii69

Los obreros de "El Pocero" convocan dos manifestaciones en el Ayuntamiento para pedir licencias al alcalde. (2006, 9 November). *ABC*. https://www.abc.es/espana/castilla-la-mancha/toledo/abci-obreros-pocero-convocan-manifestaciones-ayuntamiento-para-pedir-licencias-alcalde-200611090300-1524168858707_noticia.html

Magone, J. (2004). *Contemporary Spanish politics*. Routledge.

Maldonado, J. (2017). Tendencias recientes de la política de vivienda en España. *Cuaderno de Relaciones Laborales*, 35(1), 15–41. https://doi.org/10.5209/CRLA.54982

Marcinkowski C. (2015). *The city that never was*. Princeton Architectural Press.
McGovern, S. (2008, 27 August). From boom town to ghost town. *BBC News*. http://news.bbc.co.uk/2/hi/business/7584097.stm
Naredo, J. (2010). El modelo inmobiliario español y sus consecuencias. *Boletín CF+S, 44*, 13–26. http://habitat.aq.upm.es/boletin/n44/ajnar.html
Naredo, J. (2015). Un episodio relevante: La burbuja especulativa y la crisis inmobiliaria en perspectiva. *Cuaderno de Investigación Urbanística, 100*, 77–82. https://doi.org/10.20868/ciur.2015.100.3168
Nieto, A. (2008). *El desgobierno de lo público*. Ariel.
Orgaz, L. (1995). Algunas reflexiones críticas a las recomendaciones de la comisión de expertos sobre urbanismo. *Ciudad y Territorio, 3*(103), 105–9. https://recyt.fecyt.es/index.php/CyTET/article/view/84006
Palomera, J. (2013). How did finance capital infiltrate the world of the urban poor? Home ownership and social fragmentation in a Spanish neighborhood. *International Journal of Urban and Regional Research, 38*(1), 218–35. https://doi.org/10.1111/1468-2427.12055
Palomera, J., & Vetta, T. (2016). Moral economy: Rethinking a radical concept. *Anthropological Theory, 16*(4), 413–32. https://doi.org/10.1177/1463499616678097
Pareja-Eastaway, M., & Sánchez-Martínez, T. (2017). Social housing in Spain: What role does the private rented market play? *Journal of Housing and the Built Environment, 32*, 377–95. https://doi.org/10.1007/s10901-016-9513-6
Paumgarten, N. (2013, 25 February). The hangover: The euro zone's fourth-largest economy has become its biggest liability. *The New Yorker*. https://www.newyorker.com/magazine/2013/02/25
Ponce, J. (2012). Land use planning and disaster: A European perspective from Spain. *Oñati Socio-legal Series, 3*(2), 196–220. https://opo.iisj.net/index.php/osls/article/view/157/182
Ramiro, L., & Verge, T. (2013). Impulse and decadence of linkage processes: Evidence from the Spanish radical left. *South European Society and Politics, 18*(1), 41–60. https://doi.org/10.1080/13608746.2012.757452
Roca, J., & Burns, M. (2000). The liberalization of the land market in Spain: The 1998 reform of urban planning legislation. *European Planning Studies, 8*(5), 547–64. https://doi.org/10.1080/713666428
Rodríguez, R. (2009). La política de vivienda en España en el contexto europeo: Deudas y retos. *Boletín CF+S, 47/48*, 125–72. http://habitat.aq.upm.es/boletin/n47/arrod.html
Romero, J., Jiménez, F., & Villoria, M. (2012). (Un)sustainable territories: Causes of the speculative bubble in Spain (1996–2010) and its territorial, environmental, and sociopolitical consequences. *Environment and Planning C: Government and Policy, 30*(3), 467–86. https://doi.org/10.1068/c11193r

Sánchez, S. (2016, 5 March). El despertar de Seseña. *El País*. https://elpais.com/elpais/2016/02/29/album/1456762866_786627.html#foto_gal_1

Sánchez-Martínez, T. (2002). *La política de vivienda en España, análisis de sus efectos redistributivos*. Universidad de Granada.

Soriano, J. (1995). *Hacia la tercera desamortización (por la reforma de la Ley del Suelo)*. Idelco.

Tamames, R. (2005). La autarquía española y las rémoras para el crecimiento económico posterior. *ICE, 826*, 13–24. https://dialnet.unirioja.es/servlet/articulo?codigo=1710422

Urreiztieta, E. (2006, 18 June). Paco "El Pocero": de las alcantarillas al cielo. *El Mundo*. https://www.elmundo.es/suplementos/nuevaeconomia/2006/329/1150581601.html

SECTION III

Forms and Norms of Speculative Housing

7 Speculation in the London Housing Market: Flat Break-Ups, Loft Conversions, and Overseas Buyers

CHRIS HAMNETT

Introduction

The term "speculation" has two distinct meanings. The first is speculation in the intellectual sense of a theory or conjecture without firm evidence; the second concerns speculation where assets are purchased or development undertaken in the hope of future financial gain. Financial speculation has existed for millennia, and history is sadly littered with a variety of speculative bubbles, booms and busts ranging from the Dutch Tulip Bubble of 1636–37, to the Mississippi and South Sea Bubbles of 1720, to the US subprime mortgage crisis of 2006 (Chancellor, 1999; Tett, 2009). Speculation has also been a consistent feature of urban development. While there are a number of cities (New Delhi; Washington, DC; Canberra; and others) where government has owned or acquired the land, planned the city, and overseen construction (Hall, 1998), the capitalist city is primarily a product of speculative construction and redevelopment by landowners, developers, and builders in search of profit.

The history of modern cities is littered with examples of speculation, from Renaissance Italy onward and even before; indeed, it is literally built upon them. Urban historians such as Summerson (1962), Dyos (1968), and Olson (1980) have shown how Georgian and Victorian London was the product of speculation, and Harvey (1995, 2003) has done the same for Paris. Landowners, developers, and builders saw the opportunities offered by a rapidly growing population and began development, sometimes by creating boulevards or garden squares for the wealthy or other times by throwing up slum housing for the poor and working classes. Speculation is not necessarily always a bad thing. It can simply entail taking a risk in the development process by building before sales are agreed upon. The great majority of house building in

Britain, the United States, and many other Western countries is, and long has been, essentially speculative in that most housing is constructed without a pre-contracted buyer.

It can be difficult to distinguish between speculation and investment. Whether an activity qualifies as speculative or investing depends on a number of factors, including the nature of the asset, the expected duration of the holding period, and the amount of leverage. It could be argued that all development that is not a response to a specific, pre-contracted purchaser at an agreed price and is dependent on the realization of an unknown gain is speculative. For example, while acquiring an additional property (in addition to one's principal residence) with the intention of renting it out would qualify as a bona fide investing activity, buying half a dozen condominiums with minimal down payments for the purpose of "condo flipping" would undoubtedly be regarded as speculation. It's a continuum ranging from long-term investment in property development or housing construction without a firm buyer or tenant to speculative short-term property trading or flipping with the aim of a quick profit. Lau in Chapter 8 of this volume shows one way in which property owners have begun to overcrowd and split apartments in Hong Kong. Similar problems are also seen in London, with landlords renting out ever smaller micro apartments to low-income tenants

Several authors have examined the production of the built environment under capitalism, including Harvey (1973, 1995), Fainstein (1994), Christophers (2011), and Badcock (1984). The objects and forms of speculation in the production and transformation of the built environment inevitably vary considerably over time and space depending on the history of development and specific profit opportunities available. Specifically, the historical form of the built environment, the legal system, planning legislation, and finance will all influence the form of profitable opportunities for speculation. At certain times, perhaps resulting from changes in the wider financial situation or from changes in government legislation, opportunities for profit present themselves that were not previously open. There are many potential areas for speculation in the modern city, but the one with which this chapter is concerned is that of the housing market and the production, transformation, and sale of housing stock for profit.

Housing in the Speculative City

Any city in a capitalist economy will, almost inevitably, be a speculative city to a very large extent. Given the underlying rationale of capitalism, which is to generate profit – preferably as large as possible – the built environment has long offered a rich seam of opportunities for developers and speculators in terms of its production and transformation. While property speculation and private development took place in the pre-capitalist era, the dominant forces for development were arguably the crown, the landed classes, and the church. But in a capitalist economy, most private investment takes place with a view to capital gain or the production of an income stream. There may be some forms of charitable investment and public investment in key elements of urban infrastructure that take place for reasons connected to the general public good, but the objective of private investment is, for the most part, geared towards private or corporate gain or profit, as Fainstein and Novy highlight in Chapter 1 of this volume.

This profit-making objective is particularly true where housing is concerned. In capitalist economies, housing is not just a place to live; rather, it is a commodity – produced, sold, transformed, and exchanged for profit. While some social housing is produced and distributed at below market prices, that venture is generally an exception; social housing's share of the overall housing stock has been in decline in many cities over the last twenty to thirty years, although a few cities like Singapore and Hong Kong are an exception, as Lau and Chua show in Chapters 8 and 9 of this volume. Both those cities have a high level of social housing. Speculation in the housing market takes a wide variety of forms, which differ both from country to country and over time, depending on the range of speculative possibilities available to builders, developers, owners, and landlords at any given point. Speculation is not limited purely to the production of housing but also takes place through the exchange, rent, sale, and redevelopment of the housing stock and the financing of housing purchase through the mortgage market. This latter has become increasingly important with what Aalbers (2017) has termed the "financialization of the housing market." While there have been a long series of housing market booms and busts (Hamnett, 1999), this process reached its most damaging extent in the 2000–09 boom and bust in the US housing market, driven to a large extent by the boom in subprime mortgage lending, which triggered the global financial crisis when the pumped-up market in mortgage derivatives collapsed, taking with it many major financial institutions. Nor was the speculative boom in housing restricted to the United States. There were similar housing boom and busts in Spain and Ireland, leaving both countries with many unfinished housing schemes, ruined banks, bankrupt companies, and individuals who lost their homes (Norris & Byrne, 2015; Agnello & Schuknecht, 2009; Muellbauer & Murphy, 1997). The implications in Spain are clearly highlighted by Catalán Eraso and Chu in their analysis of the El Quiñón development outside Madrid (Chapter 6, this volume).

We cannot understand the structure and operation of the housing market in capitalist economies without understanding the underlying basis of production and profit. If it is not profitable to produce, sell, or rent housing, then (outside the social or charitable sector) it will generally not be produced, sold, or rented. Issues of housing need do not generally enter into the housing market in capitalist cities. Empty sites will be kept empty until a profitable (re)development opportunity emerges. Hence the paradox of housing shortages, homelessness, and vacant property in such cities (London is a good example).

The structure and operation of the housing market will differ from country to country, over time, and even from city to city, depending on a varying mix of political, legislative, cultural, and historical factors. There is thus no universal model or template that all capitalist cities replicate in terms of housing types, design, or spatial layout. In some cities, for example Paris and Madrid, the rich tend to cluster in the central city, and the poor are relegated to the suburbs or the periphery, whereas in others such as Brussels, the inner city is predominantly the preserve of low-income groups, and the rich live on the periphery. What is common to all capitalist cities, however, is that the type, size, and quality of market housing available to different groups is very strongly differentiated by income and wealth. Put simply, the rich tend to live in the best housing and the poor in the worst. This division is a simple product of the interaction between the income structure and the price mechanism in such cities. The housing market in such cities was brilliantly compared to the seating plan of a theatre by David Harvey (1973) in his classic book *Social Justice and the City*. The rich sit in the expensive stall seats, the low-income patrons in the amphitheatre, and the poorest are unable to gain entrance at all. This structure was even truer in the Victorian city than it is today (Steadman-Jones, 1971).

But the housing market in such cities does not simply involve allocation of the existing housing stock. It also involves the production, transformation, redevelopment, and exchange of that housing stock over time in search of profit. It is important to stress that there are large variations from city to city and over time in the structure and operation of these processes. But the common characteristic is that they almost all involve the search for profit, although the structure and strength of constraints on this quest will vary. Thus, the Netherlands has historically been characterized by the operation of a very strong land planning system, and in Helsinki, the majority of the city land is owned by government, as it is in Hong Kong and Singapore (Haila, 2000). In these cases, city governments are likely to exercise very strong overall control over the structure and pace of development, as they effectively call the shots in terms of land availability. In other contexts, the (re) development process is much more in the hands of market participants or local growth machines (Logan & Molotch, 1987).

What I want to do in this chapter is to examine three very different aspects of the housing market in London to highlight the different ways in which speculation has influenced the nature of the housing stock and housing outcomes. The first is a very specific manifestation of residential speculation – the break-up and sale of privately rented apartment blocks, which was marked in London in the 1970s – and the way in which the government sought to control the problems by means of subsequent legislation. This process is an example of how speculators seek to profit from transformation of one form of housing tenure to another. It is a form of residential arbitrage, reliant on both different valuations operating in various residential markets and the ability to move property from one sector to another. The second is the growth of "loft" conversions in former industrial and warehouse buildings in inner London during the 1990s onwards, which illustrates how changes of use take place from one use (in this case, warehouses, factories, and offices) to another because it is more profitable. The third highlights the rise of overseas property investment ownership in London, where foreign owners are happy to buy and hold property, keeping it vacant, as a store of value and a hedge against uncertainty.

Flat Break-Up in London: A Case Study of Speculative Residential Arbitrage

The flat "break-up" market first emerged in London in the late 1960s. The name refers to the process whereby blocks of privately rented residential apartments, many built either in the late nineteenth century or in the 1930s and largely owned by institutional landlords such as insurance companies, were sold by their owners to speculative landlords whose interest was to sell as many of the individual flats as possible, thereby realizing substantial profit from the difference between the value of the flats in private renting and the value for owner occupation. This process seems fairly straightforward, but it requires some elaboration, particularly on the evolution of what Hamnett and Randolph (1984, 1986, 1988) termed the "value gap" between rented and open market sale value and the historical factors that led to the emergence of this gap. This term is to be distinguished from Neil Smith's (1979) "rent gap," which refers to the gap between buildings and the underlying value of land on which they stand.

Purpose-built blocks of apartments, so-called "mansion blocks," first emerged in central London in the 1870s (Hamnett & Randolph, 1988;

Figure 7.1. Typical mansion block in London. Source: Chris Hamnett.

Dennis, 2008), when they were built for the growing professional class. This wave of construction lasted until the early twentieth century but re-emerged in the 1930s, when low interest rates made private building very profitable once again, until war intervened. These two eras saw the construction of hundreds of blocks of rental apartments in both central London and the suburbs. Some of the blocks were built and owned by large private landlords, but most were owned by reputable institutions such as insurance companies or pension funds that relied on a steady and predictable income stream as a key element of their business model (Figure 7.1).

The problems with this sector began in 1915 when the British government introduced rent controls in response to wartime rent gouging by some landlords in the face of housing shortages. The real difficulties, however, only emerged in the late 1960s, following the 1965 Rent Act, which had sought to reintroduce controls in the sector in response to some widespread abuses by speculative landlords, notably Peter Rachman, who gave his name to "Rachmanism." Consequently, private renting developed a bad reputation, and many institutional landlords sought to exit the sector and the major reputational risks it engendered. But due to tenure security legislation designed to protect sitting tenants, landlords found it difficult to sell their properties with the exception of vacant ones, and a gap emerged between the tenanted value of properties and their open market vacant possession value. The tenanted value was considerably less than the open market possession value, as the existence of tenants limited the landlords' freedom to sell and to raise the rents. This "value gap" difference (Hamnett & Randolph, 1984) could often be one-third to half the open market sale value. The gap offered an arbitrage potential if it were possible to shift property from one sector to another. The size of the gap increased dramatically in the early 1970s as a result of very rapid house price inflation in London (about 100 per cent from 1970–73). The increase gave landlords a significant financial incentive to sell their properties for owner occupation. Ironically, it was the desire of large institutional landlords to divest themselves of residential property holdings because of the bad publicity that provided the raw material for another round of later speculative abuses.

Consequently, the 1970s saw the sale of a large number of privately owned blocks of flats, usually by public auction. In almost all cases, the blocks were purchased by a new breed of speculative property owners (flat breakers), whose overriding objective was to sell as many flats as possible as quickly as possible (to turn capital over quickly). There were two main ways of making these sales. The first was to offer individual flats to the sitting tenants at a substantial discount to the open market vacant possession sale price (perhaps 30 to 40 per cent reduction). The second was to wait for sitting tenants to move (unlikely, given the rent protection) or die, when the flats could be sold. This latter method was why many prospective buyers would look at the age structure of the tenants. The ideal was a high proportion of single tenants in their late 70s and 80s, which offered a good statistical probability of early vacancy. Predictably, some landlords were not keen on waiting and sought other ways to encourage their tenants to move out, ranging from financial inducements to overt forms of harassment. In the interim, and to generate good cash flows to help pay the interest on their debt finance, landlords raised service charges or cut the standard of service provision or maintenance, or both (Hamnett & Randolph, 1984, 1986, 1988).

The consequence of the attempt by new landlords to exploit the value gap by breaking up blocks and selling individual flats was that many residents experienced a variety of problems regarding services, service charges, insurance, and maintenance and building costs. They also experienced considerable difficulty in contacting landlords regarding problems, as many of the new entities (with names like Gaingold and Specmore) operated from offshore tax havens behind the façade of managing agents who dealt with tenants and their problems, taking 10 to 15 per cent of rental income and service charges. Not surprisingly, resident complaints increased substantially, as many residents felt they were being given a raw deal in terms of both costs and services, while other residents were effectively forced out by a variety of disreputable methods. Many tenants did not know the name or identity of their landlord, who operated via the managing agents from a tax haven. It was thus almost impossible to directly contact the landlord in the event of problems or disputes. Landlords were increasing their cash flow by jacking up service charges, getting inflated building repair costs from their own builders and passing them on to tenants, overcharging for insurance, and various other scams.

The growing number of complaints led to increasing political protests, particularly from the articulate residents in central and inner London, many of them in Conservative-controlled parliamentary seats. Eventually, the government established a Committee of Inquiry into the scale, extent, and nature of the problems. As the only academic in Britain to have done research on the issue, I was fortunate to be asked to become a member of the committee and act as its research director. The committee produced a report (The Nugee Report on the Management Problems of Blocks of Flats) some two years later in 1984 that led to the Landlord and Tenant Act, 1987, which received all-party support in the Houses of Parliament and was passed into law. The principal objective of the legislation was to limit the extent to which landlords could profit by exploiting tenants or long leaseholders by overcharging for services or maintenance costs, failing to provide services, and so on. One of the key provisions of the act was the requirement for all service charge notifications to tenants and leaseholders to include a United Kingdom address at which legal notices could be served by aggrieved residents. Previously, it had been possible for landlords based in an overseas tax haven to simply hide behind the façade of non-contactability. The absence of a UK legal address meant that residents were not obliged to pay a service charge or other demand. Today, approaching forty years on from the Nugee Report, the great majority of private rental mansion apartments have now been sold for homeownership. Those that are still rented are likely to be rented under the recent shorthold legislation, which permits landlords to give tenants a specified period of notice and reclaim the property. Significantly, this form of housing market transformation generally took place without any physical change. The tenure change was sufficient to create or extract surplus value. Ironically, a number of large insurance companies, such as Legal and General, are now moving back into residential rental property investment to provide a long-term stable income stream.

Loft Conversions and Flat Conversions in London

The second issue to be addressed is the more recent one of "loft conversions" in London. Again, this type of speculation is an example of a form of residential arbitrage, whereby property is transformed from one sub-market to another with a significant increase in value in the process. The process of loft conversion is well known from the early work by Zukin (1989) on Soho and similar areas in New York. Essentially, the process involved the conversion for residential use of former industrial buildings in downtown New York that had become vacant. Many of these buildings, often built in the late nineteenth century, have now become extremely desirable and attractive apartments. A very similar process took place in London, but with some interesting twists.

In London, the process was focused on what can be termed the "City fringe." This area comprises a broken ring of nineteenth century Victorian former industrial areas surrounding the City of London, including Clerkenwell, Hoxton, Shoreditch, and Bermondsey. In nineteenth century London, as in New York, these areas were the locations of light manufacturing industry such as textiles, watches, jewellery, and book production. Many of the buildings utilized cast iron frames and brick and glazed exteriors with large open-plan floor areas. With de-industrialization from the 1960s onwards, many of these areas became run down and semi-derelict. A similar process affected many riverside warehouses in Docklands and elsewhere as a result of the decline and subsequent closure of London docklands, although many of these buildings had already been converted in the 1980s. The key issue for both owners and planners became what to do with the buildings for which there appeared no ready market in the 1970s and 1980s. A potential solution appeared with the advent of deregulation in the City of London from 1986 onwards, which dramatically increased the presence of big overseas banks and the demand for office space. Developers saw an opportunity to convert old industrial buildings and warehouses in the City fringe into cheap secondary office space for small users who did not want, or could not afford, the high price of purpose-built offices. A number of buildings were acquired, but the economic recession of the early 1990s meant that the demand for secondary office space in the City fringe rapidly evaporated. The stock of old empty factories and warehouses increased with no potential market until Harry Handelsman, the CEO of the aptly titled Manhattan Loft Corporation, saw a 1930s former industrial print building (1-10 Summers Street) up for auction in Clerkenwell, London EC1. The building had been bought for conversion into offices, but the owner had become bankrupt. Handelsman purchased the 45,000 square foot building (Figure 7.2) for what is now the astonishingly low sum of £450,000 (£10 per square foot). Architects CWZG were brought in, and after gaining planning permission, the building was rapidly converted into "raw" loft space. Each apartment was supplied with water, electricity, and sewage connections, but was left vacant for each buyer to fit out as they desired.

The big question was how to market converted apartments in a former industrial building in a rundown inner city area. The masterstroke was to appoint a public relations company, which organized a number of gritty modelling photo shoots in the building that were then promoted in cutting-edge style magazines. The apartments were quickly sold for an average of £100 per square foot. Today, apartments for sale in this iconic building would command £1000–1,500 per square foot or more. As a result of Handelsman's brilliant eye for a potential opportunity, many other loft conversions in the area followed, and today Clerkenwell is one of the prestige areas for loft conversions in London. The whole area has been revitalized and is now seen as one of the most exciting areas to live in London, with the ability, as in Soho, New York, to walk to work or into the West End of London in thirty minutes. A large number of other redundant or empty former industrial Victorian buildings in inner London were subsequently converted into apartments, including many old factories and print works such as the Ziggurat building (Figure 7.3). The attraction for residents was the proximity to central London and the aesthetics of the high ceilings, large windows, exposed brickwork, beams, and ironwork.

The loft conversion market is now a well-developed aspect of the inner London housing market, but it owes its genesis to a speculative purchase at an auction by a developer who believed it would be possible to replicate in London a phenomenon he was familiar with in Manhattan. It should also be stressed that the change of use from office/commercial to residential was contingent upon a change in government land use planning regulations that permitted this kind of change of use without the need for a major redrawing of land use categories. This land use transformation is a classic example of how a combination of changing planning legislation and changing economics associated with a recession put in place the circumstances that permitted developers to see the profit potential of changing from one land use to another. Today, many of the old factories, warehouses, and offices in inner London have been converted into residential use because they fetch a much higher price than as offices or factories. Indeed, there are examples of important 1960s office blocks being converted to residential use (Hamnett & Whitelegg, 2007).

Figure 7.2. 1-10 Summers Street, a 1930s former industrial print building.
Source: Chris Hamnett.

Figure 7.3. The Ziggurat building. Source: Chris Hamnett.

Figure 7.4. A Victorian school converted into apartments, London. Source: Tim Butler.

The loft conversion process in London is a geographically specific example of a more general process of land use conversion into housing. It can be seen across London in a variety of now redundant former uses – old schools, churches, hospitals, telephone exchanges, military barracks, warehouses, police stations, and so on (Figure 7.4). The ring of now disused former Victorian mental hospitals around the periphery of London have proved very suitable for conversion, particularly given their solidity of construction, their high design values, and the open space suitable for new construction or parkland for residents. In London, almost everything that can be converted is converted. One of the most telling examples is the conversion of the old Jewish Soup Kitchen for the Poor on Brune Street in the City of London into luxury loft apartments selling for over £1 million. This building, as its name indicates, was originally built to provide food for poverty-stricken Jewish immigrants (Figure 7.5).

Both the processes discussed above contain a large element of speculation in that capital was invested with no clear guarantee of return. Arguably, flat break-ups represent a purer form of speculation in that the process

Figure 7.5. The Jewish Soup Kitchen for the Poor converted into luxury loft apartments. Source: Chris Hamnett.

operated to profit at the expense of the existing residents, who ended up either paying substantially higher rents and service charges, and living with poorer quality of services, or being encouraged to buy or move out. However, some sitting tenants would have been able to buy their flat at a discount to the open market value. The loft conversion process could not adversely affect existing residents, as there were none. Instead, the developers' profits were achieved by creating residential units out of former industrial buildings or warehouses for which there was little or no demand. This form of built form transformation is arguably beneficial in that it has created many new housing units out of what was previously unused, or derelict, or low-value space. It is possible to also include a variety of other forms of speculative residential development, for example, flat conversions whereby houses are split into a number of smaller units. The motivation in all these cases is profit maximization. Developers are generally not philanthropists, and some are rapacious. However, without property developers, it is very likely that the physical form of cities would be much more static. As noted earlier, the flat break-up process did not create any new housing units or even make any physical changes. It merely involved a shift of both ownership and housing tenure from rental to ownership in order to unlock potential profits for the landlords, who created nothing apart from a change in the legal form of ownership but were able to extract considerable profits from the process.

A final example of how property can be transformed into a higher value form is via the process of "flat conversion." This process is a fairly simple one whereby a property built for single family residence, usually of between two and four floors depending on the size of the house, is split into a number of separate apartments, often with the addition of a new back extension, which, typically, would include a small kitchen and bathroom for each new apartment. Thus a three-to-four-floor Victorian house with two main rooms on each floor can be converted with the aid of the back extension into three to four separate apartments. In many cases, the initial conversion was also accompanied by a tenure change, with the apartments being sold rather than rented. The process initially got underway in areas of inner London dominated by three-to-four-floor Victorian houses that easily lent themselves to conversion. However, in recent years (and as property prices in London have increased), the process has spread further out into areas of Edwardian two-storey housing, where the property has simply been split into a ground floor and a first floor apartment. Arguably, the process has responded to the growth of smaller, one- and two-person households, as the resultant one-to-two-bed conversions are generally not suitable for families. As in the previous examples, however, the rationale for the conversions has been predominantly financial, as developers can generate a greater return by purchasing a house, splitting it into separate apartments, and reselling them, rather than retaining the house as a single family property. For a time in the 1980s and 1990s, flat conversions represented the largest single net addition to the housing stock in London, considerably more than new builds. The process was initially encouraged by the existence of "home improvement grants" from 1969, which gave owners and landlords a grant for each unit created.

At the other end of the conversion process, we see illegal conversions of backyards or sheds in poor areas of London into low-quality accommodation (I hesitate to use the term "housing") for immigrant workers and migrant groups, who have to endure high levels of overcrowding and shared facilities such as toilets, bathrooms, and kitchens. In this respect, parts of inner East London are seeing a return to the type of housing exploitation of low-income groups seen in the nineteenth century and in the 1950s, when housing conditions were particularly bad. It is difficult to label this process as pure speculation. It is more simply the sweating of an asset to exploit its profit potential to the maximum. Local authorities are engaged in tracking down examples of illegal conversions and multiple occupancy, but they are difficult to pin down. It is, however, a classic response to a rapidly rising population outpacing growth in the number of new housing units. Landlords and developers seek to profit by subdividing and splitting accommodation into more smaller units for tenants on limited incomes. Recently, changes in English planning legislation have allowed developers to convert existing commercial buildings to residential use without minimum size restrictions, with the result that profit-hungry developers and landlords are trying to cram in as many small units as possible, some only 15 square metres (Kenber, 2019). This development is somewhat similar to the process of unit splitting described by Lau (Chapter 8, this volume) in Hong Kong.

Speculative Overseas Buyers

The final example is that of speculative overseas buyers. This phenomenon has grown considerably in scale and importance in recent years, particularly in the more attractive and expensive central and inner west areas of London where there is a significant international investment market. London has long been attractive to wealthy overseas buyers seeking a place to live in London. It has also attracted increasing numbers of overseas investors from Singapore, Hong Kong, Malaysia, and China, attracted by a stable legal system and property market, and relatively high rents. Such buyers are willing to use rents to cover the mortgage and outgoings, in the hope of substantial long-term capital gains as yields are often low (4 to 5 per cent). An apartment that costs £1 million to buy may rent for £1,000 per week or £50,000 per annum, so after management costs, the owners see less than 5 per cent even before financing costs. Supporters of overseas financial investment argue that the buyers who typically buy off-plan and put up a 20 per cent deposit help to finance housing construction in London. That may be, but for the most part, most ordinary Londoners cannot afford to purchase or rent such properties, so the extent to which they actually help to increase the housing supply is questionable. Even if they do help builders finance construction, it is debatable whether the housing helps local needs (Ley, 2017; Wilson & Barton, 2017)

Of more concern in recent years, however, is the growth of what is often called "buy to leave." This phenomenon involves overseas buyers purchasing property primarily to act as a store of value or "safe haven." The objective is not to derive rental income and not necessarily to see substantial capital growth, but simply to have a place to park money overseas. Many of these buyers are from Russia or China or other countries where there is uncertainty about political stability and a desire to get some money out of the country and diversify their asset base and security. In this respect, the property is being used as a proxy bank vault, and the owner may rarely visit and chooses to keep it empty. This practice is leading to concern that, as well as helping to push up prices in London, it is also resulting in the depopulation of some parts of central London: the "lights out" areas, where the density of non-resident overseas owners is precipitating the closure of local restaurants and other facilities. Whether this process can be termed speculation is tricky. It certainly involves the use of housing as a quasi-financial asset, turning parts of London into the housing equivalent of bank vaults filled with inert gold blocks that clog up the housing market but perform no useful housing purpose (Fernandez et al., 2016).

This bank deposit type of housing, which is rarely or sporadically occupied, is clearly not contributing in any way to the housing needs of the city. On the contrary, it is removing part of the housing stock from use. It represents the transformation of housing into a pure financial asset that operates in a similar way to art in a bank vault: it is a pure store of value detached from any use value. An interesting analysis of high-value property purchases in London indicates that a high proportion of them (36 per cent in central London) were registered to overseas buyers in 2014–16 (Wallace et al., 2017). Also, it can be argued that the existence of high levels of overseas demand are helping to push up property prices in London and other cities (Foroohar, 2017; Scanlon et al., 2017; Hamnett & Reades, 2019).

Conclusion

The examples outlined above highlight a number of main ways in which profit-driven speculation has transformed London's housing stock over the last forty years. They do not represent the totality of the various forms of transformation. I have not, for example, considered dockland warehouse conversion in detail. Nor have I looked at the ways in which large parts of London's former council housing stock have been converted into homeownership or private rental since Margaret Thatcher initiated the "right to buy" for tenants in the 1980s. While Thatcher saw it as a way to widen homeownership and increase the Tory vote, I doubt she anticipated that many units would subsequently be converted into private rentals. What is clear is that, in a profit-driven free market, new forms of speculation are always emerging as the structure of the housing market, supply and demand, legislation, policy, and finance all change. The search for profits from housing is never ending. If money can be made from housing in an unregulated market economy, it will be.

The consequences of a purely market- and price-based housing system are very predictable. There is essentially a hierarchy of housing in terms of size, location, condition, desirability, and price, which is then mapped onto income and affordability to produce the conventional system of the rich living in the nicest housing in the best areas and the poorest living in the worst housing in the poorest areas. But the essence of speculation is that the form and dimensions of the housing system often change over time as new opportunities become available. Thus, in many older northeastern and midwestern American cities in the postwar era, a combination of immigration, car ownership, suburbanization, and urban renewal led to the deterioration or abandonment of many inner city neighbourhoods as the rich and middle classes moved out. The consequences can be seen in Washington, DC; Cleveland; Pittsburgh; Detroit; Buffalo; and other cities. A handful of American cities, such as New York, San Francisco, and Boston, have seen widespread gentrification as capital and the middle classes returned to the inner city, but this movement has been the exception rather than the rule. Gentrification has been more widespread in London and other cities (Hamnett, 2003, 2021), but while some of it is related to landlord or developer speculation (particularly where flat break-ups and loft conversions are concerned), much of the original gentrification was essentially small scale and buyer led. Today, this situation has changed, as most of the older period property has already been gentrified, and developers and speculators have turned their attention to different types of opportunity. One of the most recent has been the redevelopment of former council estates, such as the Aylesbury Estate in Southwark, where the local authority has decanted all the tenants and sold the site to a developer, who then clears and rebuilds with 80 to 90 per cent market housing and a minute amount of so-called affordable housing (Lees, 2014). This process highlights how speculation has pushed its way into what remains of the social rented housing sector with the agreement of local councils under the guise of increasing the number of housing units.

REFERENCES

Aalbers, M. (2017). The variegated financialisation of housing. *International Journal of Urban and Regional Research*, 41(4), 542–54. https://doi.org/10.1111/1468-2427.12522

Agnello, L., & Schuknecht, L. (2009). *Booms and busts in the housing market: Determinants and implications* [Working paper series no. 1071]. European Central Bank. https://www.ecb.europa.eu/pub/pdf/scpwps/ecbwp1071.pdf

Badcock, B. (1984). *Unfairly structured cities*. Basil Blackwell.

Chancellor, E. (1999). *Devil take the hindmost: A history of financial speculation*. Plume.

Christophers, B. (2011). Revisiting the urbanization of capital. *Annals of the Association of American Geographers*, 101(6), 1347–64. https://doi.org/10.1080/00045608.2011.583569

Dennis, R. (2008). "Babylonian flats" in Victorian and Edwardian London. *The London Journal*, 33(3), 233–47. https://doi.org/10.1179/174963208X347709

Dyos, H.J. (1968). The speculative builders and developers of Victorian London. *Victorian Studies*, 11, 641–90. https://www.jstor.org/stable/3825462

Fainstein, S. (1994). *The city builders: Property, politics and planning in London and New York*. Blackwell

Fernandez, R., Hofman, A., & Aalbers, M. (2016). London and New York as a safe deposit box for the transnational elite. *Environment and Planning A: Economy and Space*, 48(12), 2443–61. https://doi.org/10.1177/0308518X16659479

Foroohar, R. (2017, 16 April). Chinese buyers fuel Brooklyn real estate boom. *Financial Times*. https://www.ft.com/content/93d89320-2063-11e7-b7d3-163f5a7f229c

Haila, A. (2000). Real estate in global cities: Singapore and Hong Kong as property states. *Urban Studies*, 37(12), 2241–56. https://doi.org/10.1080/00420980020002797

Hall, P. (1998). *Cities in civilization*. Weidenfeld & Nicolson.

Hamnett, C. (1999). *Winners and losers: Home ownership in modern Britain*. UCL Press.

Hamnett, C. (2003). Gentrification and the middle-class remaking of inner London, 1961–2001. *Urban Studies*, 40(12), 2401–26. https://doi.org/10.1080/0042098032000136138

Hamnett, C. (2021). *Gentrification: An Advanced Introduction*. Edward Elgar.

Hamnett, C., & Randolph, W. (1984). Landlord disinvestment in housing market transformation: Analysis of the flat break-up market in central London. *Transactions of the Institute of British Geographers*, 9(3), 259–79. https://doi.org/10.2307/622233

Hamnett, C., & Randolph, W. (1986). Landlord disinvestment and housing market transformation: The flat break-up market in London. In P. Williams & N. Smith (Eds.), *Gentrification of the city*. George Allen and Unwin.

Hamnett, C., & Randolph, W. (1988). *Cities, housing and profits: Flat break-up and the decline of private renting*. Heinemann.

Hamnett, C., & Reades, J. (2019). Mind the gap: Implications of overseas investment for regional house price divergence in Britain. *Housing Studies*, 34(3), 308–406. https://doi.org/10.1080/02673037.2018.1444151

Hamnett, C., & Whitelegg, A. (2007). Loft conversion and gentrification in London: From industrial to postindustrial land use. *Environment and Planning A: Economy and Space*, 39(1), 106–24. https://doi.org/10.1068/a38474

Harvey, D. (1973). *Social justice and the city*. Edward Arnold.
Harvey, D. (1995). *The urbanization of capital*. Blackwell.
Harvey, D. (2003). *Paris: Capital of modernity*. Routledge.
Kenber, B. (2019, 5 July). Landlords make millions from flats the size of parking spaces. *The Times*. https://www.thetimes.co.uk/article/landlords-make-millions-from-flats-the-size-of-a-parking-space-nm5tw72ss
Lees, L. (2014). The urban injustices of New Labour's "new urban renewal": The case of the Aylesbury estate in London. *Antipode, 46*(4), 921–47. https://doi.org/10.1111/anti.12020
Ley, D. (2017). Global China and the making of Vancouver's residential property market. *International Journal of Housing Policy, 17*(1), 15–34. https://doi.org/10.1080/14616718.2015.1119776
Logan, J., & Molotch, H. (1987). *Urban fortunes: The political economy of place*. University of California Press.
Muellbauer, J., & Murphy, A. (1997). Booms and busts in the UK housing market. *The Economic Journal, 107*(445), 1701–27. https://doi.org/10.1111/j.1468-0297.1997.tb00076.x
Norris, M., & Byrne, M, (2015). *Asset price Keynesianism, regional imbalances and the Irish and Spanish housing booms and busts* [Working papers 201514]. Geary Institute, University College Dublin.
Olson, D.J. (1980). *The growth of Victorian London*. Peregrine.
Scanlon, K., Whitehead, C., & Blanc, F. (with Moreno-Tabarez, U.). (2017). *The role of overseas investors in the London new build residential market: Final report for Homes for London*. London School of Economics. https://www.lse.ac.uk/business-and-consultancy/consulting/consulting-reports/the-role-of-overseas-investors-in-the-London-new-build-residential-market
Smith, N. (1979). Toward a theory of gentrification: A back to the city movement by capital, not people. *Journal of the American Planning Association, 45*(4), 538–48. https://doi.org/10.1080/01944367908977002
Steadman-Jones, G. (1971). *Outcast London*. Penguin Books.
Summerson, J. (1962). *Georgian London*. Penguin.
Tett, G. (2009). *Fool's gold: How unrestrained greed corrupted a dream, shattered global markets and unleashed a catastrophe*. Little Brown.
Wallace, A., Rhodes, D., & Webber, R. (2017). *Overseas investors in London's new build housing market*. Centre for Housing Policy, University of York. https://eprints.whiterose.ac.uk/117771/8/GLA_version_University_of_York_data_report_amend_060617aw_no_track_changes.pdf
Wilson, W., & Barton, C. (2017, 17 July). *Foreign investment in UK residential property* [House of Commons Briefing Paper, 07723]. https://researchbriefings.files.parliament.uk/documents/CBP-7723/CBP-7723.pdf
Zukin, S. (1989). *Loft living: Culture and capital in urban change*. Johns Hopkins University Press.

8 Speculative Subdivision of Private Rental Flats in Hong Kong

MANDY LAU

Introduction

Housing development in Hong Kong is full of paradoxes. As a market-friendly city characterized by a neoliberal policy environment, Hong Kong has witnessed high levels of house price appreciation over the years. As many scholars have argued, Hong Kong is dominated by a "tenacious culture of property" (Ley & Teo, 2013) and a "property-based" mode of regulation (Smart & Lee, 2003). Government ownership of land means that the Hong Kong government can generate much revenue through land leasing, premiums, and development charges, which has aroused suspicions of a "developer bias" in policy formulation to maximize land revenues (Forrest & Yip, 2014; Haila, 2017).

Yet, Hong Kong is also characterized by a large public housing program – around one-third of the population currently reside in public rental housing, while around 15 per cent of the population reside in subsidized sale flats, meaning that almost half of the population are living in the public housing sector (Transport and Housing Bureau, 2019). Forrest and Yip (2014) have explained this paradox through the social wage thesis – the low-rent regime of public housing supports low-income service sector workers, who would otherwise generate substantial pressure on social security. At the same time, commitment to public housing construction helps boost the political legitimacy of the government, as argued by some local scholars (Forrest & Yip, 2014, p. 564).

Despite the existence of a large public housing sector, there have been major troubles in the private rental sector, especially the emergence of large numbers of poor-quality subdivided units since the late 2000s. Subdivision of private flats is not new to Hong Kong. In the post-war years, it involved subdividing rooms with fabric board partitions (known as "partitioned rooms"). These rooms were not self-contained, which meant sharing toilets and kitchens among many private renters (Yip & La Grange, 2006, p. 1005). In recent years, however, self-contained subdivided units have become widespread. These new forms of subdivision often violate building codes, involving provision of extra toilets and cooking areas, overloaded electrical sockets, and lack of proper drainage, all of which pose safety and hygiene problems (Society for Community Organization, 2013).

Whether or not this subdivision phenomenon can be labelled as speculation is open to debate. On one hand, these practices are aimed at securing quick profits, some of which involve unethical profit-making through violation of building codes. Through subdivision of existing flats into multiple subunits, landlords are able to capture higher returns – rents per square metre of subdivided units are often higher than rents for whole flats. In the absence of rent control or security of tenure, tenants often face rent increases within a short period of time and are threatened by the possibility of eviction (Lau, 2019). Landlords operating illegally subdivided flats are at risk of prosecution, although in reality these practices are tolerated by the government, since it would be difficult for the government to accommodate tenants displaced by a crackdown.

On the other hand, these practices are viewed by some people as natural market responses to growing demand from low-income households, providing much-needed shelter for service sector workers, especially migrant households from the mainland of China. Unlike flat break-ups in London in the 1970s (Hamnett & Randolph, 1984), which involved tenure change without creation of new housing units, the subdivision phenomenon in Hong Kong has indeed increased the quantity of rental flats, though at the expense of housing quality. Some even venture to say that landlords of subdivided flats are "doing a favour" to low-income households, who would otherwise end up as street sleepers.

Instead of sweating over the labels for these practices, this chapter explores the following paradoxes: Why do so many people need to rent subdivided flats, despite the existence of a large public housing system? Why do people claim that there is not enough land for affordable housing development when there is evidence of continued allocation of land for construction of large, luxury apartments, which are favoured by speculators? This chapter seeks to make sense of these paradoxes by drawing connections between speculative practices in the wider housing market and profit-maximization practices in the low-end rental market.

Dual Role of the Government in Land Supply

Understanding housing supply in Hong Kong involves understanding land ownership and allocation practices. In Hong Kong, all land is owned by the government, except a small plot of land in the Central district. Indeed, the large public housing program in Hong Kong has been possible mainly due to the government's dominant control over land ownership and development rights (Chiu, 2007, p. 73). Land for private housing is sold to developers through the leasehold system – most leases are renewable, subject to payment of a reassessed annual rent. Land is mainly disposed of by public auction, supplemented by tendering or private treaty.

In the past, the government sold land on a regular basis. However, as the Asian financial crisis in 1998 pushed down property prices, the government introduced a special land application list system in 1999, under which the auction or tender of listed land slots would only be triggered when the price proposed by developers met the requirement of the government. Furthermore, in order to shield private property owners from further drops in house prices, the government suspended the sale of the Home Ownership Scheme (HOS) flats throughout the 2000s, which effectively stopped supply of affordable, subsidized sale flats for lower-middle-income groups.

As property prices continued to drop, the government stopped regular land sales in 2002, making the land application list system the only way of land disposal until the government started to sell land again on an irregular basis in 2010. Following the rapid rise of property prices in recent years, the government decided to scrap the land application list system in 2013. This change means that, throughout the 2000s, land supply for private housing has been mainly initiated by developers rather than the government.

Private flat supply, especially that of small- and medium-sized flats, dropped to very low levels throughout this whole decade. However, a substantial number of large-sized luxury flats were built during this period. This situation could possibly be explained by the inflow of large amounts of capital from Chinese investors from the mainland into Hong Kong's real estate market. This trend was facilitated by government immigration policies, especially the introduction of the Capital Investment Entrant Scheme in 2003, which enabled applicants who made a capital investment in Hong Kong of at least HK$10 billion to gain residency. As Hui and colleagues (2011) argued, these policies have driven up demand for luxury housing and contributed to the rapid growth in residential property prices.

Although recent trends in luxury property development in Hong Kong are well known, there has not been any explicit attempt to draw a link between these practices and the crisis that has emerged in the private rental sector. Instead, private rental problems are often blamed on a short supply of public housing. The government has been keen to posit public housing construction as the inevitable solution to the housing challenges of low-income households, while remaining silent on the question of distribution of land resources, especially in urban locations preferred by low-income households. This stance was certainly the one taken by the Long Term Housing Strategy Steering Committee:

> Since rental is one of the key concerns of the IHHs [inadequately housed households], particularly for those living in SDUs [subdivided units], the Steering Committee recommends that PRH [public rental housing] should be the primary housing solution for eligible households. (HKSAR Government, 2013, para. 5.22)

There is room to question the validity of the above assumptions, which tend to portray the government as a benevolent state that is working hard to provide more affordable housing for its citizens. Critical perspectives in the housing literature have problematized taken-for-granted assumptions of a benevolent state, arguing that the state might in fact be actively fostering and maintaining the conditions that generate inequalities and facilitate profit-reaping by privileged groups (Jacobs, 2015a, 2015b). In other words, this body of literature calls for more critical analyses of government policymaking to expose less benign motivations of governments and the many ways in which they may be implicated in the production of ongoing social inequalities and marginalization processes. Loïc Wacquant, for example, has highlighted the state's dual role as simultaneous producer and alleviator of social inequalities:

> The state practices laissez-faire at the top, at the level of circulation of capital and production of inequality, but it turns interventionist and intrusive when it comes to managing the consequences of inequality at the bottom, for the life spaces and life chances of the precarious fractions of the post-industrial working class. (Wacquant, 2013, p. 9)

In other words, Wacquant argues that the state's so-called commitment to alleviating social inequalities involves tinkering "downstream," disguising the fact that it is responsible for producing inequalities "upstream" (p. 8). Similar views have been raised by other scholars, who have questioned the apparent "busy work" of governments that look as if they are actively solving housing affordability problems, even though such policy activities have had little impact on long-standing problems (Gurran & Phibbs, 2015, p. 718). This body of work suggests that governments may actually be more interested in maintaining the coalitions necessary for them to stay in power (Levine & Forrence, 1990, p. 170). Nevertheless, since governments are often lobbied by interest groups representing underprivileged citizens, their political legitimacy tends to be sustained through a range of "busy work," which can give the appearance of earnest intervention without material interruption of the status quo (Gurran & Phibbs, 2015, p. 718).

The rest of this chapter examines the relevance of the above theoretical insights for the subdivided housing problem in Hong Kong. How has the supply of flats of different sizes changed over the years? This analysis is based on a mix of data sources, including secondary data, demographic data, data on subdivided units from the Census and Statistics Department (CSD, 2011, 2015, 2016), and data on the private domestic stock from the Rating and Valuation Department (RVD, 2017). In addition, policy and consultation documents are also analysed to identify key themes and discourses, especially in relation to the government's *Long Term Housing Strategy* (HKSAR Government, 2013, 2014).

Subdivided Housing in the Low-End Rental Market

The private rental sector in Hong Kong has declined over the years, from around 24 per cent of total stock in the 1980s to around 15 per cent since the 1990s (La Grange & Pretorius, 2002, p. 723). This decline has been linked to an expansion of homeownership, as well as an increase in public renting. As mentioned, a significant proportion of low-income households reside in the public rental sector. Low-income households with no access to public housing, however, have no choice but to compete for a limited supply of private rental stock.

Demand for small rental flats has grown due to large numbers of immigrants from the mainland of China – according to official statistics, new arrivals from the mainland constitute the most important growth driver of local population. The cumulative figure of new arrivals from the mainland of China (known as "One-way Permit Holders") was 221,000 persons from 2006 to 2010 and 220,000 persons from 2011 to 2015, with around 40 per cent of the new arrivals renting their accommodation in the private sector (Research Office, 2017, 2018). Supply of private rental flats has not caught up with this growing demand, however, while private rents rose substantially from the mid-2000s to the early 2010s.

Rental affordability problems have been reflected in the growing length of the public housing waiting list, which doubled from around 100,000 applicants in 2001 to around 200,000 applicants in 2011. Unlike other places characterized by state retreat from social housing provision (Pawson, 2006), the Hong Kong government has maintained its commitment to public housing supply over the years. This policy is different from other places like Australia (Hulse & Burke, 2015; Hulse & Yates, 2017), where the private rental sector has assumed the primary role of accommodating low-income households due to the meagre provision of public housing.

Yet, despite the size of the public housing sector in Hong Kong, inadequate rental housing has proliferated in the city. In 2014, for the very first time, the Census and Statistics Department conducted a dedicated survey on housing conditions of subdivided units as part of its regular series of Thematic Household Surveys. The same survey was repeated in 2015. In these survey reports, subdivided units (SDUs) were officially defined as those units that are "formed by the sub-division of individual quarters into two or more units for rental purposes to more than one household" (CSD, 2016, p. 3). As mentioned in the introduction, some SDUs have observable physical partitions, with independent toilets and cooking areas for each subunit, while others are bedspace apartments, where tenants have to share toilets and cooking areas with other tenants within the quarters.

According to the survey findings, the number of households living in subdivided units in 2014 and 2015 were 85,500 and 87,600, respectively (CSD, 2015, 2016, Table 4.2). In terms of the size of these flats, according to the data collected in 2014, the majority (58.8 per cent) of households living in SDUs resided in units of 7 to 13 square metres. In terms of average area per capita, the figure for one-person households was 8.6 square metres per capita, and for two-person households, it was 5.4 square metres per capita (CSD, 2015, Table 4.5). The figures for 2015 were very similar. These SDUs tend to be concentrated in old buildings in urban locations (see Figure 8.1), with more than 75 per cent of these dwellings located in the urban area, Kowloon and Hong Kong Island (CSD, 2015, 2016, Table 4.1), reflecting the demand for accessible flats from low-income households, many of whom work long hours in the service industry and cannot afford to travel long distances.

Furthermore, the survey illustrated that the main reason for renting SDUs is that these are more affordable than whole flats. This finding can be interpreted by examining the rents for whole flats in recent years. In Hong Kong, the Rating and Valuation Department classifies all properties into one of five classes: Class A (saleable area less than

Figure 8.1. A typical old building in the inner urban area of Hong Kong.
Source: Photo by Author.

40 square metres); Class B (saleable area of 40 to 69.9 square metres); Class C (saleable area of 70 to 99.9 square metres); Class D (saleable area of 100 to 159.9 square metres); and Class E (saleable area of 160 square metres or above). One would expect Class A flats to be affordable to lower-income households, but even these small flats have become increasingly unaffordable in recent years. The rental index of Class A flats had increased from 90.1 in 2006 to 137.1 in 2011 (52 per cent increase), and by 2016 it reached 184.8 (105 per cent increase over ten years). This increase is higher than the overall increase for flats of all classes, suggesting high demand for small flats in the context of affordability problems.

Indeed, for a household belonging to the lowest two income decile groups in 2011, household income would be below HK$8,300 (CSD, 2011, Table 2.15b).[1] Taking the average rent of urban Class A flats, which was HK$240 per square metre in 2011, such households would have to

---

[1] The analysis in this chapter utilizes Census data that excludes foreign domestic workers (FDWs), since FDWs in Hong Kong typically live in their employers' homes.

206   Mandy Lau

downsize to units of around 14 square metres in order to maintain a rent-to-income ratio of 40 per cent. If they wanted to maintain a rent-to-income ratio of 30 per cent, they would have to further downsize to around 10 square metres. This calculation echoes the government's survey data on the typical sizes of subdivided units, which indeed has been found to be 7 to 13 square metres. Thus, the data in this section provide a brief picture of the market conditions that have underpinned subdivision of rental flats in recent years. It is not clear, however, why there has been an imbalance between supply and demand for small flats, given that there has been continued production of public rental housing in Hong Kong, unlike other places that have been characterized by a state retreat from social housing provision.

A possible explanation for the proliferation of subdivided units in Hong Kong is the undersupply of *low-rent* flats in the private market. However, it is not easy to gauge changes in supply of low-rent flats in the private market. Although official data is available from the Rating and Valuation Department regarding changes in the private domestic stock, these figures do not differentiate between flats of different rent levels. The only differentiation is between private domestic stock of different classes, meaning stock of different sizes (Class A, B, C, D, and E, by square metre size, as explained above).

For the purpose of this discussion, it is most appropriate to focus on changes in the Class A stock, since these are comparatively small-sized flats and thus are most likely to accommodate low-income households. It would be reasonable to assume that low-income households are more likely to occupy the *older* stock of Class A flats, which are of lower quality and have lower rents. Again, such analysis is constrained by lack of data, since the data from the Rating and Valuation Department do not differentiate between flats of different ages either. Nevertheless, it is possible to construct an approximate picture by combining multiple sources of data, including examining changes in supply of *new* Class A flats (which are likely to be occupied by lower-middle- to middle-income households, who are not able to afford larger flats), changes in demolition of Class A flats (that is, loss of *older* Class A stock), and comparing these changes to the trends for rental flats of larger sizes.

Changing Supply of Small-Sized Class A Flats

Figure 8.2 illustrates the number of new completions of Class A private domestic flats from 2003 to 2016. The year 2003 is chosen as the starting point, since data before 2003 include village houses, which are low-rise

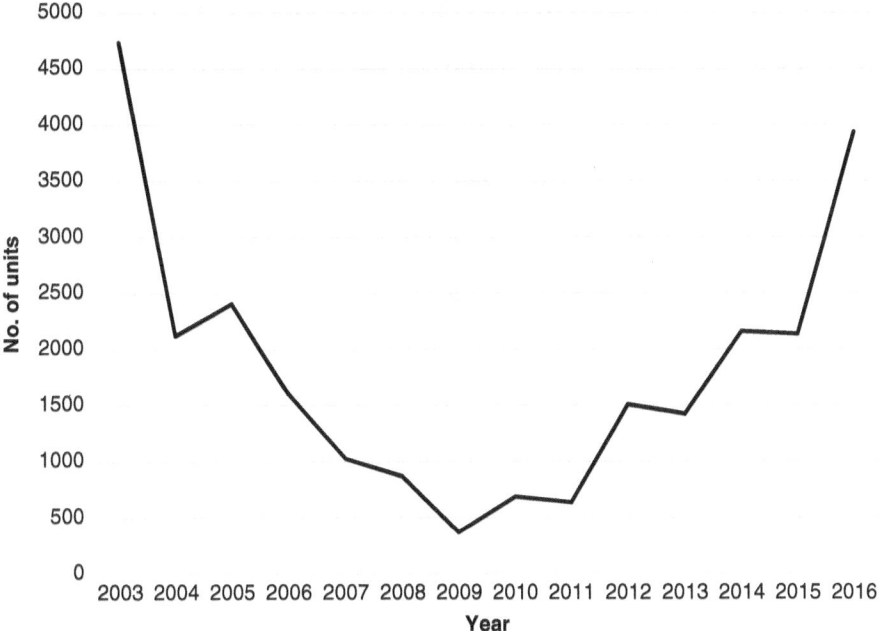

Figure 8.2. New completions of Class A private domestic flats in Hong Kong, 2003–2016. Source: Adapted from Rating and Valuation Department (RVD, 2017).

dwellings located in the suburban areas of Hong Kong. Comparison of data after 2003 helps ensure greater consistency.

Based on the figures from 2003 onwards, it is clear that new completions have fallen substantially over the years, with a sharp drop from over 4,000 completions in 2003 down to around 2,000 completions in 2004. Since then, new completions have continued to fall, with the lowest figures recorded from 2008 to 2011, whereby annual completions were less than 1,000. The figures climbed back to around 1,500 in 2012 and reached almost 4,000 by 2016.

To some extent, the slow growth of small-sized Class A flats reflects the slow growth of all private domestic completions, which fell from over 25,000 completions in 2003 to below 10,000 in 2008 and remained more or less below 10,000 until around 2014. Yet, the share of Class A flats among all new completions has also declined. In 2003, Class A completions accounted for around 18 per cent of all completions (4,738 out of 26,397); while by 2008, the share of Class A completions had fallen to just 10 per cent (871 out of 8,776) and remained below 10 per cent until 2012.

Indeed, the share of large-sized flats in the same period (2008 to 2012) was comparatively high. Class D and Class E flats (any flat with a saleable area of 100 square metres or above) can be considered as large-sized flats in the context of Hong Kong. Prior to 2008, the share of Class D and E flats remained below 10 per cent. However, Class D and E flats accounted for as much as one-third of all completions in 2009 (2,417 out of 7,157) and remained above 10 per cent until 2013. This finding suggests that developers focused on producing large-sized flats in the late 2000s to early 2010s, while supply of more affordable, small-sized flats fell to extremely low levels. Limited supply of new small-sized flats over the last decade may have driven lower-middle-income households into the older stock of Class A flats, thus competing with low-income households for the existing older stock – a possibility that will be examined in later sections.

The main limitation of the above data is that the figures only reflect changes in new flat supply but do not differentiate between flats that are owner-occupied and those for lease. If the majority of new completions are owner-occupied, then the supply of new rental flats would be even lower. In order to understand more specifically the changing supply of new *rental* flats, it is necessary to examine data on the mode of occupation after completion.

Figure 8.3 illustrates the number of units that were leased among all newly completed Class A flats from 2003 to 2016. The figures are based on data from the Rating and Valuation Department (RVD). The data need to be interpreted with caution, since the number of units includes only units that were valued by the RVD and reported as wholly occupied. Also, newly completed units may not be immediately valued by the RVD; hence the numbers in each year may include completions from the past few years. Nevertheless, these figures offer a good approximation of the ratio of owner-occupied versus rental flats in each particular period of time.

Based on Figure 8.3, it is clear that the proportion of lettings was relatively low prior to 2008. Since 2009, the proportion of lettings has remained above 30 per cent, and in many years has exceeded 50 per cent of all completions in that year. This finding suggests an increasing demand for small-sized private rental flats, possibly from middle-income households who have increasingly been unable to afford homeownership.

Furthermore, it seems that there is also a *spatial* dimension to this growing trend of private renting. The data from the RVD are further

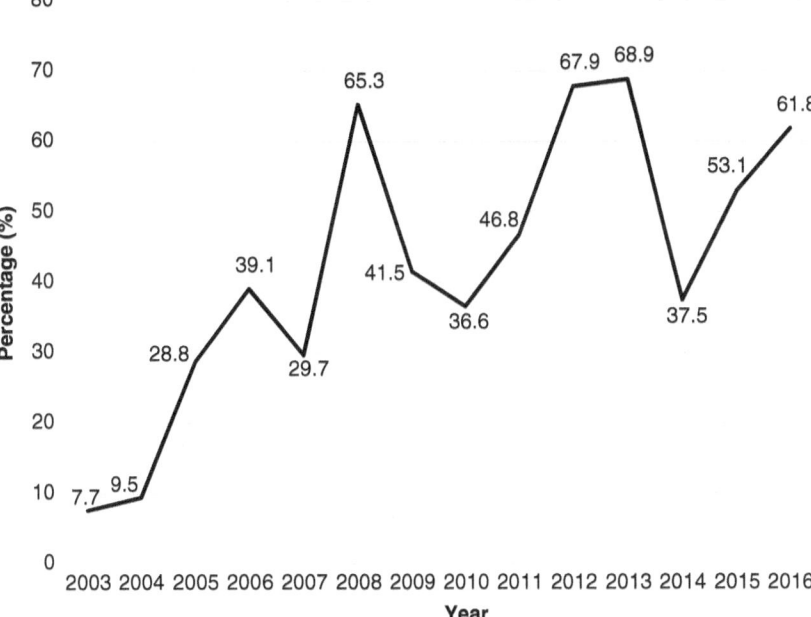

Figure 8.3. Units that were leased among all newly completed Class A flats in Hong Kong, 2003–2016. Source: Adapted from Rating and Valuation Department (RVD, various years).

differentiated between lettings in the main urban area (Kowloon and Hong Kong Island) and the suburban area (New Territories). Figure 8.4 illustrates the proportion of all lettings in each year that are located in the urban area.

The data in Figure 8.4 suggest that not only has there been an increase in the proportion of flats leased after completion, but there has also been an increase in the proportion of lettings located in the urban area. The proportion of urban lettings was around 10 to 20 per cent prior to 2008, but since 2008, it has risen to above 30 per cent, and in many years, above 60 per cent of all leased flats that year. This finding suggests that location matters for renters of small flats – not only are these households seeking more affordable, small-sized flats, but they are also targeting rental flats that are located in the urban area, with close proximity to jobs and amenities. Nevertheless, as mentioned earlier, these are new rental flats that are more likely to be occupied by lower-middle- to middle-income households. In order to assess changing

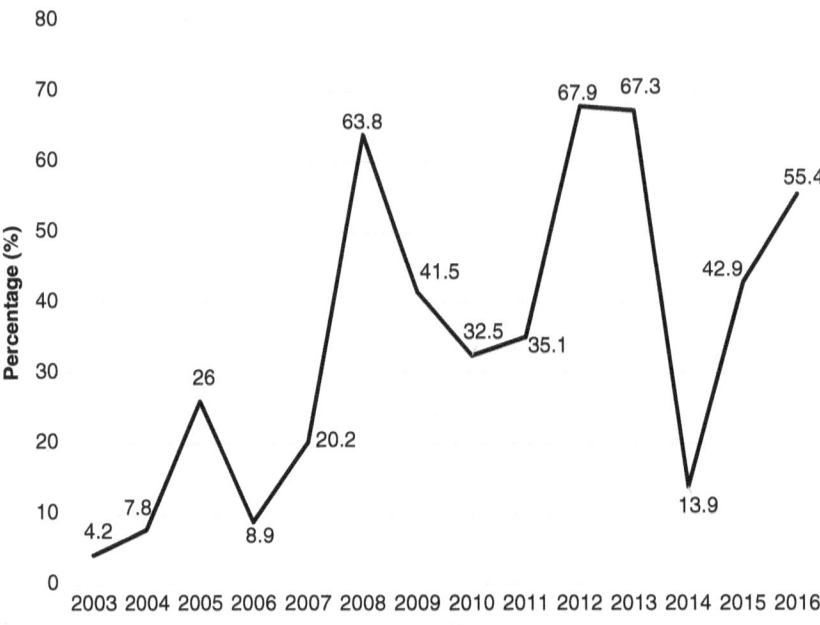

Figure 8.4. Percentage of all lettings in each year located in the urban area, Hong Kong. Source: Adapted from Rating and Valuation Department (RVD, various years).

supply of small flats for low-income households, it is also necessary to examine changes in the older Class A stock.

Demolition of Older Class A Stock

Limited supply of new small-sized flats, especially in the years from 2009 to 2013, together with high demand for urban flats, suggests that competition for urban Class A flats has been significant, which helps explain substantial rent increases among Class A flats. Theoretically, households can rely on the existing stock of Class A flats if they are not able to rent a new flat. Yet, given the aging housing stock in Hong Kong, there has also been a loss of Class A stock over the years due to demolitions in the urban redevelopment process, which is illustrated in Figure 8.5.

Again, the *spatial distribution* of Class A demolitions also matters. Data from the Rating and Valuation Department indicate that the

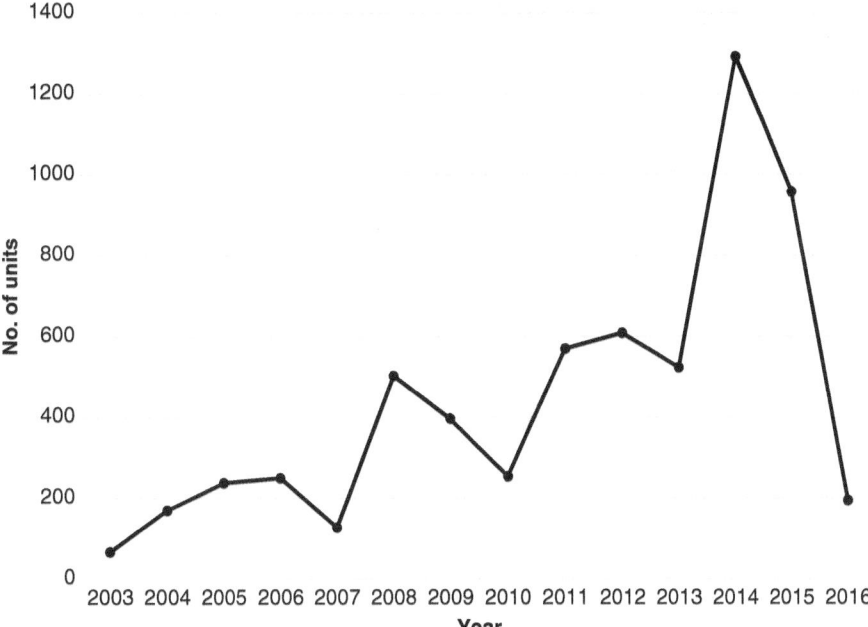

Figure 8.5. Loss of Class A stock over the years due to demolitions in the urban redevelopment process, Hong Kong. Source: Adapted from Rating and Valuation Department (RVD, 2017).

majority of demolitions across all years are located in the urban area. This trend is not surprising, since the majority of the older stock was built in the inner urban area. The implication is that the supply of small-sized flats in urban locations, which are preferred by low-income households, has been further diminished by demolition processes in recent years.

If we combine the trends in new completions and demolitions, then it becomes clearer why there has been an overall undersupply of small Class A flats. Based on the data from the RVD, in the thirteen years from 2003 to 2016, the total stock of Class A flats has grown by just 16,086 units (a 4 per cent increase), less than the combined growth of Class D and E flats (large flats with saleable area of 100 square metres or above), which increased by 13,534 units and 4,642 units, respectively. Indeed, the undersupply situation has been most serious in the years from 2008 to 2013. The most critical year was 2009, when the number of Class A demolitions (391 units) was even more than new Class A completions in that year (373 units). Together with the loss of Class A stock through conversions to non-residential use, the total loss resulted in a net drop in Class A stock from 2008 to 2009.

Furthermore, the number of households in the lowest two income deciles grew substantially, from 445,081 households in 2006 to 473,431 in 2011 – an increase of 28,350 households in five years (CSD, 2011, Table 2.15b). By contrast, data from the RVD indicate that the stock of Class A flats only grew from 350,455 units in 2006 to 352,056 units in 2011 – just 1,601 units in five years. Thus, considering increasing demand from the lowest two income deciles, there is evidence that the growth in the number of low-income households has exceeded the growth in Class A stock in the same period, which helps explain the proliferation of subdivided units.

What is worth noting, though, is that the government has continued to build public rental housing for low-income households over the years. For example, in the five years from 2006–07 to 2010–11, the government built around 69,000 public rental units. Although this figure is low compared to production levels in past years, it is still larger than the growth in the number of households in the lowest two income deciles. In other words, the surge in subdivided flats does not seem to be attributable to insufficient supply of public housing alone. Considering that the scale of the subdivided unit problem is larger than the shortfall in supply of small rental flats, a further question could be explored: Is it possible that proliferation of subdivided units has been driven by competition for small, urban flats from middle-income households who are not able to afford larger flats?

Competition for Small, Urban Flats from Middle-Income Households

Theoretically, one might expect middle-income households to rent Class B flats (saleable area of 40 to 69.9 square metres) or larger, which would be affordable to them due to their higher incomes. Indeed, the stock of Class B flats has experienced the strongest growth among all classes, with an increase of 87,900 units from 2003 to 2016 (a 58 per cent share of overall growth in stock in this period). Yet, average rents of Class B flats have grown considerably over the years, especially in urban locations. Urban locations include Kowloon and Hong Kong Island; since rents in Kowloon are comparatively cheaper, they can be used as a reference point to gauge the changing affordability of Class B flats. In 2003, average monthly rents of urban Class B flats (using Kowloon as a reference point) was around HK$120 (US$15) per square metre; in 2006, the rent had increased to HK$155 (US$20) per square metre; and by 2011, it had doubled to HK$240 (US$30) per square metre. In other words, even for the smallest property size within Class B (that is, 40 square metres), the average monthly rent would be around HK$6,200 (US$800) in 2006 and around HK$9,600 (US$1,200) in 2011.

Median household income, however, has not caught up with growth in rents. According to the Census data in 2006, median household income was HK$17,100, while in 2011, median household income was HK$20,200. In other words, if a middle-income household wanted to rent a small Class B flat of 40 square metres, the rent-to-income ratio would be 36 per cent in 2006 and as high as 48 per cent in 2011. Therefore, it is not unreasonable to assume that, during the period between the late 2000s and early 2010s, some middle-income households have traded off by living in smaller Class A flats, where rents per square metre are similar to those of Class B flats but overall rents are lower due to smaller flat size. The implication is that the growing unaffordability of Class B units has very likely increased the competition for small Class A flats, resulting in increasing competition between lower-income and middle-income households.

Of course, if low-cost homeownership were available to these middle-income households, they might choose the option of buying a subsidized owner-occupier unit rather than renting on the private market. However, government production of subsidized owner-occupier flats, known locally as Home Ownership Scheme (HOS) flats, declined to historically low levels in the mid- to late-2000s. In the five years from 2006–07 to 2010–11, there were only 5,690 completions of HOS flats. It is not surprising that low supply of subsidized owner-occupier flats has been insufficient to cater to the demand for affordable homeownership from middle-income households, who have therefore turned to private renting to meet their housing needs.

Further analyses of the data reveal a high proportion of unoccupied Class D and E flats after completion. Taking the five-year period from 2007 to 2011 as an illustration, the number of Class D and E completions was 6,904 flats. Yet, the number of Class D and E flats reported as wholly occupied was only 2,052 (that is, only around 30 per cent). This figure suggests that many of the Class D and E flats were not even for residential purposes, but most likely were held vacant for investment purposes, possibly for speculative gains by investors with large amounts of capital. Again, this finding indicates the possibility of a domino effect, whereby production of large-sized flats for investment purposes, without sufficient production of medium-sized flats for residential purposes, has displaced some middle-income households to smaller-sized flats, thus increasing the competition between middle-income and low-income households in the context of a limited supply of small flats.

Lack of Affordable Options for Middle-Income Groups

The analyses above revealed that the subdivided housing problem in Hong Kong cannot be explained by insufficient public rental housing alone. Instead, the findings highlighted the interconnectedness of the housing problems experienced by different groups of renters, especially the potential displacement of low-income renters by higher-income renters who are not able to afford homeownership and are also not able to afford larger rental flats that have become increasingly unaffordable in recent years. What is interesting, though, is that, despite the high degree of politicization of the subdivided housing problem, the range of solutions that have emerged have been extremely narrow. Indeed, there seems to have been a sole focus on increasing public housing production, with the assumption that this measure alone would tackle the problem effectively.

This interpretation is fairly narrow and does not take into account other factors that have contributed to the subdivided housing crisis, such as worsening affordability for middle-income households and speculative property investment in the luxury flat market, which were illustrated earlier. To some extent, the prevailing housing discourse has been reinforced by some non-governmental actors, including political groups whose proposed solutions are quite closely aligned to the government's framing of the housing problem. This view is particularly noticeable in the responses of different actors to the consultation for the *Long Term Housing Strategy* in 2013–14. Responses from pro-grassroots political parties tended to involve lobbying for higher public housing targets, given that this measure was perceived as the primary solution to the subdivided housing problem. For example, in response to the government's proposal of building 28,000 public housing units over a ten-year period, many political parties proposed higher supply figures as their preferred solution:

> We propose to increase public housing production to 33,000 per annum: 28,000 public rental units, and 5,000 subsidised owner-occupier housing. This will target the housing needs of lower to middle-income households. (HKSAR Government, 2014, para. B127)

The suggestion of building more than 30,000 public housing units per annum has been echoed by the consultation responses from other pro-grassroots political parties (see, for example, HKSAR Government, 2014, para. B101, B131). It seems that more critical responses have mainly come from grassroots organizations, who have challenged existing land use allocations more explicitly, as illustrated in the following written representations from subdivided housing concern groups:

> After the Urban Renewal Authority completes the land acquisition process for redevelopment sites, thirty percent of the land should be set aside for building public housing. This will resolve the myth of shortage of urban land, and will address the housing needs of grassroots citizens. (HKSAR Government, 2014, para. B021)
>
> We ask the government to set aside thirty percent of the land for every urban redevelopment project for building public housing. This will strike a better balance and allow grassroots citizens who rely on jobs in the urban area to continue to live in the urban area, which would alleviate their burdens. (HKSAR Government, 2014, para. B086)

Nevertheless, it seems that these critical views have not achieved much salience beyond the consultation processes. Prevailing societal discourses continue to focus predominantly on supply targets for public housing, with insufficient problematization of land use allocations and supply trends among different property sizes.

Furthermore, successive governments have largely avoided the obvious option of increasing supply of subsidized sale flats, despite its role in providing more affordable housing for households on lower-middle incomes. Since the suspension of the Home Ownership Scheme (HOS) flats in the early 2000s, there has been extreme reluctance to reconsider this option as a long-term policy solution. This reluctance is not just limited to the government – it is also found among many local politicians, who are keen to avoid being blamed for any fluctuations in house prices. Their reluctance is understandable from a political perspective, given the close association between HOS policy and the drastic fall in housing prices in the past. Yet, lack of major intervention with respect to this policy issue means that the housing problems of middle-income groups remain unresolved.

Conclusion

Through analysing Census data and property data across different years, this chapter has made several observations about speculative practices in the housing market in Hong Kong. First, the stock of small-sized flats has not caught up with the growth of low-income households in the lowest income deciles, which helps explain subdivision of private rental flats, especially in the low-end rental sector. Second, there is evidence that the imbalance between supply and demand for small rental flats has been aggravated by the unaffordability of medium-sized flats. These flats are supposedly affordable to middle-income households but have become increasingly unaffordable since the mid-2000s. Combined with minimal production of subsidized owner-occupier units, this trend has pushed middle-income households into competition with low-income households for small-sized rental flats. Third, a high percentage of large-sized flats remain unoccupied after completion, suggesting that these large flats are not for owner-occupation or renting but instead serve as speculative vehicles. These developments take up precious land resources, which could have been made available for construction of other types of private flats or subsidized owner-occupier units.

Although these practices have been driven by the flow of capital into the real estate market, the government is indirectly implicated in them through its refusal to intervene more boldly, especially its reluctance to prioritize land allocation for non-luxury housing development. Thus, the above analysis of the interrelationship between different segments of the private property market in Hong Kong echoes the argument of Wacquant (2013), who suggested that governments play a dual role through production of inequalities "upstream," while appearing to be busily alleviating inequalities experienced "downstream" by disadvantaged citizens. The findings in this chapter add more specifics to the discussion on property speculation in Hong Kong by flagging the implications of uneven production of flats of different sizes and the domino effects of speculative behaviour in the luxury residential market.

These observations raise a series of questions: Why is so much land, especially urban land, allocated for the development of large Class D and E flats? Considering that household sizes in Hong Kong have declined over the years, why is there a need to allocate land for large-sized flats, which are unaffordable to the average domestic user? Why does the government claim that there is insufficient land for public housing construction when land is continually set aside for luxury property development, which tends to meet speculative demand rather than user demand? Indeed, these questions have not been adequately tackled by the latest *Long Term Housing Strategy* in 2014, which merely repeats the well-rehearsed rhetoric of public housing construction. In the absence of more housing options for middle-income groups, the inter-competition between middle- and low-income households for private rental flats is unlikely to disappear overnight.

There is an urgent need for more critical approaches that challenge existing inequalities in housing and land development, which are the root causes of this uncomfortable inter-competition between middle- and low-income groups. Indeed, some grassroots advocacy groups have already pushed for the retention of prime sites in the main urban area, such as redevelopment sites that have been acquired by the Urban Renewal Authority, to be used for constructing subsidized sale flats in order to provide more affordable owner-occupier opportunities for middle-income households. Yet, there is no evidence that the Urban Renewal Authority is prepared to shift away from existing market-oriented strategies – so far, there have only been a few attempts to develop subsidized flats, which offer a smaller discount compared to government-subsidized flats.

Another approach that has been tried out in recent years is the imposition of land lease conditions. In response to public resentment against speculative luxury property development, the government announced in the 2010–11 Budget Address that it would impose flat-size restrictions on new-build developments through the lease conditions of designated land lots. In the first site that was put to tender in December 2010, the tender conditions specified a minimum supply of 800 flats of 35 to 40 square metres. Such restrictions focus on facilitating supply of small-sized flats, which could be interpreted as a more balanced approach to utilizing limited land resources. Nevertheless, these restrictions have only been imposed on several sites, and commentators have questioned whether these measures have any impact on private property prices, which have continued to surge over the last few years. Furthermore, size restriction is a compromise solution that comes with a cost – size-restricted flats are (slightly) more affordable at the expense of housing space. This development is hardly a cause for celebration.

What kinds of housing futures are likely to emerge out of the above bundle of policy responses? If supply of public rental housing does increase as planned, there would be greater housing security for lower-income households who manage to get into this sector. But what about the rest of the population, who are neither rich enough to join the property speculation game nor poor enough to join the public housing scrambling game? Will the housing system look increasingly like an hourglass – more and more public renters at the bottom, and fewer and fewer subsidized homeowners in the middle? Will society witness a steady decline of the socio-political influence of the middle class, who are not entitled to public rental housing and receive only breadcrumbs from the government – a few thousand subsidized sale flats here and there? With all their energies consumed by this mad scramble for breadcrumbs, how is this group going to achieve their non-housing aspirations?

The case of Hong Kong speaks to other places – expanding the public rental sector alone is unlikely to resolve long-standing socio-political contradictions generated by land and property speculation. Poor tenants are often perceived as the primary victims of property speculation, although in reality, nobody (except the super-rich) is immune to its painful effects. As this chapter has argued, there tends to be insufficient problematization of the status quo, not just by the government but also by political actors who focus on increasing the supply of public rental housing for the poorest, while being relatively ambivalent on the housing struggles of middle-income groups. There may be a lot of grand-sounding talk about anti-speculation measures in Hong Kong, but when it comes down to concrete policy choices, the city is still very much entrenched in a speculative mindset.

ACKNOWLEDGMENTS

The author would like to thank Ms. Leung Oi Kwan, Venus for her assistance with data collection.

FUNDING

This work was supported by the Research Grants Council (RGC) of Hong Kong under Project No. 17608615.

REFERENCES

Census and Statistics Department (CSD). (2011). *2021 population census thematic report: Household income distribution in Hong Kong*. Census and Statistics Department. https://www.statistics.gov.hk/pub/B11200572012XXXXB0100.pdf

Census and Statistics Department (CSD). (2015). *Thematic household survey report no. 57: Housing conditions of sub-divided units in Hong Kong*. Census and Statistics Department. https://www.statistics.gov.hk/pub/B11302572015XXXXB0100.pdf

Census and Statistics Department (CSD). (2016). *Thematic household survey report no. 60: Housing conditions of sub-divided units in Hong Kong*. Census and Statistics Department. https://www.statistics.gov.hk/pub/B11302602016XXXXB0100.pdf

Chiu R.L.H. (2007). Planning, land and affordable housing in Hong Kong. *Housing Studies*, 22(1), 63–81. https://doi.org/10.1080/02673030601024614

Forrest, R., & Yip, N.M. (2014). The future for reluctant intervention: The prospects for Hong Kong's public rental sector. *Housing Studies*, 29(4), 551–65. https://doi.org/10.1080/02673037.2013.878020

Gurran, N., & Phibbs, P. (2015). Are governments really interested in fixing the housing problem? Policy capture and busy work in Australia. *Housing Studies*, *30*(5), 711–29. https://doi.org/10.1080/02673037.2015.1044948

Haila, A. (2017). Institutionalisation of "the property mind." *International Journal of Urban and Regional Research*, *41*(3), 500–7. https://doi.org/10.1111/1468-2427.12495

Hamnett, C., & Randolph, W. (1984). Landlord disinvestment in housing market transformation: Analysis of the flat break-up market in central London. *Transactions of the Institute of British Geographers*, *9*(3), 259–79. https://doi.org/10.2307/622233

HKSAR (Hong Kong Special Administrative Region of the People's Republic of China) Government. (2013). *Building consensus, building homes: Long term housing strategy consultation document*. Long Term Housing Strategy Steering Committee. https://www.thb.gov.hk/eng/policy/housing/policy/lths/lthb_consultation_doc_201309.pdf

HKSAR (Hong Kong Special Administrative Region of the People's Republic of China) Government. (2014). *Long term housing strategy: Building consensus, building homes: Report on public consultation*. Long Term Housing Strategy Steering Committee. https://www.thb.gov.hk/eng/policy/housing/policy/lths/report_on_public_consultation.pdf

Hui, E.C.M., Ng, I., & Lau. O.M.F. (2011). Speculative bubbles in mass and luxury properties: An investigation of the Hong Kong residential market. *Construction Management and Economics*, *29*(8), 781–93. https://doi.org/10.1080/01446193.2011.610329

Hulse, K., & Burke, T. (2015). Private rental housing in Australia: Political inertia and market change. In R. Duffy-Jones & D. Rogers (Eds.), *Housing in twenty-first century Australia: People, practices and policies* (pp. 139–52). Ashgate.

Hulse, K., & Yates, J. (2017). A private rental sector paradox: Unpacking the effects of urban restructuring on housing market dynamics. *Housing Studies*, *32*(3), 253–70. https://doi.org/10.1080/02673037.2016.1194378

Jacobs, K. (2015a). The "politics" of Australian housing: The role of lobbyists and their influence in shaping policy. *Housing Studies*, *30*(5), 694–710. https://doi.org/10.1080/02673037.2014.1000833

Jacobs, K. (2015b). A reverse form of welfarism: Some reflections on Australian housing policy. *Australian Journal of Social Issues*, *50*(1), 53–68. https://doi.org/10.1002/j.1839-4655.2015.tb00334.x

La Grange, A., & Pretorius, F. (2002). Private rental housing in Hong Kong. *Housing Studies*, *17*(5), 721–40. https://doi.org/10.1080/0267303022000009772

Lau, M.H.M. (2019). Lobbying for rent regulation in Hong Kong: Rental market politics and framing strategies. *Urban Studies*, *56*(12), 2515–31. https://doi.org/10.1177/0042098018791951

Levine, M.E., & Forrence, J.L. (1990). Regulatory capture, public interest and the public agenda: Toward a synthesis. *Journal of Law, Economics & Organization, 6*, 167–98. https://doi.org/10.1093/jleo/6.special_issue.167

Ley, D., & Teo, S.Y. (2013). Gentrification in Hong Kong? Epistemology vs. ontology. *International Journal of Urban and Regional Research, 38*(4), 1286–1303. https://doi.org/10.1111/1468-2427.12109

Pawson, H. (2006). Restructuring England's social housing sector since 1989: Undermining or underpinning the fundamentals of public housing? *Housing Studies, 21*(5), 767–83. https://doi.org/10.1080/02673030600807720

Rating and Valuation Department (RVD). (2017). *Property market statistics. Private domestic – completions, stock, vacancy and take-up*. Rating and Valuation Department.

Research Office, Legislative Council Secretariat. (2017). *Statistical highlights issue ISSH20/16–17*. The Legislative Council Commission.

Research Office, Legislative Council Secretariat. (2018). *Statistical highlights issue ISSH18/17–18*. The Legislative Council Commission.

Smart, A., & Lee, J. (2003). Financialization and the role of real estate in Hong Kong's regime of accumulation. *Economic Geography, 79*(2), 153–71. https://doi.org/10.1111/j.1944-8287.2003.tb00206.x

Society for Community Organization (SoCO). (2013). *2012/13 Research report on cage homes, cubicles, and sub-divided flats*. Society for Community Organization.

Transport and Housing Bureau. (2019). *Housing in figures: 2019*. HKSAR (Hong Kong Special Administrative Region of the People's Republic of China) Government.

Wacquant, L. (2013, 26 November). *Constructing neoliberalism: Opening salvo* [Plenary address]. The Australian Sociological Association, Brisbane. http://www.antoniocasella.eu/nume/Wacquant_constructing_neoliberalism_2013.pdf

Yip, N.M., & La Grange, A. (2006). Globalisation, de-industrialization and Hong Kong's private rental sector. *Habitat International, 30*(4), 996–1006. https://doi.org/10.1016/j.habitatint.2005.10.005

9 Contradictions of State and Household Investments in Public Housing in Singapore

CHUA BENG HUAT

The public housing authority, the Housing and Development Board (HDB), is one of the government agencies in Singapore most visited by foreign dignitaries and study teams. The national public housing program has been much studied, but never replicated, by other states because of its unique features.[1] The national housing program promises and delivers housing to 90 per cent of Singaporean citizens and permanent residents, of which more than 80 per cent own a ninety-nine-year lease on their high-rise flats. This practically universal provision has been motivated by the concern for social and political stability; home-ownership gives every citizen a stake in the nation. The program has been enabled by the fact that the state owns nearly 90 per cent of the land of the island nation through inheritance from the British colonial administration; draconian public appropriation of private land holdings, especially during the first two decades of state formation; and, finally, extensive land reclamation along the coasts and around a set of small islets. Land has thus been highly nationalized and used for infrastructure development and public housing estates.

The political ideological motivation behind developing a nation of homeowners is not unique to Singapore. Similar motivation has characterized the great sell-off of council housing in Britain during the Thatcher years (Saunders, 1990) and in Franco Spain (Catalán and Chu, Chapter 6, this volume). Nor is state ownership of land unique to Singapore; for example, the Hong Kong government also owns all the land on the island. The Singapore housing program differs from all these instances by two determining features. First, the Singapore state sells the subsidized housing unit directly to the citizen-owner without

---

[1] For greater details regarding Singapore's public housing program see Chua (1997), Castells et al. (1990), and Wong & Yeh (1985).

the mediation of a private property developer. Any increased value accrued to the housing unit goes directly to the homeowner rather than to a private speculative developer (see Fainstein and Novy, Chapter 1, this volume). Second, in the Singapore program, as discussed later, there is a ready availability of mortgage for all Singaporean public housing purchasers through a closed circuit of financial transfer between the HDB, the mortgage holder, and the purchaser's compulsory social security savings, bypassing commercial financial institutions and fluctuating market mortgage rates. The two features in combination significantly reduce the cost and financial burden of the public housing homeowner.

Alongside the public housing estates, there is a much smaller private housing sector, about 10 to 15 per cent, that acquires land through the following three methods. First, private developers vie for the remaining 10 to 15 per cent of freehold, privately held land at very high cost. Second, like the Hong Kong government (see Lau, Chapter 8, this volume), the Singapore state releases land parcels, with ninety-nine-year leases, through publicly conducted closed-bid auctions for residential developments by private developers. However, unlike Hong Kong, which derives a significant part of its annual budget from such land sales, the Singapore government channels the proceeds of the sales into its national reserves away from routine government expenditure. Finally, a developer may make a general offer to purchase the entire existing housing estate, locally known as an "en bloc" sale, for intensified residential redevelopment; homeowners are incentivized to the collective sale because the selling price far exceeds selling individually (Sim et al., 2002). If the existing estate is on ninety-nine-year leasehold land, the developer would have to pay a hefty development charge to the state to refresh the lease to ninety-nine years. Strict regulations apply to land leased for residential developments. A developer will have to complete the development within three years of acquiring the lease, and all residential units must be sold within two years of completion. All unsold units are subject to a heavy punitive tax. Developers are thus prevented from land banking for potential enhanced capital gains at some future date and at the same time reduce supply, creating demand and price hikes. Freehold lands are not subjected to these regulations.

Unlike the public housing sector, which is restricted to only citizens and permanent residents, there is no restriction on citizenship status in the private sector. Understandably, prices in the private sector per square foot far exceed those in the public housing sector. The local real estate industry broadly divides the private sector into two tiers, namely, the mass market and the high-end market. The mass market consists largely of ninety-nine-year leasehold condominiums outside the city core areas, targeting residents in public housing who aspire to move into imagined privacy, social status, and the luxuries of gated communities, locally known as "HDB upgraders." The high-end market consists of landed properties of terraced, semi-detached and detached houses or bungalows and luxury apartments in the city core. Given the political and economic stability of Singapore, there is good evidence that the very high end of the private sector attracts highly speculative investments from overseas, similar to conditions found in all global cities (see Hamnett, Chapter 7, this volume). Since the global recession in 2008, houses and flats at Sentosa Island, Singapore's "resort" island, saw sales at losses of up to 40 per cent of the original prices (Lee, 2017). The focus of this chapter, however, is not on the speculation activities in the private sector, except when the sector intersects with the public housing sector. The primary concern of this chapter is the "speculative" activities in the public housing sector.

Public Housing Homeownership

Of the 90 per cent homeowner households, 85 per cent of them hold a ninety-nine-year lease on their flats. The high rate of ownership is facilitated by the easy access to mortgages through the compulsory social security savings of all workers in Singapore. Every Singaporean wage earner must compulsorily save a certain percentage of the monthly wage, with a matching contribution from the employer, as their personalized social security savings for retirement. This fund is called the Central Provident Fund or CPF (Low & Aw, 1997). Individuals are permitted to make pre-retirement withdrawals from their CPF savings to pay both the down payment and the monthly mortgage for their public housing flats. The entire transaction is carried out in a closed circuit: an individual purchases a flat from the HDB, which holds the mortgage, and the CPF pays the monthly mortgage on his or her behalf directly to the HDB. As the monthly CPF savings are generally in excess of the monthly mortgage sum, the entire process is cashless, and consequently, many public housing residents do not know the monthly cost for their accommodation. No commercial financial institutions are involved in the mortgage market of the public housing sector. On the part of the state, unlike a public rental system, in which the rent collected constitutes an insignificant portion of the development cost of the housing estate and each cycle of construction is a drain on the national economy, income from the sale of flats ensures the recovery of a very significant portion of the developmental cost. The recouped capital can then be ploughed back into the next cycle of new housing production, thus enabling the overall subsidy to the system to be maintained at a tolerable margin. Between 1975 and the mid-1980s, government subsidy for the HDB was generally below S$2 billion annually during the first decade of the twenty-first century (Heng, 2015), and the government has spent S$28 billion in the program since its inception (The Economist, 2017). This sum is a small price to pay for housing the nation.

As we shall see, while the pre-retirement withdrawal of CPF has facilitated homeownership, it has had serious financial consequences for the individual homeowners and the national public housing system as a whole. For now, it should be noted that, since prices for new flats are set by the HDB, in principle it should maintain price stability across time. Yet, new public housing prices kept rising until affordability became a political issue in the late 2000s, causing the long-ruling People's Action Party (PAP) government to lose a significant level of popular electoral support in the 2011 general election. This price rise was the result of a formula used by the HDB to price new flats with reference to the market for "resale flats."

After a mandatory period of residency, usually five years, an existing leaseholder is free to sell the flat in the open market to another citizen or permanent resident. The flats in the open market are locally known as "resale flats." However, the government promises to keep new public housing flats at a level that is affordable to 90 per cent of eligible households and also promises that it will periodically raise the monthly income ceiling for eligibility, in step with the general economic growth, so as to include as many households as possible. Therefore, logically, eligible households should purchase the subsidized new flats directly from the HDB, instead of purchasing older flats with shortened leases. Yet, the resale flats find a ready market for several reasons. First, permanent residents are not entitled to purchase new subsidized flats. Second, households with a monthly income that exceeds the limit of eligibility and is excluded from government subsidy are restricted to purchasing resale flats at market values. Third, resale flats tend to be in housing estates that are nearer to the city core and with established amenities of everyday life, such as schools, medical clinics, commercial services, and different modes of public transportation. Last, but not least, purchasing a resale flat avoids the three-to-five-year wait on the queue for new subsidized flats.

On the sellers' side, the incentive to sell the existing flat is further encouraged by the fact that the seller can, in turn, purchase a second, and final, new subsidized flat from the HDB. This provision is motivated by the presumed need of families to adjust their housing needs across the family life cycle. The seller either uses the tax-exempt proceeds of the sale as enhanced capital to finance an upgrade to a larger flat or downsizes to a smaller flat and retains the surplus from the sale as profit, depending on the family's spatial needs. In the first thirty years of the public housing program, upgrading was a common phenomenon, as Singapore was a developing economy with large family sizes and a young population. However, by the end of the twentieth century, Singapore had transitioned into an aging society with a very low birth rate; consequently, downgrading has picked up speed, and the HDB is constructing more small flats to accommodate empty-nest older families and even single aged members of society. In both instances, the financial interests of the sellers thus dovetail with the housing desires and/or needs of the purchasers of resale flats. Furthermore, in spite of the reduced length of leases, resale flats consistently fetch better prices than equivalent new, and better designed, flats in new public housing estates. As a result, there has been a very active resale market. For example, more than 8,000 units of resale flats were transacted in eight consecutive quarters until the end of 2009 (Phang & Helble, 2016). The incentive to sell existing flats increases as the gap between the prices of the existing resale flats and new flats widens; "the correlation between volume and the resale price–new price differential is 93%" (Edelstein & Lum, 2003, p. 348).

Meanwhile, instead of price stability, prices for new subsidized public housing flats have also risen in tandem due to a pricing formula disclosed to the public by the government after questions were raised by political opposition parties in the early 1990s regarding the actual levels of subsidy, implying that the government might in fact be profiting from providing public housing. The government declared that new flats were priced at a 20 per cent discount off the resale market prices for equivalent-size flats, regardless of the actual construction costs. Questions of actual subsidy remain unanswered. The formula had a disastrous consequence, because it created a vicious cycle of price inflation across the board: the prices of resale flats form the base of the prices of new flats, which in turn becomes the higher base for the prices of resale flats, and the cycle continues with the two prices chasing each other upwards. The resulting rates of inflation of public housing prices can be gleaned from these figures: in 1972–73, a five-room flat was sold by HDB for S$30,000, while its resale price in 2016 was S$720,000; in 1983–84, a new five-room flat was sold by HDB for S$84,000, while its resale price in 2016 was approximately S$600,000; in 1990–91, a new HDB five-room flat sold at an average of S$110,000, while the average resale price was S$550,000 in 2016. The variation in prices of five-room flats is due to the location and size of the flats. Flats built before the late 1980s tend to have larger floor areas than those built from 1990 onwards. Obviously, the HDB had been raising the prices of new flats, presumably based on the 20 per cent market discount formula.

Clearly, in Singapore, the ownership of a ninety-nine-year lease, combined with the profit-making opportunity provided by the resale market, has transformed the public housing flat into a vehicle for capital accumulation for the leaseholder. To the extent that close to 85 per cent of the residents in the one million public housing flats are owners of a ninety-nine-year lease, the opportunity to accumulate wealth through public housing homeownership may be said to be relatively universalized or "democratized"; real estate is not the game of only the wealthy in Singapore. In practice, however, the opportunities are captured largely by the upper-middle-class end of the public housing population, the so-called "HDB upgraders." For this group of households, who are adept at using HDB regulations, the economic gains have been very substantial, especially for households who had entered the public housing sector early. Illustrative of this phenomenon is the real property ownership history of an engineer's family: Lim bought his first five-room public housing flat in 1975 for S$35,000 and sold it in 1985 for S$123,000 minus a 10 per cent levy paid to the HDB; in turn, he bought a five-room equivalent private sector condominium for S$430,000 and sold it in 1992 for S$620,000; then he bought a five-room equivalent Housing and Urban Development Corporation (HUDC) condominium – a higher quality public housing unit for middle-class families who have incomes beyond eligibility for public housing but have insufficient funds to be able to afford private condominiums – for S$430,000 and sold it in 1996 for S$760,000; next, he bought a five-room HDB resale flat for S$480,000 and sold it in 2015 for S$520,000; finally, he bought his second new four-room (downsizing because both children were married) public housing flat directly from HDB for S$296,000. Over the period from 1975 to 2015, Lim made a total of S$540,000, all within public housing flats except for one.

As prices in the public housing sector rise, so too do prices in the small, but expensive, private sector. In the interests of a more comprehensive understanding of property investment in Singapore, the following case is illustrative of investment in private sector properties. Yeo, a contemporary of Lim, entered the housing market only in 1985, due to late marriage. As his income was beyond the eligibility ceiling for public housing, he had to buy in the private housing sector. Here is his "housing career": in 1985, he bought his first townhouse for S$450,000 and sold it for S$500,000 in 1991; in turn, he bought a semi-detached house, with 5,000 square feet of land, for S$1.15 million. This flat remains his current residence and is estimated to be valued at more than S$6 million. Like most two-income professional families, Yeo invested in real estate: in 1995, he bought a condominium for S$1.1 million, which was sold en bloc for S$2.4 million in 2004; in turn, he bought a condominium for

S$1.8 million, which was sold en bloc for S$4.2 million in 2007; then he bought two condominiums at S$1.65 million and S$3.2 million, financed by aggregated gains from the two en bloc sales; in 2009 he bought another condominium for S2.1 million. Due to the strategic choice of locations, all the investment condominium units have been let without disruption, with rents that more than cover the monthly mortgages. Yeo's current real estate holdings, including his principal home, is estimated to be approximately S$14 million, from a total investment of S$3.5 million, taking into account renovation costs for all the housing units.

Yeo's ownership of multiple properties is not exceptional. Indeed, it is a relatively common practice among upper-middle-class Singaporeans. Although no official data is available, an indirect indication of its ubiquity is the fact that, under pressure from the upper-middle-class public housing residents, the government, from the mid-1980s, has permitted owners of HDB flats to invest in private properties but not in additional public housing flats. Such practice is common because property is a relatively "easy" mode of investment. It is a long-term investment that does not require constant attention to the market conditions, unlike playing the stock market. The only concern is the availability of renters who can afford rents that are in excess of the monthly mortgage payments. Given the massive presence of multinational corporations, many of which have their regional operational headquarters in Singapore, there is a ready rental market of global expatriate managers who are able and willing to pay high rents for quality condominiums because their accommodation costs are part of their remuneration packages. As seen from the two examples, clearly the higher end of middle-class Singaporeans have made housing a vehicle for investment, and while the quantum of profit is very significantly higher from investment in the private sector, it is nevertheless possible to make profit from public housing ownership, even when a household is only permitted to own one public unit at any one time. Furthermore, those who are not in a position to invest in additional properties are nevertheless aware of the rising value of their public housing flats. Thus, it can be said that Singaporeans are generally "property minded" (Haila, 2017).

Housing Asset–Based Social Security and Pressure to Make Capital Gains

Haila (2017) is correct in suggesting that this property mindedness is not due to any Asian or Singaporean "cultural propensity" but is the result of specific legal and institutional factors that contextualize property ownership in Singapore. She has identified three factors: first, the ownership of public housing and its resale for profit; second, the possibility of enhanced capital gains in the above mentioned en bloc sales of private condominium estates; and third, investment in additional properties as a hedge against retirement needs. This last reason is because, in both public and private homeownership, Singaporeans have been making pre-retirement withdrawals of the retirement social security fund, the CPF, to pay for their flats or houses. The CPF system is not a national pension system. It is a non-redistributive compulsory personalized social security savings system in which one is as wealthy or poor as one's savings at retirement. Without a guaranteed pension, an individual Singaporean is thus compelled to have his or her own retirement plan and is thus under intense pressure to grow wealth during active working years. Investment in properties is one path to growing wealth, hence the widespread property mindedness.

Encouraging public housing homeownership has been the explicit policy of the government behind the continuous extension of public housing homeownership since 1968. Current Prime Minister Lee Hsien Loong reminds the citizens:

> The most important thing we [the PAP government] do for Singaporeans, of course, is to help every family own a home – the HDB flat. The house is much more than a secure roof over their heads. The house in Singapore is also a major way for us to level up the less successful and to give them a valuable asset and a retirement nest egg ... That's why we are making sure that HDB flats are affordable even to lower-income households. (H.L. Lee, 2011)

With the pre-retirement withdrawal of the CPF by homeowners, housing has become the asset in an asset-based social security system (Chia, 2011), and the depletion of a potential retirement fund is a source of concern. Indeed, since the early 1980s, local economists had already warned that the hefty CPF withdrawal for housing might leave a large number of Singaporeans without sufficient funds to finance their retiring years (Central Provident Fund Study Group, 1986, pp. 51–5; Asher, 1991; Asher & Nandy, 2008). However, the government had been relatively unconcerned because, with the exception of one brief short dip in prices during the 2008 global recession (Phang, 2013, p. 82), the annual rate of increase of public housing prices has persistently far outstripped the annual interest accrued to CPF savings, making public housing a good investment. Nevertheless, potential retirement funds have undoubtedly been severely reduced, if not depleted. Thus, in examining the Singapore homeownership system, Hailer raises the question:

"'How do retired people live when their pension savings are tied to housing?' One solution is to buy several properties and become landlord" (Haila, 2017, p. 504), a solution that is illustrated by the above two case studies of Lim and Yeo.

However, Haila's solution of multiple property ownership to generate rent as a livestream of income to live on during retirement is only available for a small portion of the Singapore population. In 2014, it was reported that more than 45,000, approximately 4 per cent, of public housing owners own private properties (Heng, 2014). If we add to this number the approximately 15 per cent of private property owners presumed to be able to own additional properties, Haila's solution would apply to only 20 per cent of the homeowner population. But for the overwhelming remaining 96 per cent of public housing owners, the public housing flat is their only significant asset. These public housing homeowners face a common dilemma endemic to the housing-asset social security system: being "asset rich, cash poor" (Doling & Ronald, 2010, p. 170) without the necessary means to monetize their housing investment to fund their retirement needs, creating a situation of relative poverty in spite of homeownership. In Singapore, for public housing homeowners who are unable to enhance their own wealth by strategic property transactions, the responsibility of translating their housing asset into adequate retirement funds falls on the government.

Strategies of Monetizing Housing Assets

Having encouraged the entire nation to invest in public housing ownership, from which it has gained very significant political capital and legitimacy, the long-ruling People's Action Party Singapore government has to bear the responsibility for protecting the quality and price of the public housing flats and ensure that the investments in the flats pay long-term dividends. To maintain the prices of public housing flats, prices must not be allowed to fall below their investment values, that is, the HDB selling price, with homeowners ending up with negative equity. Such a serious fall in public housing prices would not only bring financial trouble to homeowners but would also cause a political crisis for the ruling government. Prices of existing flats had been supported and/or enhanced by the earlier mentioned 20 per cent market discount pricing formula for new public housing flats relative to prevailing prices of equivalent resale flats, which created an unintended vicious cycle of price inflation of both new and existing public housing flats. As an estate ages, the condition of its flats and the general estate environment inevitably deteriorates, thus eroding the property values of the flats. In 1990, to support the property values of older flats against all subsequent generations of better designed flats and estates, the government established a highly subsidized estate upgrading scheme to improve the flats, amenities, and environment of older estates; citizens only bore 10 to 20 per cent of the cost, while permanent residents had to bear the full cost of the upgrading (Chua, 2003).

To enable the public housing homeowner to monetize the capital that is invested and accumulated in the flat, the most direct way is, of course, to sell the existing flat, downgrade to a smaller flat, or, if possible, move in with an adult child and keep the profit for retirement needs. The HDB has, however, developed an alternative – a "lease/buy back" scheme. A homeowner can sell all but thirty years of the remaining lease to the HDB, in return for a monthly income, without having to vacate the flat. As homeowners are most likely to buy a ninety-nine-year lease flat in their early thirties, there will still be more than sixty years left in the lease when they reach current mandatory retirement age at sixty-five. Keeping the last thirty years of the lease would enable the homeowner to age in place for the remaining years of his or her life. However, neither sales scheme has been popular because, firstly, they are not as lucrative as renting out a flat. Secondly, homeowners remain tenaciously traditional in their attitude in wanting to "pass down" their flats as inheritance for their children, even though the latter would have already owned their own public housing flats; indeed, one future worry of the HDB is the surplus of flats in the face of an aging population and a radically low birth rate. An alternate and preferred strategy to generate retirement income is to rent out extra rooms or the entire flat for a livestream of monthly income, as rental regulations have been relaxed to accommodate new families awaiting their public housing flat allocation as well as the sharp increase of foreign labour population. By 2014, about 44,000 rooms and 40,000 whole flats in HDB estates were rented out (Heng, 2014).

Creative Destruction

All the above strategies for maintaining competitive values of existing older housing units and processes of enabling rental returns cannot prevent the inevitable decline in market value of existing flats due to the constantly shortening of the ninety-nine-year lease. The same applies to the ninety-nine-year leasehold condominiums in the private sector. In both cases, a flat with less than fifty years lease is unlikely to obtain a mortgage from the banks. As mentioned, private condominiums are subject to the possibility of en bloc sale, which generally means enhanced capital gains for the homeowners. The HDB has developed a parallel program of en bloc acquisition of older housing estates for redevelopment under the so-called Selective En bloc Redevelopment Scheme (SERS), also with increased financial advantages to the homeowners. In both cases, older housing blocks are destroyed to make way for new more densely packed estates with taller buildings.

Being a small island nation, there is persistent pressure on Singaporean state planners to maximize the carrying capacity of every square inch of land to accommodate an expanding population and sustain economic growth. Thus, in 2001, the plot ratio for all land was increased by a multiple of three from the existing density in anticipation of intensification of land use in future redevelopment (Urban Redevelopment Authority, 2001). To intensify land use in public housing estates, the HDB initiated the SERS in 1995. The scheme targeted for redevelopment selected older estates with four-to-twelve-storey housing blocks, which had been developed during the 1960s and 1970s in the city and its immediate vicinity. Between 2012 and 2015, about 350 blocks in seventy-eight locations were demolished (Teoalida, n.d.). In the largest SERS exercise, 3,480 flats and shops in 31 blocks, some of which were more than fifty years old, were slated for demolition. As public housing is built on state land, the state reserves the right to repossess the land. While the level of compensation for affected homeowners may be subject to negotiation, the right to repossession is not.

Under SERS, new thirty-to-forty-storey blocks are first constructed in the vicinity of the blocks targeted for demolition. Affected households are then relocated into these new blocks to minimize disruptions to their neighbourhood routines. Homeowners are compensated at the prevailing market prices for the old flats. With the 20 per cent market discount formula, this compensation is generally more than the price for the new ninety-nine-year lease flats; any remainder is profit. With such favourable conditions, few affected families have protested about being resettled. The former minister of national development, Khaw Boon Wan, noted:

> With every new HDB town becoming more modern and better designed, there is a need to ensure that the older towns do not end up too far behind. They [affected households] will get a new modern flat with a fresh 99-year lease, with greenery on their doorstep, and panoramic views of the city and surrounding areas. I am sure they will find this attractive and exciting. (Yeo, 2014)

His sentiments were echoed by a seventy-four-year-old resident: "My neighbours and I are all really happy. Why wouldn't you want a new flat?" Those who lament having to move are comforted, saying: "At least we [long-term neighbours] can all move together and won't be alone" (Yeo, 2014). SERS thus appears to be a perfect solution to the problem of declining values.

Unsurprisingly, it quickly became the expectation of public housing homeowners to be eventually resettled under SERS. Sensing the danger of this development, the government quickly quelled this expectation before it became politicized. The current minister of national development, Lawrence Wong, warned Singaporeans: "Do not assume that all old HDB flats will be automatically eligible for SERS." He pointed out that the scheme is "only offered to HDB blocks located in sites with high redevelopment potential ... typically sites where the land has not been well utilized. It is also subject to the availability of suitable replacement sites for residents and the Government's financial resources," which is why to date "only 4 per cent of HDB flats have been identified for SERS since it was launched in 1995." As in the normal course of events, "for the vast majority of HDB flats, the leases will eventually run out, and the flats will be returned to HDB, which in turn surrenders the land the flats are on to the State. As the leases run down, especially towards the tail-end, the flat prices will come down correspondingly" (The Straits Times, 2017). Minister Wong's clarification has cast a chill over the entire nation of homeowners.

Political Perils of the State-Regulated Market

The combined effects of the above policies have practically guaranteed public housing homeownership as a fail-safe investment for all citizens, except those too poor to buy even the smallest public housing flat. Ironically, the same factors have also created a systemic inflationary pressure that causes public housing prices to rise inexorably, with serious repercussions on their affordability for first-time entrants into the market. This contradiction has serious political consequences for the PAP government. The "perfect storm" materialized at the close of the first decade of the twenty-first century, almost fifty years after what appears to be a virtuous system in which practically the entire nation has made wealth through homeownership.

Due to Singapore's very stable domestic conditions, foreign direct investment (FDI) continued to flow into the country. Between 2006 and 2008, the total FDI grew from S$370.49 billion to S$510.58 billion (Department of Statistics Singapore, 2019). To meet the increased demand for workers created by this capital inflow, the population, of which one in four was an immigrant, increased from 4.35 million to 5.18 million between 2005 and 2011 (Department of Statistics Singapore, 2006, p. 19; 2012, p. 9). The increase in population, combined with a slowdown in supply of new flats from the HDB, led to an acute housing shortage and price inflation during the latter half of the 2000s. The resale price index rose 86 per cent in the six years from 2005 to 2012. For example, "the median price of a resale five-room flat in Ang Mo Kio (an older estate) increased from SG$327,000 to SG$609,000. This increase of SG$282,000 was more than four times the median annual income of resident households" (Phang, 2013, pp. 81–2); correspondingly, "private home prices had surged 60%" between mid-2009 and mid-2013 (Ong, 2014a). Due to the 20 per cent market discount price formula, prices of new flats also increased in tandem. The mismatch between the rapid inflation of housing prices and the tepid rates of income increase was common knowledge, as reflected by this very rough estimate from the following citizen:

> In 1981, I earned $800 plus as a fresh graduate. At that time, one of my colleagues bought a five-room HDB flat for $35,000. Now, a graduate's pay has risen about four times, but HDB flat prices have risen more than 11 times. (C. Lee, 2011)

Affordability of public housing became a generalized anxiety, especially for new entrants into the housing market, such as newly married young families.

By 2009, the government realized that the rapid inflation of public housing prices would be among the multiple and mounting discontents that would be politicized in the forthcoming 2011 general election. Instead of touting "public housing as asset," Prime Minister Lee Hsien Loong re-emphasized public housing as a necessity for the long term rather than for quick turnaround for profit (Lee, 2010). Meanwhile, the government took some small steps to address the affordability issue. It increased "additional housing grants" to first-time homeowners to offset the rising costs and lengthened the mortgage period for twenty- and twenty-five-year mortgages to thirty years. However, these minor adjustments were grossly inadequate. The 2011 May general election delivered the PAP the worst election results in its more than sixty years in power. It lost six parliamentary seats instead of the usual one or two and garnered only 60 per cent of the popular vote. Given that the promise of affordable public housing to all citizens had been absolutely fundamental to its legitimacy and longevity, the PAP government immediately undertook more radical measures to cool the housing market in order to regain its political ground.

The new minister of national development, Khaw Boon Wan, who was responsible for housing policies, immediately removed the 20 per cent market discount formula that was partially responsible for the vicious cycle of price inflation across all housing sectors; prices for new flats were set by the HDB without reference to the resale market. He simultaneously increased the supply of new housing units from 9,000 in 2009 to 25,000 for 2011, and by 2014, more than 50,000 new housing units were placed on the market. First-time homeowners were counselled publicly to delay their purchase of a flat and wait for the new supply. Generous cash grants from the state were provided, not only to new homeowners but also to lower-middle-class households that needed to upgrade their housing. The cost of these subsidies from 2005 to 2013 was S$1 billion.

On the other hand, to reduce competition for resale public housing, additional constraints were placed on permanent residents, including (1) not being permitted to purchase a resale flat for the first three years of residency; (2) having to dispose of all other properties, including those in their country of origin, within six months of purchase; and (3) having to obtain permission to rent out the flat from the HDB every year, rather than every three years, for a limit of five years. Considering permanent residents owned only 5 per cent of the total public housing stock of nearly one million units, and rented out only 2,000 out of 40,000 flats eligible to be rented, these constraints had a marginal impact on the housing market. However, they were of greater political symbolic significance, as the presence of permanent residents in the resale market had become a lightning rod for public anger. Politically, these measures served to inform the citizens that undeserved privileges for permanent residents had been removed (Chang, 2012).

Correspondingly, to reduce multiple property ownership among Singaporeans and foreign investors, commonly conceived as property speculation, the down payment for second and subsequent property purchase was sharply increased from 10 to 30 per cent of the unit cost. Additional stamp duty was also imposed on property purchases – a 15 per cent levy on all foreigners, 5 per cent on permanent residents buying their first flat, 7 per cent on Singaporeans purchasing second flats, and 10 per cent for subsequent properties. The greatest dampening effect is the limit imposed on the personal debt of Singaporeans. In 2013, the total debt of an individual, including existing mortgages, car loans, and credit cards, was capped so that it could not exceed 60 per cent of his or her monthly income. Banks were not permitted to make loans beyond this total debt-servicing ratio. The combined result of these financial regulations had a chilling effect on housing sales. By mid-2013, the prices of all properties, public and private, began to inch lower by an average of 1 per cent every quarter for four consecutive quarters (Tan, 2014) and continued to fall for the next four quarters. In the private condominium sector, sales in the first quarter of 2014 dropped more than 50 per cent from the same period in the previous year (Ong, 2014b). Prices kept falling at a slow rate every quarter, cumulatively reaching approximately 15 per cent, until the third quarter of 2017, when both prices and sales volume began to show signs of picking up. It would appear that the government had swiftly wrested back control and reoccupied its place as the price-setter for the public housing market, and by extension, it had affected the prices in the entire housing market for now. By the 2015 general election, public housing affordability disappeared as a political issue, and the PAP won a landslide victory, recovering its popular electoral support of close to 70 per cent.

The cooling measures may have deflated the potential housing bubble for now, but they have not resolved the fundamental contradictions in the universal housing-asset social security system. For the housing asset to be able to fund the retirement needs of the homeowner, the nominal price of the flat must necessarily improve from the time of purchase to retirement; the price must at least keep up with annual inflation rate, if not do better. Over the approximately thirty-year period between purchase of the flat and retirement, compounding the annual rates of increase, even without factoring in the profit motive of the homeowner, the monetary value of the flat would be quite hefty, as reflected in the prices of resale flats. As the public housing market is a closed one constituted of citizens and permanent residents, the gains made in the resale flat by existing homeowners are in fact transferred as a financial burden to the purchasers, who are generally of a younger generation and often new entrants into the housing market. As the state is the monopoly supplier of housing to the population, it can move quickly to deflate resale prices through increased supply and pricing of new subsidized flats. Yet, the government is unable to price new flats at levels that would aggressively bring down the price of resale flats. To do so would cause a forced write-down of the nation's capital that is embedded in the total public housing stock and, at the individual level, potentially jeopardize the lives of present and future retirees, with severe economic and political consequences for the ruling government. Consequently, instead of pricing new public housing flats at affordable levels relative to the actual financial abilities of the new entrants into the housing market, the flats are priced at levels affordable only with significant cash grants from the government in order to maintain the values of existing flats at "tolerable" levels. Ultimately, existing homeowners will continue to seek financial gains from the value of their public housing flats, while the government acts to restrain the rate of price increases and adds a hefty cash grant as part of the subsidies for new public housing flats. Selling of new public housing flats is thus, in effect, a very significant social transfer, which is not reflected in the social welfare budget. The balancing of prices of public housing within the retirement needs of existing homeowners and affordability for new entrants into the housing market thus requires constant vigilance on the part of the public housing authority.

Conclusion

The social democracy of the early PAP government caused it to be committed to the universal provision of affordable public housing. However, instead of providing rental housing like the social housing created in immediate post-war Europe, the government has encouraged the citizens in the entire nation to purchase subsidized public housing on a ninety-nine-year lease by drawing on their compulsory social security savings. Every public housing flat thus holds the retirement capital of its owner. This universalized public housing homeownership program shows that property ownership of public housing is, like all property ownership, more than just a consumption good. It is also an investment good and thus subject to profit motive. However, being highly regulated in its market transaction, a public housing unit is not open to speculative flipping by its owner. For the overwhelming majority of ordinary Singaporeans, the drive to accrue property value and accumulate capital through public housing ownership is, therefore, due less to quick profit speculation than the necessity to prepare for the point in time when the housing unit can be monetized to meet retirement needs, particularly in view of extended longevity in a developed Singapore.

On the part of the government, being able to provide housing for all the citizens, except for the top 10 per cent of income strata, has delivered to the ruling People's Action Party massive political legitimacy and longevity in parliamentary power; the party has governed Singapore without interruption since 1959. However, having encouraged Singaporeans to invest in their public housing flats, the PAP government is obliged to bear the responsibility of ensuring the security of the investment. For this reason, administrative rules and regulations have been introduced to ensure that the prices of existing public housing units are protected and increased. Using the same rules and regulations, Singaporeans have strategized to improve their capital accumulation through public housing homeownership, which has inflated the cost of public housing and raised concerns about its affordability for future generations of new homeowners. When affordability has become a political issue, countermeasures have been taken to cool the inflationary housing market, but these measures have not been allowed to cause prevailing prices to drop to levels that would destroy the national capital formation embodied in the entire public housing stock and also jeopardize the financial interests and the retirement funding of existing homeowners. Thus, when cooling measures begin to threaten the interests of existing homeowners, other measures are taken to prevent the market from falling precipitously. Such measures include cutting the supply of available housing units and easing housing mortgages and loans. The government is thus permanently engaged in balancing a set of contradictory demands: (1) supplying sufficient new flats and keeping them affordable for first-time homeowners and low-income families without turning public housing into a welfare entitlement; (2) preventing an oversupply of new flats that might hurt market values of existing and resale flats; and (3) increasing property values of existing flats and resale prices to ensure that retirees have sufficient funds for retirement, while closely watching the build-up of inflationary bubbles that might jeopardize affordability of resale prices to potential buyers. Failure to maintain a balance of the competing demands through periodic intervention in the market will incur a political cost. In sum, in spite of the housing market sector being severely circumscribed and controlled by actions of the government/state, rather than by a free market, profit-making through public housing ownership is, perhaps ironically, practically guaranteed by the state, dovetailing the needs of ordinary Singaporeans.

REFERENCES

Asher, M.G. (1991). *Social adequacy and equity of the social security arrangements in Singapore*. Times Academic Press.

Asher, M.G., & Nandy, A. (2008). Singapore's policy responses to aging, inequality and poverty: An assessment. *International Social Security Review*, 61(1), 41–60. https://doi.org/10.1111/j.1468-246X.2007.00302.x

Castells, M., Goh, L., & Kwok, R.Y.-W. (1990). *The Shek Kip Mei syndrome: Economic development and public housing in Hong Kong and Singapore*. Pion Limited.

Central Provident Fund Study Group. (1986). Special issue – Report of the Central Provident Fund Study Group. *Singapore Economic Review*, 31(1), 1–108.

Chang, R. (2012, 26 July). PRs in the HDB market: Boon or bane? *The Straits Times*. https://ifonlysingaporeans.blogspot.com/2012/07/prs-in-hdb-market-boon-or-bane.html

Chia, N.C. (2011, 1 March). *Retirement financing options for Singaporeans: Issues and challenges* [Paper presentation]. Launch of the Singapore Research Nexus, National University of Singapore.

Chua, B.H. (1997). *Housing and political legitimacy: Stakeholding in Singapore*. Routledge.

Chua, B.H. (2003). Maintaining housing values under the condition of universal home ownership. *Housing Studies, 18*(5), 765–80. https://doi.org/10.1080/02673030304260

Department of Statistics Singapore. (2006, March). 2005 in brief. *Statistics Singapore Newsletter*. https://www.singstat.gov.sg/-/media/files/publications/reference/newsletter/ssnmar2006.pdf

Department of Statistics Singapore. (2012, March). 2011 in brief. *Statistics Singapore Newsletter*. https://www.singstat.gov.sg/-/media/files/publications/reference/newsletter/ssnmar2012.pdf

Department of Statistics Singapore. (2019). Stock of foreign direct investments in Singapore, annual. https://data.gov.sg/dataset/foreign-direct-investment-in-singapore-by-country-region-stock-as-at-year-end-annual

Doling, J., & Ronald, R. (2010). Home ownership and asset-based welfare. *Journal of Housing and the Built Environment, 25*, 165–73. https://doi.org/10.1007/s10901-009-9177-6

Edelstein, R.H., & Lum, S.K. (2003). Housing prices, wealth effects, and the Singapore macroeconomy. *Journal of Housing Economics, 13*(4), 342–67. https://doi.org/10.1016/j.jhe.2004.09.006

Haila, A. (2017). Institutionalization of "the property mind." *International Journal of Urban and Regional Research, 41*(3), 500–7. https://doi.org/10.1111/1468-2427.12495

Heng, J. (2014, 12 June). Let HDB landlords enjoy their rent. *The Straits Times*. https://www.straitstimes.com/opinion/let-hdb-landlords-enjoy-their-rent

Heng, J. (2015, 18 September). HDB incurs $2.02b deficit in last FY. *The Straits Times*. https://www.straitstimes.com/singapore/hdb-incurs-202b-deficit-in-last-fy

Lee, C. (2011, 25 October). Housing affordability key to good parenting. *The Straits Times*, 24.

Lee, H.L. (2010, 29 August). National Rally Day speech. https://www.pmo.gov.sg/Newsroom/prime-minister-lee-hsien-loongs-national-day-rally-2010-speech-english

Lee, H.L. (2011, 20 October). Speech by Prime Minister Lee Hsien Loong at the debate on the president's address, 20 October 2011 at Parliament. https://www.pmo.gov.sg/newsroom/speech-prime-minister-lee-hsien-loong-debate-presidents-address-20-october-2011

Lee, X.E. (2017, 2 May). Losses in "at least half of Sentosa Cove home sales." *The Straits Times*. https://www.straitstimes.com/business/property/losses-in-at-least-half-of-sentosa-cove-home-sales

Low, L., & Aw, T.C. (1997). *Housing a healthy, educated and wealthy nation through the CPF*. Times Academic Press.

Ong, C. (2014a, 1 July). Too early to relax property cooling measures, says MND. *The Straits Times*. https://www.straitstimes.com/singapore/housing/too-early-to-relax-property-cooling-measures-says-mnd

Ong, C. (2014b, 4 July). Is the time ripe to lift property cooling measures? *The Straits Times*. https://www.straitstimes.com/opinion/is-the-time-ripe-to-lift-property-cooling-measures

Phang, S.Y. (2013). Public housing – Appreciating assets? In K.S. Hock & L. Chan-Hoong (Eds.), *Singapore perspectives 2012*. Institute of Policy Studies.

Phang, S.Y, & Helble, M. (2016). Housing policies in Singapore. [ADBI Working paper, No. 559]. Asia Development Bank Institute (ADBI). https://www.econstor.eu/bitstream/10419/161439/1/852480318.pdf

Saunders, P. (1990). *A nation of homeowners*. Unwin and Hyman.

Sim, L.L., Lum, S.K., & Malone-Lee, L.C. (2002). Property rights, collective sales and government intervention: Averting a tragedy of the anticommons. *Habitat International*, 26(4), 457–70. https://doi.org/10.1016/S0197-3975(02)00021-8

Tan, M. (2014, 2 July). Home prices continue to dip in Q2. *The Straits Times*. https://forums.condosingapore.com/showthread.php/22193-Home-prices-continue-to-dip-in-Q2

Teoalida. (n.d). Housing Singapore: List of HDB SERS sites. https://www.teoalida.com/singapore/serslist/

The Economist. (2017, 6 July). The high life: Why 80% of Singaporeans live in government-built flats. *The Economist*. https://www.economist.com/asia/2017/07/06/why-80-of-singaporeans-live-in-government-built-flats

The Straits Times. (2017, 24 March). Don't assume all old HDB flats will become eligible for Sers, cautions Lawrence Wong. *The Straits Times*. https://www.straitstimes.com/singapore/housing/dont-assume-all-old-hdb-flats-will-become-eligible-for-sers-cautions-lawrence-wong

Urban Redevelopment Authority (URA). (2001). *Concept plan 2001*. Urban Redevelopment Authority.

Wong, A., & Yeh, S.H.K. (Eds.). (1985). *Housing a nation: 25 years of public housing in Singapore*. Housing and Development Board.

Yeo, S.J. (2014, 28 June). Queenstown area set for biggest Sers project to date. *The Straits Times*. https://ifonlysingaporeans.blogspot.com/2014/06/queenstown-area-set-for-biggest-sers.html

Afterword

ALAN SMART

This is an opportune time for a book on the speculative city, although perhaps it has always been a good time. Real estate speculation is on the minds and agendas of urban residents and managers around the world. In cities with particularly high housing costs, there are widespread concerns about foreign speculators driving up prices and distorting the kind of housing produced, resulting in landscapes characterized by simultaneity of empty luxury housing and growing numbers of homeless on the streets or in tiny subdivided flats (see Hamnett, Lau, chapters 7 and 8, this volume). Precariously employed youth compete for a shrinking supply of (relatively) affordable housing. The impact of urban speculation is intensified by new technologies, including Airbnb, securitization of property investments, and cheaper information and money transfer systems that allow ordinary citizens to more easily purchase foreign property. The rich case studies in this book provide a broad context for thinking about these issues and dissecting speculation to find its global similarities and diversities.

Speculation has been central to urbanization, if not since inception, at least for many centuries, as the editors, as well as Susan Fainstein and Johannes Novy (chapter 1, this volume), remind us. Simultaneously dealing with the urgency, novelty, and historical continuity of speculation is one of the many virtues of this book. Only with careful attention to the urban past can we decide what might be new about speculation in contemporary cities. For Fainstein and Novy (chapter 1, this volume), there has been an intensification of speculation since the twentieth century. The share of mortgages in bank lending in seventeen OECD (Organisation for Economic Co-operation and Development) countries rose from 30 to 60 per cent between 1870 and 2010, while in the United Kingdom, mortgage lending was 16 per cent of total lending in 1928, compared to 63 per cent in 2007 (Hofman & Aalbers, 2019). Fainstein and

Novy (chapter 1, this volume, p. 23) stress the blurring of distinctions between property and other investments. Investors can now buy and sell shares of a piece of property without involvement in development and management. Invention of the corporation as a legal person freed capital investment without liability; new financial technologies since the 1970s have facilitated wide public involvement in property investment through vast pension funds. The traditional illiquidity of real estate has been greatly reduced, allowing it to take its place in the pantheon of core investment asset classes (Hofman & Aalbers, 2019).

Our futures are dependent on the directions and dreams of real estate markets. Beliefs about inevitable urban decline can prompt disinvestment, sometimes institutionalized as the redlining of problem areas, which generates a market for speculative ideas about revitalization through urban renewal and other governmental programs. Alternatively, real estate booms can generate their own self-reinforcing dynamics, "irrational exuberance," or simply urgency to get a foot into the property market before it becomes too unaffordable. Urban planning involves authoritative forms of representation that choose, or mediate, between contesting place-narratives, whether a neighbourhood is a slum needing revitalization or a vibrant ethnic community. Urban speculation shares these characteristics. A convincing plot about bottomless demand in East Asia for real estate in safe overseas harbours or about the attraction of lofts and inner city life among the "creative class" channels housing markets if the story is convincing, or thought to be convincing, to other investors.

City branding is a key dimension of local governmental storytelling. Governments speculate their assets, hoping to increase future revenues and attract external investments. In tax-increment financing, assumptions are made about possible future increases in tax revenues resulting from public-private cooperation on infrastructure. Public-private cooperation has become increasingly central to urban governance in North America and elsewhere (Fainstein and Novy, chapter 1, this volume, p. 26). In Hong Kong, Singapore, and China, however, distinct forms of urban speculation are enabled by heavy governmental control over land; private speculation is thereby focused by government decisions about land supply and public housing provision (Woodworth, Lau, Chua, chapters 5, 8, and 9, this volume).

As Chua Beng Huat (chapter 9, this volume) demonstrates, ordinary people become involved in real estate speculation to finance their own livelihoods or retirements. When public housing homeowners in Singapore cannot enhance their wealth by strategic property transactions, the "responsibility of translating their housing asset into adequate retirement funds falls on the government." The Singapore government actively intervenes in housing markets to protect prices and ensure continual modest increases. Such policies and practices encourage housing bubbles and reduced affordability, creating complex pressures on Singapore's government to both use public housing resales as a basis for retirement and restrict the excesses of real estate development.

Max Woodworth (chapter 5, this volume) shows that involvement of ordinary people and small-scale developers with informal finance helps shape urban growth in China. By turning urbanization into a "mass speculative event, significant numbers of people are drawn into the city's growth for personal pecuniary gain and become invested in the fortunes of the local state's urbanization agenda" (p. 150). The wealth effect, where gains on the stock market increase consumption, thereby stimulating the economy, has been shown to be smaller than the housing wealth effect, perhaps because of the immediacy for ordinary people of knowing that their home has increased in value, even when they don't intend to sell (Smart & Lee, 2003). The high level of second mortgages, which housing inflation encouraged, frequently used for luxuries like boats and holidays, was an important factor in the subprime mortgage boom and collapse.

Escalating housing prices can also facilitate individual real estate speculation. In Hong Kong in the late 1890s, "news about the threat of 'poor Europeans' being dispossessed by wealthy Chinese" appeared in the local English press, "prompting debates over the need to implement new legislation to protect the interests of the 'white middle class'" (Chu, 2012, p. 114). One response was an effort to create a "European Reservation" in Kowloon to complement the one already existing at the Peak (currently the world's most expensive housing area). This episode presages a narrative that has attracted massive media attention in recent decades. Hong Kong's negotiated 1997 return to Chinese sovereignty created great concern, even panic, caused by speculation about disastrous futures among the wealthy and middle classes, many of whom sought a safe haven in Canada, Australia, and elsewhere. Selling a modest flat in Hong Kong could purchase much more house in these countries. The efforts of Hong Kong people to avoid a risky future, or at least to have an insurance policy in the form of a second passport, created a political and cultural confrontation that continues to this day. In Canada, the assets of Hong Kong migrants, combined with their pursuit of prestigious neighbourhoods with good schools, encouraged them to buy in areas previously controlled by wealthy Vancouver Anglo elites. This phenomenon created a moral panic about "monster homes" destroying culturally valued landscapes solely for the pursuit of profit.

Hong Kong migrants, and the property developers behind them, were accused of seeing place simply as having a monetary value, rather than the use values of the established (elite, Anglo) community, and of destroying this carefully cultivated sense of place through cutting down trees and demolishing homes to replace them with "monster homes" (Smart & Smart, 1996). The perception of speculative real estate activity by Hong Kong migrants "greatly exacerbated racism and contributed to the racialization of space and the ongoing struggles over spatial hegemony" in Vancouver (Mitchell, 2004, p. 68). Similar narratives about money from the mainland of China are endemic in contemporary Hong Kong, Sydney, and elsewhere. Accusations of immoral and unpatriotic speculation directed at ethnic minorities have a long and tragic history, as Max Weber (2013) noted in his discussion of "pariah capitalism" and Daniel Chirot and Anthony Reid (2011) showed in their edited volume comparing the overseas Chinese in Southeast Asia to Jews in Eastern Europe.

We should not, however, restrict our thinking about the speculative city to real estate investment. Contemporary forms of urban entrepreneurialism are strongly influenced by heightened levels of intercity competition and the need for cities to find ways to forge roles for themselves in a globalized and increasingly digitized world. Encouraging external speculation on a city as an emerging global, liveable, or creative city is a key reason for sponsoring mega-events. Olympics or Expos can unleash massive amounts of speculative redevelopment of undervalued urban space (Olds, 1998; Zhang and He, chapter 4, this volume). The branding of cities, their marketing through condensing slogans and labels, tries to encourage speculation in particular cities or regions. As the leaders of Dubai and Doha speculate about new paths to prosperous futures for their cities beyond fossil fuels, international investors speculate on their prospects and vulnerabilities (Alraouf, chapter 3, this volume). Beyond selling places, however, there is a higher level of speculation, one that aims to profitably speculate on the very nature of the city.

Ugo Rossi and Arturo Di Bella (2017) diagnose start-up urbanism 2.0 as a new variant of entrepreneurial urbanism. It involves transformed unions between the urban and the technological. Rossi and Di Bella suggest that local public-private partnerships promote environmental interventions precisely to enhance the milieu, the context, of start-ups in order to create a more vibrant start-up scene and encourage aggregation economies like that in Silicon Valley. This union involves new "urban-technological fixes," which promise intelligent solutions to contemporary crises and challenges. Entrepreneurial proponents, in the public and private sectors, proclaim a new urban revolution is emerging, based on the pursuit of the common good through the development of a more collaborative ethos rather than (just) the crass realization of profit, tapping into the inherent dynamism and creativity of city living. Although data-based urban management is presented as a win/win solution that solves problems of both efficiency and ecology, the dominance of private sector contracts and proprietary technologies means that it can be, in practice, a way of coopting private creativity (which can become intellectual property rights under certain circumstances), an attack upon and exploitation of what Michael Hardt and Antonio Negri (2009) call the urban "commonwealth," which produces "the positive externalities" created in contemporary cities.

According to Hardt and Negri (2009), these positive externalities are the product of "biopolitical labor." Urban vitality diminishes when the common – the positive collective outcomes of the externalities of work and community found in sociocultural systems of communication, scientific knowledges, and metropoles – is destroyed or made into private, often branded, property (p. 145). The common "exists in and is put to work by broad, open social networks. The creation of value and the accumulation of the common, then, both refer to an expansion of social productive powers" (p. 83). Tapping into social networks through surveillance and social media results in the channelling of big data into the development of artificial intelligence (AI) systems, so that, as a result, enclosing the urban commons is not just local, nor are its consequences parochial. Rather, the tech giants, particularly the BAT (Baidu, Alibaba, Tencent) of China, are using urban big data in a national version of testbed urbanism (Halpern, 2015), developing urban management platforms that can be exported. By doing so, they are speculating on the idea of the urban itself, in the creativity of urban situations, while selling lucrative management services and software (Zhang and He, chapter 4, this volume). Knowledge-based urban development (Alraouf, chapter 3, this volume) may be seen as facilitating new oligopolies. In the new age of capitalist trusts, a handful of global firms dominate intellectual property concentrations. They are widely seen to patrol "kill zones" around their core areas of interest. In these zones, start-ups are acquired or sabotaged by offering competing services free or as part of anti-competitive bundles of services. Speculative exploitation of big cities as a pre-eminent source of big data is leading to oligopolies that damage the milieus and ways of thinking they draw on for new innovations.

Digitally mediated speculation returns us to the problem of global homogenization, even if in a rather different way than in the "Coca-colonization" version of American cultural imperialism. Global algorithms create a different, but fundamentally threatening, form of global convergence, with automated inequalities lacking in transparency and often revealing hidden biases. Machine learning versions of AI remove the need for specifically programmed algorithms, other than those that afford learning from a source of sufficiently big data. In discussions of the risk of "autonomous killer robots," one proposal is that autonomous systems should be explainable: "Humans should be able to understand how a machine took a decision when things go wrong" (Taming, 2019, p. 17). It seems reasonable to apply this principle to machine learning AI that deploys policing resources or allocates welfare, given the damage that these autonomous systems can also do.

Only one or a few AI platforms may dominate once initial competition is resolved, resulting in common management platforms dominating urban futures wherever governments can afford to buy into the systems. This tendency seems to amplify Fainstein and Novy's (chapter 1, this volume) conclusion that "the physical form of the speculative city does not vary much from place to place." At the same time, property speculation also "produces uneven development. When property markets are hot, small businesses and low-income people are pushed out. In slumps, vacancies and abandonment take hold."

Financial technologies are also changing the speculative terrain. More broadly, there are claims that our economies, societies, cities, and lives have become progressively more financialized. This financialization thesis is key to claims that cities have become more speculative. For Mayra Mosciaro and colleagues (chapter 2, this volume), financialization demands more liquid commodities for comparing to other investments (p. 45). Financial penetration of the everyday lifeworld is seen in the way investors conceptualize real estate investments as "just another asset class," while more homeowners see their decisions largely in investment terms. More generally, financialization can be defined as "increasing dominance of financial actors, markets, practices, measurements and narratives, at various scales, resulting in a structural transformation of economies, firms, states and households" (Aalbers, 2016, p. 2).

Exchange values eclipse the use values of homes in governmental decisions (Logan & Molotch, 2007), encouraging us to see our places in commercial terms, so we might "cut our losses" rather than work to save a troubled neighbourhood. Financialization is one current within entrepreneurial urbanism, leading to a situation in which "entrepreneurial strategies are increasingly realized through financially mediated means and in conjunction with credit market actors, agencies, and intermediaries" (Peck & Whiteside, 2016, p. 5).

Again, claims for novelty need caution. Speculative housing provision was key to Fordism from the Great Depression to the 1970s:

suburbanization enhanced consumer demand and fostered self-reinforcing growth. New Deal programs made private homeownership available to more of the US population through government mortgage guarantees and road-building programs. Increased savings in the postwar period fuelled the housing boom. Residential mortgage debt increased from US$17.7 billion to US$208.7 billion between 1946 and 1965, facilitating homeownership for more than 60 per cent of the population (Florida & Feldman, 1988). Suburbs were the clearest example of the second level of urban speculation – not in particular places but in a particular kind of place, low-density automobile-based suburbs – by government as well as private developers and builders. The suburbs were also ground zero for the subprime mortgage meltdown, which brought down the world's financial system and substantial portions of the US middle class. Those tempted into speculative consumption based on second mortgages were first to lose when the bubble burst. While big banks and other financial institutions were "too big to fail," ordinary people had to be protected from "moral hazard," the risk of encouraging risky investment through insurance and bailouts (Smart, 2013).

I prefer a regulationist reading of financialization. The key assumption for regulation theory is that capitalism is a force for change without inherent regulatory principles (Aglietta, 1998). A regime of accumulation is a system of production, distribution, exchange, and consumption. Capitalism is a diverse family of regimes of accumulation, where most production and distribution are organized by formally equal individuals contracting to buy and sell products for profit and provide labour for wages. Crises arise from imbalances of power between those who control capital and their employees, resulting in insufficient demand for production increases that are necessary for continued growth. Declining profits and recessions lead to overproduction and underconsumption. The mechanisms that overcome such conflicts are the mode of regulation: institutions that try to keep distortions within limits compatible with social cohesion (Aglietta, 1998).

Robert Boyer (2000) sees two outcomes of financialization. With a critical mass of assets, there may be a virtuous system of growth where raising the rate of profit at the expense of wages can adequately fuel demand, because demand is based more on returns to assets rather than wages. If financialization occurs in an economy dominated by wages, a shift to greater profits has a negative effect due to inadequate demand, leading to instability (Boyer, 2000). When asset-based incomes are greater than wages, however, a push for increased rates of profit may be consistent with growth. Most nations lack the conditions for stable financialized growth regimes, so financialization leads to financial instability, such as seen in the 1997 Asian financial crisis and earlier in most of the Global South, and after 2007, in the Global North. The only likely exceptions Boyer identifies are the United States, Britain, and Canada, where wealth in relation to households' disposable income is particularly great. The 2007 crisis doesn't disprove Boyer's thesis but rather suggests adequate regulatory regimes are far from being in place; monetary institutions continue to increase instability by allowing bubbles to form.

Promotion of homeownership fostered capitalist values of individual property ownership and encouraged hard work to support expanded consumption. Mortgages and other consumer debt to fill homes with the requirements of modernity, such as washers and dryers, illustrate a different meaning of financialization as a process of colonizing or penetrating people's lifeworlds. Social talk about housing prices both reflects the "housing myth" that prices always go up (Aalbers, 2015) and reinforces it, at least until something like the subprime crisis undermines it. Yet, after a drop in homeownership rates, financialization in housing continues, and homes as financial assets continue to powerfully shape life chances and economic development.

Hong Kong is an early example of a finance-driven regime of accumulation. Throughout the 1990s, an average of over 30 per cent of government revenues came from land sales and related taxes (see Lau, chapter 8, this volume, for current issues around land sales). Revenues that indirectly accrue from real estate magnify their importance. An average of 68 per cent of fixed capital formation between 1980 and 1987 was from investment in property. The repercussions include heightened inequality and social exclusion, encouraging the population to "get in on the action" despite the consequences of unaffordable housing. Hong Kong is a useful case study because, as a small, liberal city-state, it has never been able to rely on domestic consumption to drive economic expansion. It has always had to make its way on a global stage of trade and finance. Real estate has for a long time been a central preoccupation of investors, government, and citizens alike. While these characteristics do not make Hong Kong a typical case, the city could serve as an early warning system for some possible implications of trends that are less well developed in most other localities. If so, we have serious challenges in our futures, such as unaffordable housing, now even more expensive per square metre than in London.

Annelore Hofman and Manuel Aalbers (2019, p. 91) agree with Alan Smart and James Lee (2003) that one limitation of Robert Boyer's regulationist theory of financialization, as well as a limitation of many other analyses of finance-dominated regimes, is its neglect of real estate.

Consequently, the authors argue that the United Kingdom, and likely other countries, can now "best be characterized as a finance- *and* real estate-driven regime rather than merely a finance-led regime" (Hofman & Aalbers 2019, p. 90). But they disagree with Smart and Lee (2003) that it is useful to consider the stabilizing mode of regulation to also be based on property in Hong Kong, arguing that it is better to see real estate "as part of the accumulation regime, which is embedded in a neoliberal mode of regulation" (p. 91). However, this view neglects the vast control of the Hong Kong government, much greater than in the United Kingdom, over land and real estate, and the way in which the government often responds to accumulation and legitimation crises by modulating public housing provision and by making the world's most unaffordable housing system (Lau, chapter 8, this volume) socially and politically sustainable by maintaining one of the world's largest public housing systems. Chua's account of Singapore (chapter 9, this volume) also suggests that real estate operates as much as a mode of regulation as a regime of accumulation. For local governments in the mainland of China, real estate has been a key driver of accumulation, but there are glimmerings of comparable developments where the provision of affordable housing has become indispensable to the continued expansion of finance- and real estate–driven accumulation regimes. Rebalancing from exports and investment to domestic consumption seems to be recapitulating a kind of Fordism. Whether the property and consumption dependence of China's contemporary growth regime is sustainable, in a context of rapidly increasing inequality and poorly developed pensions, remains to be seen. The tensions and contradictions of the current situation are certainly apparent: as Woodworth (chapter 5, this volume) describes, informal financial markets in China are crucial for real estate expansion in Ordos but coexist uneasily with the "central government's strong desire for macro-economic control and social stability" (p. 138). Inconsistent local government approaches to informal finance mean local officials are "prepared to turn a blind eye to illegal, usurious, or risky non-bank lending practices if they provide needed capital to local firms. Indeed, lending of all types is generally accepted until it triggers a crisis and prompts enforcement of rules that earlier were openly flouted." Finance-driven systems regimes would need more effective modes of regulation to avoid both bubbles and crashes.

Future trajectories – imagined, dreamed of, or feared – for cities are inevitably speculative, but on such speculations, massive fortunes are risked, won, and lost. The potential dystopic consequences of finance-driven regimes of accumulation are even more frightening. The key implication of Robert Boyer's model is that, for such economies to be stable, they rely more on economic demand than those with assets.

What does this portend for those without assets, no longer central to the state's growth strategies, particularly those without stable, or any, jobs, the increasing ranks of what has been called the "precariat"? Barring nightmarish *Soylent Green* scenarios, they would seem primarily to be a security concern, particularly in nations with easy access to firearms. To accompany a finance-driven regime of accumulation, we might expect, and perhaps are already beginning to see, the emergence of a wealth-based mode of regulation. Some of the features of this social formation might include what Neil Smith (1996) referred to as the revanchist city: increased security for the elite and repression for the excluded, combined with hegemonic legitimation of the necessity for greater inequality. An element of this social formation, which would seem to offer a replacement for the redistributive functions of the Fordist welfare state, could be the expansion of the employment of the working class in security roles: security guards, corrections officers, and police domestically; and border patrols, armed forces, and military contractors internationally. More progressive variants are so far mostly dreams, such as the Green New Deal, and experiments, such as guaranteed income systems. But in a world of ever more capable AI and robots, relying on wages rather than returns on assets to support demand seems increasingly non-viable, and new visions are urgently needed. How will our cities be transformed to meet new needs and new possibilities? We can only speculate.

REFERENCES

Aalbers, M.B. (2015). The great moderation, the great excess and the global housing crisis. *International Journal of Housing Policy*, 15(1), 43–60. https://doi.org/10.1080/14616718.2014.997431

Aalbers, M.B. (2016). *The financialization of housing: A political economy approach*. Routledge.

Aglietta, M. (1998). Capitalism at the turn of the century: Regulation theory and the challenge of social change. *New Left Review*, 232, 41–90. https://newleftreview.org/issues/i232

Boyer, R. (2000). Is a finance-led growth regime a viable alternative to Fordism? A preliminary analysis. *Economy and Society*, 29(1), 111–45. https://doi.org/10.1080/030851400360587

Chirot, D., & Reid, A. (Eds.). (2011). *Essential outsiders: Chinese and Jews in the modern transformation of Southeast Asia and Central Europe*. University of Washington Press.

Chu, C. (2012). *Speculative modern: Modern forms and the politics of property in colonial Hong Kong*. [Doctoral dissertation, University of California, Berkeley]. https://escholarship.org/uc/item/3r14d2r5

Florida, R., & Feldman, M. (1988). Housing in US Fordism: The class accord and postwar spatial organization. *International Journal of Urban and Regional Research*, 12(2), 187–210. https://doi.org/10.1111/j.1468-2427.1988.tb00449.x

Halpern, O. (2015). *Beautiful data: A history of vision and reason since 1945*. Duke University Press.

Hardt, M., & Negri, A. (2009). *Commonwealth*. Harvard University Press.

Hofman, A., & Aalbers, M.B. (2019). A finance- and real estate-driven regime in the United Kingdom. *Geoforum*, 100, 89–100. https://doi.org/10.1016/j.geoforum.2019.02.014

Logan, J.R., & Molotch, H.L. (2007). *Urban fortunes: The political economy of place*. University of California Press.

Mitchell, K. (2004). *Crossing the neoliberal line: Pacific Rim migration and the metropolis*. Temple University Press.

Olds, K. (1998). Urban mega-events, evictions and housing rights: The Canadian case. *Current Issues in Tourism*, 1(1), 2–46. https://doi.org/10.1080/13683509808667831

Peck, J., & Whiteside, H. (2016). *Economic Geography*, 92(3), 235–68. https://doi.org/10.1080/00130095.2015.1116369

Rossi, U., & Di Bella, A. (2017). Start-up urbanism: New York, Rio de Janeiro and the global urbanization of technology-based economies. *Environment and Planning A: Economy and Space*, 49(5), 999–1018. https://doi.org/10.1177/0308518X17690153

Smart, A. (2013). Housing support for the "undeserving": Moral hazard, fires, and laissez-faire in Hong Kong. In M. Schlecker & F. Fleischer (Eds.), *Ethnographies of social support* (pp. 17–37). Palgrave Macmillan.

Smart, A., & Lee, J. (2003). Financialization and the role of real estate in Hong Kong's regime of accumulation. *Economic Geography*, 79(2), 153–71. https://doi.org/10.1111/j.1944-8287.2003.tb00206.x

Smart, A., & Smart, J. (1996). Monster homes: Hong Kong immigration to Canada, urban conflicts, and contested representations of space. In J. Caulfield & L. Peake (Eds.), *City lives and city forms: Critical research and Canadian urbanism* (pp. 33–46). University of Toronto Press.

Smith, N. (1996). *The new urban frontier: Gentrification and the revanchist city*. Routledge.

Taming terminators: How to tame autonomous weapons. (2019, 19 January). *The Economist*. https://www.economist.com/leaders/2019/01/19/how-to-tame-autonomous-weapons

Weber, M. (2013). *The Protestant ethic and the spirit of capitalism*. (S. Kalberg, Trans.). Routledge.

Contributors

Manuel B. Aalbers is professor of human geography at KU Leuven (Belgium), where he leads a research group on the intersection of real estate, finance, and states. He is the author of *Place, Exclusion, and Mortgage Markets* (2011) and *The Financialization of Housing: A Political Economy Approach* (2016), as well as the editor of *Subprime Cities: The Political Economy of Mortgage Markets* (2012). He has also published on redlining, social exclusion, neoliberalism, corporate financialization, the privatization of social housing, neighbourhood decline, and gentrification.

Ali A. Alraouf is an architect and urban designer focusing on research within the domain of theory, criticism, and creativity in architecture and urbanism. Alraouf acts as head of the capacity building, training, research, and development unit at the Ministry of Municipality and Environment (MME) in Qatar. He is a professor at HBK University in Qatar Education City and the leader of the Green Urbanism and Planning Group at Qatar Green Building Council (QGBC).

Marta Catalán Eraso is an architect and urban designer. She completed her PhD in the Division of Landscape Architecture at the University of Hong Kong, where she was also a faculty member. Her current research focuses on urban segregation and unequal living conditions, with a particular interest in transnational architectural and urban practices.

Cecilia L. Chu is an urban historian and associate professor in the Division of Landscape Architecture at the University of Hong Kong. Her research focuses on the social and cultural processes that shape the built environment and the production of their meanings and values. She is the author of *Building Colonial Hong Kong: Speculative Development and Segregation in the City* (2022). She is an editorial board member of the *Journal of Urban History* and the *Journal of the Royal Asiatic Society Hong Kong*.

Chua Beng Huat is concurrently professor of the Urban Studies Program, Yale-NUS College, and the Department of Sociology, National University of Singapore. He has an abiding interest in public housing policies and issues since a short stint as the director of the social research unit in the public housing authority of Singapore in the mid-1980s. His most recent book, *Liberalism Disavowed: Communitarianism and State Capitalism in Singapore* (2017), includes the chapter "Disrupting Private Property Rights: National Public Housing Program."

Susan S. Fainstein is a senior research fellow in the Harvard Graduate School of Design, where she was a professor of urban planning until 2012. She also taught at Columbia and Rutgers Universities and at the National University of Singapore. Her books include *The Just City* (2010); *The City Builders* (2001); *Restructuring the City* (1983); *Urban Political Movements* (1974); and various edited volumes. Her research focuses on planning theory, urban regeneration, and comparative public policy.

Chris Hamnett is emeritus professor of geography at King's College London and a visiting professor in the Department of Urban Planning, Renmin University, Beijing. He has held visiting appointments at Nuffield College Oxford; Sciences Po, Paris; George Washington University; Netherlands Institute of Advanced Studies; and UESTC, Chengdu. He has authored several books, including *Cities, Housing and Profits* (1989); *London: Unequal City* (2003); *Ethnicity, Class and Aspiration* (2011); and *Gentrification: Advanced Introduction* (2021).

Shenjing He is professor of urban studies in the Department of Urban Planning and Design at the University of Hong Kong. She has published widely on various topics of urban and housing studies, including urban redevelopment/gentrification, enclave urbanism, urban governance, housing inequalities, and rural-urban interface. Shenjing recently launched a research project to investigate the emerging forms of neighbourhood order, for example, gated communities featuring privileged access to education service, and another project examining multidimensional housing inequalities in pandemic-stricken megacities.

Mandy Lau is associate professor in the Department of Urban Planning and Design at the University of Hong Kong. She received her PhD and MPhil from the Department of Land Economy, University of

Cambridge, and her BSc in sociology from the London School of Economics. Her major research interests include affordable housing and intergenerational relations. Lau serves on the International Editorial Advisory Board of *Housing Studies*. She is secretary of the Asia-Pacific Network for Housing Research.

Mayra Mosciaro is an urban geographer working on financialization-related topics. In 2018, she defended her PhD as part of the Real Estate/Financial Complex research group. In her thesis, she investigated the relationship between real estate, state, and finance in Brazil and Italy, focusing on major urban redevelopment projects in the cities of Rio de Janeiro and Milan. Recently, as a postdoc, she has also engaged in debates associated with the financialization of infrastructures of social reproduction (especially health care) and its impacts on accessibility and provision.

Johannes Novy works as a senior lecturer in urban planning in the School of Architecture and Cities at the University of Westminster. His research interests cover urban and planning theory, urban (development) politics, urban tourism, and leisure consumption. In addition to being active in teaching and research, Johannes is a founding member of the Berlin-based urbanist collective *u-Lab, Studio für Stadt und Raumprozesse* and a member of the curatorial board of the International Building Exhibition Stuttgart Region *IBA2027*.

Alvaro Pereira works on research projects related to political economy, law, and territorial planning. He obtained his master's and PhD degrees at the Faculty of Law of the University of Sao Paulo and worked as a postdoctoral researcher at the Faculty of Architecture and Urbanism of the University of Sao Paulo. Currently, he is a professor of public law at the Law Department of the Federal University of Sao Paulo.

Alan Smart is a professor emeritus in the Department of Anthropology and Archaeology at the University of Calgary, Calgary, Canada. His research interests include political economy, housing, urban anthropology, anthropology of law, borders, zoonotic diseases, smart cities, and posthumanism. He is the author of *Making Room: Squatter Clearance in Hong Kong* (1992), *The Shek Kip Mei Myth* (2006), *Posthumanism* (co-author, Josephine Smart, 2017), and numerous articles.

Max D. Woodworth is associate professor of geography at Ohio State University whose research focuses on the intersection of urbanization and resource development. He has explored these themes through a long-term project focused on the transformations of China's Ordos region in the 2000s as it became a dominant hub in the country's gigantic coal-mining industry. His work has been published in the *Journal of Asian Studies*, the *International Journal of Urban and Regional Research*, *Cities*, and *Area*, among other journals.

Yunpeng Zhang is a postdoctoral research fellow based at KU Leuven, Belgium. His research explores the politics and lived experiences of managed speculative urbanization and the mechanisms of durable inequalities in China. Funded by the Research Foundation – Flanders (FWO), his ongoing research project investigates the rapid development of platform technology in China and the roles played by China's uneven geographies.

Index

Aalbers, Manuel B., 113, 181
Abu Dhabi, 70–1, 75, 78, 82–4
accessible spaces, 28
accoutrement, 77
additional development rights, 7, 53–7, 59, 64
administrative centralism, 161
advanced economies, 109
advanced industrialized countries, 134
affordable housing, 26–7, 37, 40–1, 196, 200, 202, 215
aging population, 225, 230
Al Jazeera, 90
Allon, Fiona, 10
Alraouf, Ali A., 7–8, 98
Andromeda Tower, 36
Ang Mo Kio, 233
Anhangabaú, 54
anti-speculation measures, 218
apartments: purpose-built, 183. *See also* mansion blocks
Arab solidarity, 75
Arab Spring, 75, 85, 101
Asia, 27, 109, 116
Asian cities, 28
Asian financial crisis, 201
Asia-Pacific region, 116
asset accumulation, 5, 11

asset-based regime of accumulation, 15
asset-based social security system, 228
asset classes, 23, 45
assetization, 45
Atlantis Resort, 80
Australia, 204
Austria, 28, 37
autocratic regimes, 75, 85
Aylesbury Estate, 196

Baer, William, 12
Bahrain, 70–2, 75–6, 87
bailouts, 124
bandwagon effect, 140
bankruptcies, 10, 181, 187
Battery Park City, 31
Belo Horizonte, Brazil, 47
Bermondsey, United Kingdom, 187
Bilbao effect, 25
blue collar workers, 9
bondholders, 24
boom and busts, 4, 22, 181
Boston, 196
Brazil, 7, 47, 49, 50, 55–6, 61, 65
Britain, 159, 180, 186, 221. *See also* United Kingdom
Brussels, 182

Budapest, 109
budgetary resources, 61
budget deficit, 86
Buffalo, 196
building rights, 55, 59, 62
business cycle, 22

Cairo, 89; Dubai by the Nile, 89; New Capital City, 89
Calatrava, Santiago, 60
Canary Wharf development, London, 33, 35
capital accumulation, 4, 12, 14, 87, 110, 112, 128, 226, 236
capital gains, 144, 151, 181, 194, 222, 228, 230
capitalist system, 11–12, 14, 110, 158
capital markets, 10, 45, 55, 112–14, 142
capital switching, 45, 110–14, 116, 119, 121, 127–8
carbon: footprints, 89; revenues, 71
casino-style capitalism, 14, 150
Castilian plateau, Spain, 155, 169
Catalán Eraso, Marta, 10, 181
Certificate of Additional Building Potential (CEPAC), 47–8, 53–64. *See also* Urban Operation, Brazil
Chengdu, Sichuan Province, China, 109, 142
Chicago, 73
China, 9, 109–11, 113–14, 117, 119, 123–5, 134–6, 138–9, 140, 142, 147, 150–1, 194, 200, 203; arable land, 135; Autonomous Region Government, 148; bureaucracy, 9; cash compensation for relocation, 145; central government, 123, 135; China Banking Regulatory Commission, 142; Communist Party, 115, 116, 162; construction land, 135; economic reform, 111, 117, 139, 142; 4 trillion RMB investment package, 124; fragmented authority, 115, 122; land-based speculative urbanization, 116; land-centred regime of accumulation, 110; land finance (*tudi caizheng*), 135; local state, 9, 33, 46, 56, 64, 115–16, 135, 150; market-oriented economy, 9; Provisional Regulations of the PRC on Bank Oversight (mutual assistance associations) (*huzu hui*), 138; rotating credit and savings associations (ROSCAs), 138–9
Chu, Cecilia L., 10, 181
Chua Beng Huat, 13
circuits of capital, 23, 111, 113; quaternary, 113; secondary, 3, 111–12, 119; tertiary, 111–12, 119
citizens: disadvantaged, 13, 216
citizenship, 77, 86–7, 102, 222
city branding, 9
city-making, 143, 146
Clerkenwell, 187–8
Cleveland, 196
closed-bid auctions, 222
coalitions, 45, 54, 61, 86, 150, 203
collaborative development, 77
collective consumption, 35, 117
collective identity, 101, 157
commercial banks, 124, 160
commodity production, 4, 111
community benefits, 25
community facilities, 40
Companhia de Desenvolvimento Urbano da Região Portuária (CDURP), 48, 51, 57–60, 64
concert halls, 25
concrete gold (Betongold), 23
condo flipping, 180
condominium, 9, 23–4, 180, 222, 226–8, 230, 235

construction: industry, 159; sector, 10, 141, 156, 160
cooling measures, 235, 237
corporate bonds, 24, 124
corporate towers, 9
corruption, 14, 86, 148, 155–6, 159, 160–1, 169, 170; 2018 Corruption Perceptions Index, 86
Cortés, Juanjo, 164, 166
council housing, United Kingdom, 195, 221
Court of Audits, 163
crash, 8, 14, 22, 84
creative cities, 71, 93, 96–7, 120–1, 127–9
creative class, 71, 94
creative district, 9
creative industry, 120, 127
creative labour, 127
credit markets, 24, 46
creditor, 10, 141, 144, 146, 149–50
crisis landscape, 168
crisis of capitalism, 15
cultural centres, 9, 125
cultural consumption, 111
cultural diversity, 121
cultural facilities, 6, 7, 123
cultural industry, 127, 129
cultural logics/rationalities, 11, 14, 157
culture-oriented urban function, 127
culture production, 129
Curitiba, Brazil, 47
CWZG, 188

Danube, Austria, 34, 36, 37
day-care facilities, 26
debt instruments, 24
debts, 14, 23–4, 53, 82, 84, 119, 135, 141, 155, 164, 185, 234; debt-servicing ratio, 234
default, 22, 84, 157

deflation, 22
deindustrialization, 22, 187
DEKA, 37
democracy, 74, 159
demolition, 27, 84, 118, 121–3, 125, 128, 145, 206, 210–11, 231
Deng Xiaoping, 117; southern tour, 117
depositor, 140–3, 149
depository insurance, 142
deregulation, 134, 160, 187
deserts, 70, 72, 79–80, 89
Detroit, 196
developing countries, 26–7
development rights, 38, 53, 55–6, 58, 201
development zones, 118, 147
discounted home prices, 145
discount formula, 225, 231, 234
disdained uses, 21
disintermediation, 24
disinvestment, 27
displacement, 7, 21, 26, 51, 62, 64, 124, 214; displaced households, 119; resettlement cost, 124
dispossession, 6, 123, 135, 140
Doha, Qatar, 8, 70–1, 74–5, 79, 91, 93–8, 100–2; Education City, 96–8, 100; knowledge-based economy, 96–8, 100; Museum of Islamic Art (MIA), 96; National Library, 96; Qatar National Museum, 96–7; Qatar Science and Technology Park, 96
domestic consumption, 120
domestic investment, 135
Donau City, Vienna, 28–9, 34, 36–8; Danube Flats, 37; Danube Platform (Donauplatte), 36; DC Tower, 37; IZD (Internationales Zentrum Donaustadt) tower, 36
Donaupark, 34

Dongsheng, 9, 144–5, 147–9
Donis, Fernando, 89
down payment, 141, 180, 223–4
dual housing market, 118–19
Dubai, 8, 27, 70–1, 75–7, 79–90, 95, 101–2; Burj-al-Khalifa complex, 81; Burj Khalifa Tower, 80; Center for Advanced Defense Studies (C4ADS), 86; Dubai Internet City, 81; Dubai Marina, 81; Dubai Media City, 81; Dubai Sports City, 81; fragmented planning, 89; Healthcare City, 81; International City, 81; Mall of the Emirates, 80; Mercato, 80; minister of state for happiness, 88; Mohammed Bin Rashid City, 89; money-laundering paradise, 85–6; New Capital City, 89; Palm Jumeirah, 81; Sheikh Zayed Road, 80
Dubai model, 8
Dubai Strategic Plan (2015), 79
Dutch Tulip Bubble (1636–37), 179
Dyos, Harold James, 179

East London, 193
East–West hub, Gulf region, 75
economic crisis, 148, 163
economic management, 112, 114
economic model, 158–9
educational facilities, 96, 168
educational services, 95
Ejin Horo, 145
elites, 8, 84, 96, 113, 116–17, 120, 126, 136, 150–1
el Pocero, 162. *See also* Hernando, Francisco Contreras
El Quiñón, 10, 155–7, 161–4, 166–71, 181; class tensions, 10, 155–7, 161–4, 166, 167–71, 181; collective future visions, 163; ONDE2000, 164, 166

Elsheshtawy, Yasser, 80, 82, 87
empty buildings, 86
entrepreneurial governance, 7, 54
entrepreneurialism, 35, 45. *See also* urban entrepreneurialism
entrepreneurial state, 39, 113
entrepreneurial strategies, 5, 46
entrepreneurial urbanism, 46
environment sustainability, 121
Europe, 6, 26–9, 34, 156, 159, 161, 236
European Union (EU), 159–60
event-media-corporate complex, 109
everyday life, 112, 224
eviction, 155, 200
excess supply of capital, 24
exchange value, 24, 62, 121, 128, 144, 147
expatriates, 78, 82, 86, 93–4, 102, 227
experts, 29, 48, 138
extraction-driven economic growth, 139
extra-institutional lending, 138
Ezquiaga, José María, 163

Fainstein, Susan, 6–7, 29n5, 51, 180–1
family life cycle, 224
farmers, 9, 116, 143, 144
favela, 49, 51, 60
feudal systems, 22
fictitious capital, 53, 61
finance-led development, 6, 14–5
financial assets, 7, 46–7, 55–6, 62, 64, 195
financial capital, 3–4, 46, 76, 112–13, 143, 157
financial capitalism, 3, 46
financial channels and technologies, 4
financial engineering, 46, 48, 50, 55, 63
financial institutions, 23–4, 45, 112–13, 124, 134, 136–8, 181, 222–3

financialization, 3–7, 10, 14, 45–7, 62, 112, 114, 134, 150–1, 157, 170, 181
financial logics, 5, 9, 112, 158
financial markets, 5, 10, 37, 45, 47, 138
financial meltdown, 124, 149
financial networks, 5, 136, 141, 144–5
financial products and services, 47, 112–13, 148, 156
financial regulations, 139, 234
financial risk and security, 6, 9, 11, 14, 64, 147, 170
financial system, 10
first-time homeowners, 233, 237
fiscal measures, 159
fiscal revenues, 117
flat break-ups, 11, 191–2, 196, 200
flat conversion, 192–3
flexibilization, 137
floor area ratios (FARs), 25, 55
floor areas, 25, 55, 125, 187, 225
foreclosure, 22
foreign direct investment (FDI), 232
foreign owners, 183
formal banks, 138–9, 141–3, 145, 148
fragmented property relations, 121
freehold lands/plots, 22, 222
Fuentes, Manuel, 163

garden city, 40
gated communities, 28, 223
gated regions, 81–2
GDP per capita, 127, 143
gentrification, 3, 6–7, 9, 23, 27, 39–40, 60, 62–4, 84, 129, 196
George, Henry, 21, 39
ghettoize, 27
ghost apartments, 25, 40
ghost city/town, 155
ghost town, 146, 168
global cities, 9, 73, 79, 223
global economy, 76, 135, 160

global financial crisis, 3, 14, 24, 70–1, 83, 87, 109, 134, 181
globalization, 61, 73, 80–1, 134–5
Global North, 7, 47, 65
global oil crisis, 72, 78
global recession, 223, 228
Global South, 7, 47
global value chain, 115
González, Isidoro, 166
government-controlled economy, 22
grassland restoration, 145
grassroots, 129, 214–15, 217; citizens, 215; organizations, 214; pro-grassroots political parties, 214
Greece, 158
green amenities, 26
growth machines, 45, 54, 126, 183
Guanabara Bay, Brazil, 49
Guangzhou, China, 109, 149
guaranteed loans, 25
Guizhou, China, 142
Gulf Cooperation Council (GCC), 72, 75, 87
Gulf region/states, 8, 71–2, 74–8, 86, 89–91, 101–2; conflicts, 15, 60, 75, 98, 111–16, 128, 137; economic prosperity, 71, 73, 77, 79; gradual urban development, 72; tribal rulers, 72

Haila, Anne, 39, 227, 229
Hamburg, Germany, 109
Hamnett, Chris, 11–12, 183
Handelsman, Harry, 187
Hardt, Michael, 244
Harvey, David, 3, 4, 9, 23, 35, 64, 110–14, 182
HDB upgraders, 223, 226
He, Shenjing, 9, 41
hedge, 24, 183, 228
hegemony, 115
Helsinki, Finland, 182

Hernando, Francisco Contreras, 155, 157, 162–4
high-end market/development, 25, 222–3
high-rise, 24, 28, 30, 36, 40, 90, 164, 221
high-value-added industries, 118
historic brownstones, 22, 30, 32
historic preservation, 25, 36
HKSAR Government, 202–3, 214–15
home improvement grant, 193
Hong Kong, 12–13, 73, 112, 180–2, 194, 199–212, 214–18, 221–2; aging housing stock, 210; Capital Investment Entrant Scheme, 201; Census and Statistics Department (CSD), 203–5, 212; Home Ownership Scheme (HOS), 201, 213, 215; land application list system, 201; Long Term Housing Strategy, 202–3, 214, 216; luxurious flats, 13; One-way Permit Holders, 203; private rental sector, 199, 202–4; Rating and Valuation Department (RVD), 203–4, 206–12; Thematic Household Surveys, 204
Hong Kong Island, 204, 209, 212
hot money, 23, 135
house price inflation, 11, 185, 225, 229, 233–4
housing bubble, 155, 160, 163, 235; burst of, 164, 170
housing needs, 12, 182, 195, 213–15, 224
housing shortage, 182, 184, 233
housing stock, 118, 129, 180–3, 193, 195, 235; domestic, 203, 206
Howard, Ebenezer, 40
Hoxton, United Kingdom, 187
Hsing, You-tien, 115
Huangpu River, Shanghai, 128
Hudson River, Manhattan, 29, 30

human rights, 88
hydrocarbon-based economy, 90, 92–3

iconic architecture, 8, 81. *See also* starchitecture
iconic development, 70, 72, 81–2. *See also* spectacular urbanism
ideological indoctrination, 110
idle savings, 144–5
illiquidity, 4
immigrants, 34, 86, 191, 193, 203, 232
immoral speculators, 10, 14
inadequately housed households (IHHs), 202
individual capitalists, 112
industrial buildings, 11, 22, 187, 192
industrial heritage, 122
industrialist, 9, 144
industrial land, 118, 120–3, 127–9
industrial landlords, 120, 122, 127–9
industrial manufacturing, 111, 120–1
industrial parks, 123, 127, 147
industrial production, 112, 116, 119
industrial relocation, 115, 118
inflation, 39, 126, 225, 233, 235
informal economy, 137, 146
informal finance, 9, 137–40, 144, 146–51; bubble, 150; circuits, 136, 145; schemes, 144, 149; system, 149
informal housing, 27
informality, 137
informal lending, 136, 138–41, 143, 148, 150
informal networks, 147
informal settlements/urban spaces, 51, 80
information asymmetries, 149
infrastructural investments, 49
infrastructure: finance, 5; networks, 111, 121, 124
inheritance, 221, 230

Index 263

inner city/urban area, 54, 61, 118, 182, 188, 196, 205, 211
Inner Mongolia, China, 134, 136, 142
institutional landlords, 11, 183–5
insurance pools, 23
intellectual property, 89
inter-class struggles, 113
interest rates, 23, 138, 140–1, 146, 159, 184
international capital flows, 7, 60
International Garden Festival, 34
International Monetary Fund (IMF), 158, 164
International Union of Architects, 89
internet and computer technology (ICT), 24
interpersonal loans, 9, 140–1
investment portfolios, 23
investors, 4, 6, 11, 21–4, 33, 36, 45, 48–9, 53, 55, 57, 62, 64, 81–2, 85–6, 124, 140, 143–7, 194, 201, 213, 234
inward investments, 118
Ireland, 181
Iron Curtain, 34
Islamism, 75

Jersey City, 7, 28–34, 40
Jewish Soup Kitchen for the Poor, 191–2
Jones Lang Lasalle, 124–6

Kangbashi, Ordos, 9, 145–7
Kanna, Ahmed, 80, 83
Keshavarzian, Arang, 81
Khaw Boon Wan, 231, 234
knowledge-based urban development (KBUD), 8, 71, 77–9, 95–8, 100–2
knowledge capital, 77
knowledge-driven industries, 79
knowledge economy, 8, 71, 75–7, 79, 90–1, 93, 95, 102

knowledge workers, 8, 71, 78–9, 94, 102
Kowloon, 204, 209, 212
Kuwait City, 70, 75

labour contracts, 137
labour deficit, 93
La Défense, 35
laissez-faire, 202
land acquisitions, 59, 140, 215
land banking, 23, 222
land development rights, 64
land enclosures, 114, 120
land governance, 119
land market, 22, 50, 115
landowners, 38–9, 161
land ownership, 49, 50, 58, 64, 114, 201
land recommodification, 110
land sales, 27, 201, 222
land speculation, 124, 160
land tenure, 114, 119
land use, 7, 12–13, 39, 50, 110, 114–15, 118, 120–1, 126, 188, 191, 215, 231
land values, 36, 39, 110, 116, 119
large-scale urban projects, 61
Lau, Mandy, 12–13, 180–1, 194
Le Corbusier, 40
Lee, Hsien Loong, 228, 233
Lee, Kuan Yew, 38
LeFrak, Samuel, 32
LeFrak Company, 32
Lincoln Tunnel, 32
liquefied natural gas (LNG), 70
liquid asset, 46, 134–5
Location, 21, 25, 30, 36, 196, 209, 225
Logan, John, 63
Loïc Wacquant, 13, 202, 216
London, 11, 26, 38, 79, 81, 179–80, 182–8, 191, 193–6, 200; Committee of Inquiry on flat-breakup, 186;

London (*cont'd*)
  foreign property owners, 183;
  Georgian and Victorian London, 179; loft conversion, 11–12, 187–8, 191–2, 196; low-quality accommodation, 193; Victorian houses, 11, 193
Long Island, New York, 34
long-term property investment, 180, 227
López, Isidro, 158–60
Los Angeles, 109
Louvre, Paris, 83
lower-income households, 205, 217, 228
lower-middle-income households, 208
low-rent flats, 206
low-rise, 25, 30, 32, 38, 206
low-skilled workers, 51
low-value space, 12, 192
luxury apartments, 200, 223
luxury housing, 13, 49, 201, 216

macro-economics, 155
Madrid, 10, 155–6, 166, 168, 170, 181–2
Malaysia, 194
Manama, Bahrain, 70, 75, 95
Manhattan, 29, 30–1, 33–4, 187–8
Manhattan Loft Corporation, 187
mansion blocks, 183–4, 186. *See also* apartments: purpose-built
marketization, 6, 26, 113, 117
Martín, José Luis, 162
Masdar City, 78, 83
master plan, 33, 36, 89
maximum floor area ratios (FARs), 55
mega-event syndrome, 109
megaprojects, 6–8, 23–5, 27–8, 32, 45, 70, 77, 81, 84, 87–8, 90
Melvin Simon & Associates, 32

microfinance, 9, 140, 143
micro-lending firms, 137, 142–3
middle-class, 51, 196, 217, 226–7, 234
Middle Eastern cities, 7, 71, 73, 75, 79–80, 82, 84, 86, 90, 96, 101
migrants, 118, 122, 146, 193, 200
migrants-cum-renters, 122
Mississippi and South Sea Bubbles (1720), 179
mixed-use districts/areas, 6–7, 49, 61
mobile workers, 28
mode of regulation, 15, 199
Molotch, Harvey, 63
money-laundering, 85–6
mortgage, 14, 134, 155, 160, 170, 223, 227, 233–4, 237; derivatives, 23, 181; market, 24, 136, 157, 181, 223; rates, 222; securities, 24
Mosciaro, Mayra, 7, 23, 245
multiple property ownership, 227, 229, 234
municipal government, 31, 51, 53–6, 110, 122–3, 145, 147
Muscat, 75
Muslims, 76

National Development Bank, China, 124
national economies, 134
negative equity, 229
neoliberal ideology, 26, 28
neoliberalism, 3, 6, 23, 45, 80
neoliberalization, 134
neoliberal urbanism, 3, 15, 135
Netherlands, the, 182
New Territories, Hong Kong, 209
new town development, 118
New York, 27–9, 31–4, 38, 73, 79, 81, 94, 187–8, 196; Mack-Cali Realty Corporation, 32
non-bank finance, 24, 136, 138–9
non-bank financial networks, 136

Index   265

non-bank lending, 139, 148
non-financial sectors, 5, 10
non-governmental actors, 214
non-recourse loans, 23
non-redistributive, 228
North America, 47
Novy, Johannes, 6–7, 51, 181, 241–2, 246
Nugee Report, 186

office space, 29, 32, 187
office towers, 27, 30, 49, 125
office workers, 146
oil industry, 81
oil prices, 72, 75–6, 78, 86
oil-producing economies, 71
oil revenues, 70, 75–6, 78
Olson, D.J., 179
Olympics, 109–10
Oman, 72, 75
ONDE2000, 164, 166
open space, 191
Ordos, 9, 134, 136–7, 139–51; coal-mining companies, 137; lending schemes, 141, 143, 146; money houses (*qianku, qianzhuang,* or *yinbei*), 138–43
Organized Crime and Corruption Reporting Project (OCCRP), 85
over-accumulation, 111–12
overbuilding, 15, 24, 146
overinvestment, 22
overseas buyers, 194–5
overseas financial investment, 194
overseas property investment ownership, 183
owner occupation, 183, 185

Paes, Eduardo, 52
Paris, 35, 51, 79, 109, 179, 182
Park Slope, 32
pawn broking, 140

pawnshops, 137
Penn-Central warehouses, 32
pension funds, 23, 57, 63, 184
People's Bank of China, 138, 142, 144
People's Republic of China (PRC), 123, 125, 135
peri-urbanization, 161
Perrault, Dominique, 36
petroleum revenue, 8
Pittsburgh, United States, 196
place marketing strategy, 60
planners, 29, 34, 52, 73, 89, 96, 121, 127, 163, 187, 231
planning legislation, 11, 180, 188, 194
plot ratio, 231
Ponzi schemes, 139–40
poor residents, 51, 119
Port of Rio de Janeiro, 49. *See also* Porto Maravilha
Porto Maravilha, 7, 45, 47–53, 56–61, 63–4; Companhia de Desenvolvimento Urbano da Região Portuária (CDURP), 48, 51, 57–60, 64; Docas S.A., 58; Fundo de Garantia do Tempo de Serviço (FGTS), 48, 57–60, 63–4; future revenue streams, 53, 60; Porto Maravilha REIT, 59 (*see also* real estate investment trusts [REITs]); Região Portuária REIT, 59 (*see also* real estate investment trusts [REITs])
Portugal, 158
post-carbon, 8, 70, 72, 78, 101
postmodernist architecture, 25
post-oil, 74, 76–7, 95, 98, 102
post-socialist, 135
poverty line, 31
predatory lending, 157
production of urban space, 4, 7, 14, 46, 61, 121
professional class, 9, 144, 184
property boom, 5, 32

property bubble, 10, 15, 22, 140, 170
property cycle, 40
property-led development, 116, 118–19, 123, 128
property mindedness, 227–8
property rights, 120, 137
property tax revenues, 56, 62
protests, 26, 163, 171, 186. *See also* social unrest
public administration, 115
public appropriation, 221
public auction, 55, 185, 201
public debt bubbles, 113
public funds, 39, 62
public good, 3, 58, 113, 125, 181
public housing, 12–14, 27, 199–204, 206, 212, 214–18, 221, 222–37; authority, 221, 236; homeownership, 13, 226, 228, 232, 236; market, 14, 235. *See also* social housing
public land, 22, 26, 47–8, 51, 58–9, 63–4, 114, 128
public-private partnerships, 6, 26, 28, 33, 40–1, 53, 57, 59
public rental system, 223
public transportation, 90, 168, 224. *See also* transportation
Pudong, Shanghai, 116, 118–19, 125
punitive tax, 222
pyramid schemes, 139

Qatar, 71–2, 75, 79, 86–98, 102; blockade against, 72, 75, 86–8, 92, 98, 101; FIFA World Cup 2022, 70, 90; labour deficit, 93; monarchy, 8, 90; National Development Strategy (QSDP), 79, 92, 94–5; National Research Strategy (QNRS), 93; Qatar Foundation, 93, 95–6, 98; Qatar Investment Authority (QIA), 93, 95–6, 98; Qatar National Museum (QNM), 96–7; Qatar National Vision 2030, 92, 95, 98; Qatar Science and Technology Park, 96
quality of life, 78, 94, 102, 121

Rachman, Peter, 184
Rachmanism, 184
Radiant City, 40
real estate holdings, 23, 227
real estate investments, 23, 45, 47, 59, 62, 85
real estate investment trusts (REITs), 23–4, 59
real estate market, 15, 37, 54, 60, 78, 86, 125–6, 135, 156, 201, 216
recriminations, 10, 148
redistribution, 3, 7, 35, 56, 118, 159
regime of accumulation, 15, 112
regulatory tools, 5–4, 61–2, 120
relative poverty, 229
Renaissance Italy, 179
rental housing, 11–13, 159, 184, 199–200, 203–4, 206, 208–9, 212, 214–17, 236
rental market, 200, 227
rent control, 28, 184, 200
rent gap, 22, 63, 183
rentier states, 101
Rentier State Theory (RST), 101
rent regulation, 27, 230
rent roll, 23
rent-to-income ratio, 206, 213
resale, 21, 23, 39, 150, 224–6, 228–9, 233–5, 237; flats, 224–6, 229, 234–5, 237; market, 39, 225–6, 234
resettlement housing, 118–19, 123
residential arbitrage, 183, 185, 187
residential developments, 33, 55, 57, 146, 155, 192, 222
residential housing properties, 11, 185, 201

resident-owners, 39
retail space, 88. *See also* shopping malls
retirement, 13, 223–4, 228–30, 235–7
returns on investment, 22, 89
rezoning, 21, 33
Rio de Janeiro, 7, 45, 47–9, 52, 61; Barra da Tijuca, 52; Copacabana, 52; Ipanema, 52; Leblon, 52; Morro da Favela, 51; Morro da Providência, 49, 51
risk-taking, 4, 41
Riyadh, 70–1
Rodríguez, Emmanuel, 158–60, 166
Rome, 109
Rossi, Ugo, 3
rural collectives, 114
rural fringes, 123, 128
Russia, 194

San Francisco, 196
Sao Paulo, 47, 54, 60, 62
Saudi Arabia, 70, 72, 86–7
schools, 21, 38, 40, 168, 191, 224
second city centre, 35
securities, 24, 55, 160
securitization, 24, 134, 157
segregation, 27, 82, 90
semi-autonomous urban development corporations, 26
semi-detached houses, 223, 226
semi-public fund, 57, 64
semi-public institutions, 60
Sentosa Island, 223
service industry, 111, 204
Seseña, Spain, 155, 161–4, 168–9
Shaanxi, 142–3
shadow banking, 5, 113
Shanghai, 9, 27, 41, 109–11, 115–29, 147; Chongming Island, 128; city beautification projects, 121; City of Design, 115, 120, 129; fragmented property relations, 121; Hongqiao transportation hub, 124; horizontal state units, 115; Jiangnan Shipyard, 122, 128; Lujiazui financial district, 125; Shanghai Port Machinery Plant, 128
Shanghai World Expo: Better City, Better Life, 127; Bidding Committee, 123; Chinese National Pavilion, 125; Expo Land Bank, 124; Expo Park, 121–2, 125, 128; Mercedes-Benz Arena, 125
Shanxi, 142–3
Sharjah, 75
Sheikh Hamad Al Thani, 95
Shell Centre, London, 188
shopping malls, 30, 49, 80, 89, 96, 102
Shoreditch, London, 187
Sichuan, 142
sideline businesses, 146
simultaneous producer, 202
Singapore: Central Provident Fund (CPF), 223, 228; compulsory social security savings, 222–3, 236; en bloc sale, 222, 226–8, 230–1; HDB upgraders, 223, 226; Housing and Development Board (HDB), 13, 39, 40, 221–34; Housing and Urban Development Corporation (HUDC), 226; housing-asset social security system, 229, 235; national housing program, 221; ninety-nine-year leasehold, 13, 221–3, 226, 230–1, 236; People's Action Party (PAP), 13–14, 224, 228–9, 232–3, 235–6; permanent resident, 221–2, 224, 230, 234–5; Selective En bloc Redevelopment Scheme (SERS), 231; single aged members, 225
single-family home, 11

skylines, 30, 37, 72–3, 93
skyscrapers, 36, 73, 80, 89, 95, 97
slump, 24, 40
slums, 26–7, 179
small businesses, 27, 40, 51, 146
small family operations, 144
small loans, 143
small-sized flats, 208–11, 217
Smart, Alan, 15, 247–8
Smith, Neil, 247–8, 52, 183, 250
snowball method, 137
social claims, 62, 64
social democracy, 236
social disparity, 82, 170
social embeddedness, 137
social equity, 12, 25
social exclusion, 163
social harmony, 158
social housing, 12, 25, 37–8, 111, 113, 160, 169, 181, 204, 206, 236. *See also* public housing
social inequalities, 3, 7, 9, 15, 129, 159, 171, 202. *See also* socio-spatial inequalities
social justice, 86, 88, 162
Social Justice and the City, 182
social protections, 134
social relations, 14–15
social security scheme, 116
social space, 116, 121
social stability, 138, 148
social unrest, 120. *See also* protests
social welfare, 13, 94, 119, 236
socio-spatial impacts, 110
socio-spatial inequalities, 63. *See also* social inequalities
socio-spatial restructuring, 111, 119, 121
soft power, 120
Soho, New York, 187–8
Soravia, 38
Sorbonne University, 83

sovereign wealth funds, 23, 39
spaces of exception, 46, 49, 54, 56, 63–4
Spain, 10, 157–60, 163–4, 167, 170, 181; Boyer Decree, 160; Communist Party, 162; decentralization of administrative control, 156, 161; financial crisis, 156; Franco era, 10, 156, 159, 221; General Plans (*Planes Generales*), 161; Housing Plan (1961–76), 158; Land Act (1998), 160, 161; land law, 160; Law of Territorial Ordinance and Urban Activity (LOTAU), 169; malpractices, 155, 162–3, 171; National Stabilization Plan (1959), 158; People's Party (Partido Popular; PP), 162, 164; Program of Urban Actuation (PAU), 162; reclassification of land, 161; Socialist Workers' Party (Partido Obrero Socialista Español; PSOE), 159, 162; Spanish Autonomous Communities, 161; United Left (Izquierda Unida; IU), 162–4; Urban Land Law (1956), 160
spatial fix, 4, 110–11, 115, 123–4, 128
spatial restructuring, 33, 110, 124
spatio-temporal fix, 45
spectacle, 6, 70–1, 74, 79–80, 82–4, 89–91, 95–6, 100–2, 123
spectacular urbanism, 70–1, 79. *See also* iconic development; starchitecture
speculative city, 4, 6, 14–15, 40, 135, 180
speculative event, 137, 144, 150
speculative gains, 14, 27, 39, 213
speculative mentality, 11
speculative overseas buyers, 194
speculative residential arbitrage, 183, 185, 187

Index 269

speculative urbanism, 6
speculative urbanization, 9, 15, 158, 167, 170
sporting events, 110
stamp duty, 234
starchitects, 25; Calatrava, Santiago, 25; Foster, Norman, 60; GTIS Partners, 60; Tishman Speyer, 60
starchitecture, 45. *See also* iconic development; spectacular urbanism
Star River property development, Guangzhou, China, 149
state capitalism, 14
state capitals, 14, 54
state-controlled corporations/firms, 113–14, 118, 124
state economy, 114, 117, 119
state intervention, 15
state-led land appropriation, 114
state-led urbanization, 150
state-owned enterprises, 39
state restructuring, 110, 114
state subsidies, 158, 170
state-subsidized housing, 159
stock exchange, 23, 55–6
subdivided flats, 12, 200, 212
subdivided units (SDUs), 199–200, 202–4, 206, 212
subdivision, 13, 199–200, 206, 215
subnational authorities, 114
subprime mortgage, 179, 181
subprime mortgage crisis, USA, 179
subsidized flats, 217, 224, 235
suburbanization, 161, 196
suburbs/suburban areas, 5, 81, 118–19, 129, 182, 184, 207, 209
Summerson, John, 179
super-rich, 25, 218
surplus capital, 111, 113, 119
surplus value extraction, 112, 128
sustainability, 75, 88–9

sustainable: community, 89; development, 78; future, 71, 90; urban growth, 163; urban region, 77
syndicalization, 23

tax anticipation notes (TANs), 47
taxation, 26
tax exemptions, 6, 8
tax-exempt proceeds, 224
tax forgiveness, 25
tax-free bonds, 6, 25
tax increment financing (TIF), 47, 55, 62
technological innovation, 119, 127
Temasek Holdings Private Limited, 14
tenacious culture of property, 199
tenure security, 184
territorial control, 110
territorial organization, 110, 115, 120, 128
territorial rationalization, 128–9
territorial states, 115, 128
terrorism, 75
Thatcher, Margaret, 195, 221
The Guardian, 89
Theurillat, Thierry, 136
Tishman Speyer, 60
Tokyo, 38, 81
tourism, 24, 37, 75, 120–1, 125
touristic venues, 49
town houses, 32
toxic assets, 10, 156, 164
tradeable commodity, 22
traditional lending, 5
traditional settlements, 70, 73–4, 91
transnational corporations, 125
Transparency International, 86
transparent securities, 4
transportation, 33, 166. *See also* public transportation

underground banks, 9, 137–8, 140–2, 145–7
underground rail networks, 124
unearned increment, 21
UNESCO Creative Cities Network, 120
uneven development, 3, 40, 63–4
United Arab Emirates (UAE), 72, 75, 79–80, 85–8, 98, 102
United Kingdom, 88, 186; Landlord and Tenant Act (1987), 186; Rent Act (1965), 184. *See also* Britain
United Nations Office at Vienna (UNOV), 34
United States, 22, 26, 28–9, 31–2, 47, 55–7, 62, 76, 78, 86, 90, 94, 112, 134, 159, 179, 180–1, 212–13
upgrading, 118, 124, 127, 225, 230
upper-middle-class, 226–7
upward social mobility, 119
urban brand, 71, 80–3, 96
urban centres, 50, 145
Urban Development Action Grant (UDAG), USA, 33
urban enclaves, 77
urban entrepreneurialism, 46. *See also* entrepreneurialism
urban fringes, 118, 123
urban frontier, 7, 52
urban futures, 6, 15. *See also* sustainable: future
urbanity, 70–1, 79–82, 84, 91, 95
urban landscapes, 6
urban land supply, 147
urban managerialism, 35, 46
Urban Operation, Brazil, 47–8, 52–65; Anhangabaú, 54; Comissão de Valores Mobiliários (Securities and Exchange Commission of Brazil, or CVM), 55; Faria Lima, 54; Porto Maravilha, 61 (*see also* Porto Maravilha)

urban periphery, 28
urban renewal, 7, 26–7, 48, 196
Urban Renewal Authority, 29, 215, 217
urban slaves, 51
urban space, 3–4, 49, 128
urban studies, 3–4, 45, 47, 134, 136, 151
urban value creation, 7
use value, 24, 144, 195

valorization, 7, 53, 59, 62–4
value gap, 11, 183, 185
Victorian city, 182
Vienna, 7, 28–9, 34–5, 37, 40; double city (Doppelstadt), 35; social-democratic urban governance, 35; Wiener Entwicklungsgesellschaft für den Donauraum (WED AG), 29, 34–7
village houses, 206
villages, 9, 91, 145, 206
virtual economy, 82, 87, 91
vulnerability, 40

wage earner, 223
Wall Street, 24, 32, 34
warehouse buildings, 51, 121, 183, 187–8, 191–2
warehouse conversion, 195
Washington, DC, 179, 196
Washington-based Center of Advanced Defense Studies (CADS), 86
wasted cities, 150
waterfront development, 28
welfare provision, 5, 63
welfare state, 12, 35
well-being, 15, 169
Werner Faymann, 37
Westchester, New York, 34
West End, London, 188

Western Europe, 47
Western norms, 77
Wong, Lawrence, 221, 232
Woodworth, Max D., 9–10, 242
working class, 26–7, 29, 157–8, 162, 164, 179, 202
working families, 10, 169
working population, 159

Yemen, 72
young families, 233

zero-carbon cities, 77
zero income tax, 86
Zhang, Yunpeng, 9, 41
Ziggurat building, 188, 190
zoning control, 115

www.ingramcontent.com/pod-product-compliance
Lightning Source LLC
Chambersburg PA
CBHW030309080526
44584CB00012B/505